*I have met the Soldiers of God. I only wish I had read this book before I had that opportunity. Howard Bushart, John Craig, and Myra Barnes have* ... *laim to be in a* holy ... *this important* topic.

*As th* ... *d, it is difficult* enou... ...*d mentality of* the e... ...*translate that* unde... *what the move-* ment ... *ialists from the* patri... *e war that the* move... *ts written from* an ou... ...*nt, SOLDIERS* OF G...

...*he Lord*

SOL... ...*. law enforce-* mer... ...*timely and* com... ...*us. Make no* mis... ...*in American* rad... ...*rving of our* clos...

...*ces*

...*rism tactics*

# SOLDIERS OF GOD

---

## WHITE SUPREMACISTS AND THEIR HOLY WAR FOR AMERICA

---

**By Howard L. Bushart, John R. Craig, and Myra Barnes, Ph.D.**

KENSINGTON BOOKS
http://www.kensingtonbooks.com

KENSINGTON BOOKS are published by

Kensington Publishing Corp.
850 Third Avenue
New York, NY 10022

First Kensington Hardcover Printing: June, 1998
First Pinnacle Printing: May, 1999
First Kensington Trade Paperback Printing: September, 2000
10  9  8  7  6  5  4  3  2  1

Printed in the United States of America

Howard Bushart: In memory of my parents and for my son Cameron. For all the gentle souls who fill my life, and for the Gypsy Rhythm Writers for their support.

John Craig: For my grandchildren Michael, Olivia, and Zachary.

Myra Barnes: For my children Jolie, Brandon and Elizabeth.

# CONTENTS

# Contents

# ACKNOWLEDGMENTS

Our most immediate thanks go to those people who gave us the information upon which *Soldiers of God* is based. Some are named in the book but many are not. Some shared their personal photographs with us, others loaned videotapes and written material, and all made sure we told their story right.

Appreciation to Ed Collins and to Bob Daly for their photographs, to Richard F. Daniels for his research, and to Simone Gers for all sorts of things.

A special thanks to our agent Richard Curtis and his assistant Laura Tucker, who got us rolling. And a very special thanks to our editor Paul Dinas and his assistants Katherine Gayle and Melanie Hulse for their expertise, encouragement, and patience.

# Introduction

*S*oldiers of God: White Supremacists and Their Holy War for America is a journey into the world of the radical and racial right and a profound departure from the reality of most Americans. To enter the world of the white supremacist is to enter a world of stringent and relentless racial divisions, a world of conspiracy and subterfuge, a world of timeless and elemental struggles on both natural and supernatural planes. It is a world condemned by the majority of Americans, even though few know exactly what the beliefs of the supremacists are.

Most of our subjects readily agree that they are outside of the American mainstream and are quite proud of that fact. The white supremacists believe that the white race is superior to all others and they have reasons, often surprising ones, for this belief. It is not merely hatred for hatred's sake but something much more.

Two things became quite clear during our research. The first was that the faith called Christian Identity seemed to encompass most right-wing groups but was never discussed at length in any secondary mainstream resources and, when it was, the term was usually applied generally and often erroneously. The other was that there was little to no discussion of the motivations of such groups, other than racism and hatred. Whereas it is true there is no shortage of racism and hatred in the movements, we realized it would be a mistake to categorically advance these factors as the sole explanations for the sometimes violent actions of organizations comprising the white supremacist movements.

Thirty years into the Great Society, although the melting pot is apparently at full boil, assimilation into one national identity is still incomplete. The backlash of the Contract with America and the Republican Revolution indicates a clear swing to the right in the collective consciousness of the United States. In the volatile climate of heated political and social debate, we find active groups of self-identified Christian patriots who are far to the right of most conservative revolutionaries, individuals who do not shrink from violence and are connected in an elusive "leaderless resistance" against what many on the far right consider an illegal and even satanic federal government.

These are the Soldiers of God and they know their identity. Their racial identity is white—Anglo, Teutonic, Saxon, Aryan—and they believe that race is in the blood. Their national identity is American. Their religious identity is Christian. And their Christian Identity is the Servant Nation, the true Israel, the inheritors of Yahweh's Kingdom and the enforcers of Yahweh's laws. They are found in the KKK, White Aryan Resistance, Aryan Nations and a host of similar right-wing organizations all following the same agenda even if their operational ideologies vary.

We interviewed members of these organizations, read their literature, reviewed hours of videotapes of lectures and lessons, attended rallies and gatherings and otherwise immersed ourselves in their world to find several common threads among the groups which constitute the racialist movement. Our research led us to understand that there is little in-depth information about the beliefs of the racial right, particularly in terms of their religious beliefs. They have been "cussed and discussed," so to speak, from every possible angle but one: they have rarely, if ever, had their beliefs presented objectively—from their point of view.

Thus, our covenant with the white supremacists such as Charles Lee and "Cadillac" John Thellin, plus many others who have been invaluable in helping us compile this work, is that we will not intentionally misrepresent them. Therefore, we have worked closely with our interviewees, coming back to them from time to time with drafts to check for content. We have not asked for their editorial approval but a simple fact check to make sure we were on target.

More than one complained about the title of this book *Soldiers of God: White Supremacists and Their Holy War for America*. Not all in the movements are soldiers or even militant, we were informed, not all are at war, and even the ones that are at war don't all get their orders from God. Not all supremacists are separatists nor vice versa, not all supremacists are rabid, and not all separatists want segregation for purely racial reasons. It isn't just *their* battle, anyway—it's for the entire white race. And it isn't only America that is at stake. Despite the objections, the title stands.

By necessity we have presented oppposing viewpoints from time to time but we have taken every precaution to avoid analysis of the groups or individual members and assiduously tried not to pass judgments. We have quoted sources and repeated conversations with as much accuracy as possible. This, at times, has proven quite difficult.

The preponderance of tracts, pamphlets, brochures, newsletters, books and Bible commentaries were privately printed, not listed in *Reader's Guide* or *Books in Print,* not available in libraries or bookstores. Many lack publishing information. Some lack authors or titles or page numbers. Valuable material was loaned to us, some of it photocopied from photocopies and almost impossible to trace. We have reproduced all of them as we found them, without adding editorial markers such as ''[sic]'' or otherwise calling attention to spelling or grammar or capitalization. Some came from web sites that no longer exist, or the items were read-only or have since been deleted. Thus, some missing information must remain missing. Likewise, the identities of some of our sources are concealed, and assumed names are used in places.

Our intention has been to produce a work which any Klansman, Aryan Nations member or other white supremacist can point to on his bookshelf and say ''That's us, all right,'' while at the same time, we trust astute non-separatist readers to draw their own conclusions.

Our sources, understandably, doubted that we would remain objective in presenting their beliefs but we have, to the best of our abilities, remained so. It is not our intention to either proselytize or marginalize but simply to say ''Here it is. This is what they believe, their values, the motivations that drive them, the world as they see it.''

We do not share those beliefs nor is it our intention to advance the separatists' or any other cause. We are not racists, Identity Christians, or white supremacists. We harbor no ambitions toward becoming propagandists or provocateurs. But we do feel strongly that problems, if they are to be resolved at all, must be examined honestly and from every possible perspective.

We also feel strongly about the free exchange of ideas and firmly believe that convictions cannot be killed by the simple refusal to hear them.

# CHAPTER ONE

# The Faces of a Faceless Movement

**"Y**ou may write the truth, you may not. We've been lied to before,'' Charles Lee says, looking up at the Houston skyline. ''It's a calculated risk. But even if you do, I doubt if your book will ever be published. The last thing the Jews who control the media want is for our message to get out.''

Charles Lee considers himself a soldier of God in a war that is well under way.

In the late spring of 1995, Lee sits beneath the sculptures of downtown Houston's theater district as we calculate the odds of getting uncensored information from inside the ranks, then the unlikelihood of getting it into print. The late morning wind still has a hint of a chill as it whips his hair away from his face, revealing a deep, crater-like scar on his forehead. An unassuming man with a mild demeanor, he seems almost shy.

A former industrial painter from the Beaumont/Port Arthur area, Lee is now Grand Dragon of the White Camelia Knights of the Ku Klux Klan of Texas and has been an active member of the racial right and the Klan for more than twenty years. His voice is soft, modulated, as he explains his beliefs directly, as matters of fact.

''I am a Christian,'' he says. ''I believe whites are superior to non-whites but that does not mean that I hate anyone. The real difference is that white Christians are the descendants of Adam and we were never meant to mix our seed with the other races of the world.''

Lee, though reared as a Lutheran, now claims the faith of Christian Identity, a doctrine entirely consistent with his beliefs on race. Christian Identity is the belief that the white race is the true Israel of the Bible. A principal tenet of the militant faction is that Jews are the direct seedline of Satan involved in a complicated conspiracy to destroy the Aryan peoples of the world. Identity is the truth which is the central organizing principle of Charles Lee's life.

"Once you know the truth," he says, "walking around on the streets of America is like walking around in a lunatic asylum. If you define sanity as knowing right from wrong, recognizing your own best interest, then almost every white person I encounter is insane. I meet white people all the time who hate me and everything I stand for. They don't seem to realize that what I stand for is them and the entire white race. They hate me, but *I'm* supposed to be the hate-monger. Maybe I'm missing something here."

Charles Lee is but one of thousands who constitute the worldwide white nationalist movements. The movements encompass numerous individual organizations which are diverse in terms of structure, agendas and beliefs. Among the groups lumped together as white nationalist are the Ku Klux Klan, White Aryan Resistance (WAR), National Alliance, Aryan Brotherhood, Posse Comitatus, any number of skinhead groups and militias, Heritage Front, National Association for the Advancement of White People (NAAWP), White Maidens, Women for Aryan Unity, Aryan Nations and numerous others. Some claim to be Christian, others make no claims to faith. Some are National Socialist, others are not. And though these groups may splinter in terms of ideology and politics, they share the unifying concept of white supremacy—the belief that the white race is superior to all other humans on earth and, even more important, the belief that the white race is targeted for systematic destruction.

Race mixing is the surest way to contaminate, and therefore destroy, a bloodline. With varying degrees of activism, combating race mingling inherent in multiculturalism and forced integration is a major component of the white separatists' agenda. Some of the milder religious groups explain that race mixing is a violation of God's law and let it go at that. Other factions are more aggressive. A flyer distributed by Aryan Nations in 1981 titled "The Death of the White Race," authored by imprisoned member David Lane, features a picture of a white woman and a black man captioned "The Ultimate Abomination." Miscegenation, the flyer states, decrees the death of a race and through the efforts of the Jewish-owned media, whose goal is to destroy the purity of the white bloodline, the white race is "the earth's most endangered species."

From this common unifying principle comes the common goal of a separate Aryan homeland. White supremacy, by necessity, includes the concept of separatism, the idea that racism—considered a natural component of human nature—cannot be overcome in an integrated society. Racism, expressed in terms of white superiority and driving the separatist agenda of the racial right, is known as *racialism* in its application to political philosophy. Racialism is built on the belief that racial "identity" must be maintained by all peoples, particularly white people. It entails the belief that conflict will always be extant whenever different races are forced to share the same territories and supports the necessity for racial homelands. Racialism is integral to separatist thinking and the supremacist world view.

Although it is safe to say that all the groups gathered under the general umbrella of white nationalism embrace the philosophy of racialism, it is equally safe to say that there are wide variations of belief among these separate entities. Even among organizations such as the Ku Klux Klan, one group does not necessarily have the same views as another. The White Camelia of Texas, for instance (Charles Lee's group), is a Christian Identity Klan while the White Kamellia of Vidor, Texas, (formerly of Louisiana) is not, although some Identity Christians are included in the ranks. Some groups in the movements believe in the basic racialist ideology but take little action outside their membership. Others are men of action. Commitment varies from group to group and certainly among individual members. And, at times, there are petty jealousies and other divisive situations which serve to create rivalries and adversarial relationships between groups. This has traditionally been the history of the white supremacist movement in America.

However, over the last fifteen years, there has been a good deal of effort expended by men such as Tom Metzger of White Aryan Resistance, Louis Beam, ex-Grand Dragon of Texas White Knights and former Ambassador at Large for Aryan Nations, and Pastor Richard Butler of Aryan Nations to bring these groups together in a more focused and concentrated effort to advance their cause, the struggle for racial survival. But even here, there are ideological differences. Beam's idea of unity, for instance, is unity of purpose and certainly not unity of organization. Metzger, on the other hand, is a tireless recruiter for WAR. Methodologies and organizational philosophies notwithstanding, the racial right sees its mission as one of absolute necessity and absolute commitment.

For Identity Christians—those who believe the white race to be true Israel—this struggle, as it has been since the creation, is a monumental task. Particularly at the present time. The responsibility to and for the race is constantly reinforced in the racialist movements. The responsibility to God, to Yahweh, through the acceptance of the burden of the chosen, pits the few against the many. According to Louis Beam in a speech at Aryan Nations in 1993, it requires an extraordinary commitment. It requires a commitment to laboring for a future which, in all probability, those present will never live to see; a commitment to working for a pure race generations from now in which the Aryan warrior will live on in his progeny. A commitment to stand up to what Beam calls "the most evil, most vile, most corrupt government on the face of the earth"—the United States Government—ZOG, the "Zionist Occupational Government" that the movements claim is run by Jews whose goal is to rule the entire world.

Beam notes that such commitment requires an internal struggle before it can ever be fully expressed in an external sense. One must come to grips with one's own mortality in a most significant way. One must work through the fears, breaking "the twin swords of prison and death" that ZOG holds over him. Once that is done, one can abandon himself to the cause, immerse himself in the struggle that the supremacists contend is much larger than the individual. And it must be, for the sacrifices are huge.

Beam speaks from experience.

The one-time helicopter gunner who served in Vietnam has a more than twenty-year history of racial activism with the Klan and Aryan Nations. Beam is also a veteran of numerous arrests, investigations and court charges. An intensive federal investigation, following the activities of The Order in the early eighties, resulted in federal indictments against a number of racialists, including Beam. The thirteen defendants—who included Richard Butler of the Church of Jesus Christ Christian, the late Robert Miles of the KKK and Mountain Church of Michigan, and David Lane of The Order, among others—were charged with conspiracy to overthrow the federal government, and some were charged with transportation of stolen money to finance that effort as well as conspiracy to assassinate a federal judge. All were subsequently acquitted.

Beam, with his wife and his young daughter from another marriage, fled to Mexico. Captured there by Mexican federal police—where his wife, Sheila, shot and seriously wounded a Mexican federal policeman during the arrest—he was brought to Arkansas to stand trial in federal court. Beam speaks of his incarceration as a positive experience, praising Yahweh for his opportunity to see his enemy "face to face" where he could learn about him and, when freed, use that knowledge against him. As always, the rhetoric stops just short of sedition. The commitment to the struggle stops short of nothing, including death.

Speaking to the congregation at Aryan Nations, Beam noted, "We're all going to die. Everyone of us in this room is going to die. Why not die for something . . . why not die for that little girl out there, for her grandchildren and great-grandchildren? Not like those yuppies who live and die for what? A stereo?"

Identity pastor Neumann Britton, at the same gathering, said, "Thirty years ago the federal government considered me one of the most dangerous men in America. Well, I've gotten worse. I've been working for the same cause as Pastor Butler since Yahweh laid his hand on me thirty-five years ago. I won't stop until we win."

Charles Lee and other Klansmen have attended meetings and are frequent visitors to Aryan Nations at Hayden Lake, Idaho. In fact, Hayden Lake has been visited by a veritable "who's who" among the racial right. Aryan Nations is a center for many organizational activities focused upon the development of a New America, an Aryan America.

Their America would be a pure land. It would have one race, one people unpolluted by the sin of miscegenation. The culture would be unsullied by the works of foreign or minority writers who have done so much to further the cause of the seed of Satan and bring America to the brink of ruin. It would be a Christian nation with no mosques or synagogues marring the land. There would be no non-white immigration, and white immigration would be limited to those clearly beneficial to the state—which is inseparable from the church. Only books and art and cinema conducive to Aryan Christian values would be allowed. In short, it would be a world such as Yahweh intended for the white Israel people.

The New America, entirely of, by, and for white Christians will not come easily nor at small cost. However, it lies on the horizon for the soldiers of God, like Hitler's dream of Aryan "Germania." If it is to be achieved at all, then the resources of the resistance movements must be pooled, united, and channeled into a common relentless will. This is the intent of those who would pull together the racial right.

The idea is to embrace a goal, or goals, upon which all the different elements can focus and toward which all can work. Thus inter-organizational cooperation is necessary. However, total unification could undermine the strategy of leaderless resistance—revolutionaries in small autonomous cells acting independently of any ruling body. This makes for creative revolution. It also creates a maddening situation for federal agents charged with monitoring such activities.

Leaderless resistance, then, becomes a loose confederation in terms of operation. As outlined in Dr. William Pierce's novel, *The Turner Diaries,* the layers of secrecy create a situation in which those in ''the organization'' receive instructions without being exposed to knowledge of where the instructions come from, thereby preventing any backtracking to the source. Such communications are couched in vague, euphemistic language so that prosecution in federal court is almost impossible even if the source is identified and conspiracy or other charges filed.

Then there are people on the fringe of the movement who, exposed to rhetoric and literature of the racial right, become involved in the loop of instruction, orientation and activism: for example, the individual who does not belong to a racial organization at all; who never speaks of his beliefs; who sits quietly at home reading *The Turner Diaries, Hunter, Liberty Bell, National Vanguard* or the various mail ministry tracts available, or *Stormfront* bulletins downloaded from the Internet and, in fact, may be studying such literature, preparing for his role in the racial holy war. This individual may, from time to time, act independently on such information and the consequences of his actions are not predictable.

''You can't hold anyone responsible for that kind of thing,'' Klansman Jim Stinson of the White Camelia, observes. ''I mean, if McVeigh read the book *[The Turner Diaries]* and built a bomb like the one in the book— that's assuming McVeigh *did* do the bombing and I'm not convinced he did—I don't see where you can reach the conclusion Pierce put him up to it.''

But that does not mean those in the movements don't appreciate the value of such actions.

''It's just another sign that people are fed up,'' says Klansman ''Cadillac'' John Thellin, also of White Camelia. ''We don't have to tell anyone what to do. And we don't. But that Oklahoma City thing, that's just the beginning. And it won't stop until things are straightened out in this country. You can listen to all that Jew talk about how it can't happen here, it will never happen here. Well, it's happening. If you don't believe it, stand back and watch."

Cadillac John Thellin lives in a modest home in a well-integrated section of South Houston. He is a large man, with what might be described as command presence. Thellin is also a biker. In fact, he speaks with pride of being the only machinist in Houston to custom-build certain hard-to-come-by motorcycle parts. His dark hair, more than liberally streaked with gray, is tied back in a ponytail hanging two-thirds of the way down his back and obscuring the Harley logo on his T-shirt. Several small dogs have the run of the house, their size incongruous with the imposing image of Cadillac John. Cadillac is animated as he speaks of the Klan.

Cadillac John is a true believer in the tenets of Christian Identity. He believes just as vehemently in the unfairness of affirmative action and the quota system, contending that such efforts are pure self-hating insanity fostered by the Jews. He believes that such programs are destructive to American society and that this destruction, the poisoning of the American mind and spirit, is much more than unexpected fallout from the implementation of the programs of the Great Society; it is a systematic plan through which all negative consequences occur by design. In Cadillac John's mind, the Klan is the thin white line of defense for the racial/political dream of the founding fathers, the only defense against the Jewish-led conspiracy to destroy America and create a One-World government.

Chain-smoking and drinking copious amounts of coffee—the pot is always brewing at the Thellins' because, like Charles Lee, he is not a drinking man—Cadillac is frank about his beliefs and his world views. "It's all right there in the Bible, every bit of it," he says. "It's right there for anyone with common sense who wants to take the time to read it. Your average American doesn't want to go to any trouble. He's happy to sit on his ass and swallow any old line of bullshit that a mud-loving preacher wants to feed him. How many Americans know anything at all about the Bible?"

Armed with ideology, white separatists carry the message into various militia groups, church congregations, classrooms, the armed forces and police departments. Once inside, the agents engage in selective recruiting —done clandestinely, of course—to spread their gospel and wait to mobilize their forces when the time is right.

These tactics are outlined in National Alliance literature and other sources readily accessible on the Internet and can hardly be considered secret. Nationalism, in this the last decade of the twentieth century, is not defined by country. Intergroup cooperation and exchange of information are crossing borders and oceans. Aryan nationalism includes South Africa and Sweden, Russia, Denmark, the Netherlands, England, Ireland, Czechoslovakia, Germany, Scotland, France, Argentina, Canada, Brazil, Italy, Spain, Croatia, Romania, Portugal, Australia, Poland and almost any nation on earth with a white population. As Pastor Richard Butler of Aryan Nations notes, "Race *is* nation."

At this point, the ideological goals of the white supremacists begin to sound at least vaguely as if they are aimed toward a one-world government of their own. Charles Lee disputes that idea.

"I'm an American and I want *my* America back," Lee says. "I'm not concerned how other countries conduct their business. Of course, if they want to follow our lead I have no problem with that."

The National Socialist wing of the supremacist movement is not so modest in terms of goals, and the exportation of National Socialism to other countries is certainly an element of their agenda. In a January 1996 article, "How Nazis Are Made" in *The New Yorker,* Ingo Hasselbach, former neo-Nazi who founded the East German National Alternative, relates getting most of his groups' Holocaust revisionism literature, anti-Jewish tracts, posters and bumper stickers from Gary Lauck of Lincoln, Nebraska. Strict German laws prohibit Nazi symbols or literature from being produced, distributed or displayed in the land that lives most intimately with the legacy of Adolf Hitler.

Gary Lauck heads up an American neo-Nazi organization named for the German Nazi Party, or National Socialist Worker's Party, Foreign Branch. The organization prints and distributes National Socialist and other white supremacist literature in eleven languages and, from America's heartland, is the major distributor of such products in Europe. It is interesting to note that Germany, the birthplace of the most formidable fascist movement the world has ever known, has stringent legal sanctions in place against anti-Semitic literature and any vestiges of Nazi Germany. It is also interesting to note how often, according to Hasselbach, the police turn a blind eye to such activities. Nazism is by no means dead in Germany even if, oddly enough, German Nazis must rely on their brethren in the country most responsible for their defeat in 1945.

As perhaps the primary exporter of racist ideology in the world, the United States is a safe haven for many Aryan extremists driven from their own countries. This does not mean these foreign racists are now neutralized. Quite the contrary. Because of U. S. free-speech rights granted by the First Amendment, "refugee" racists, who have entered the country legally, can operate rather openly. After all, it is not a crime in the United States to print racist literature and flood another country with it. Nor is it a crime for home-grown racists to do the same.

Hasselbach also related connections with Tom Metzger of WAR and with Dennis Mahon of the Ku Klux Klan, with whom he corresponded. White supremacist information sites and chat areas on the Internet are filled with messages that cross the ocean in seconds. In short, white nationalism is now white internationalism. And Louis Beam, following his acquittal on the sedition charges in Arkansas, vowed not only to unite the racial right, but to establish ties with other anti-Jewish racial organizations such as the PLO and Islamic Jihad. Whereas the overthrow of the United States government is a most ambitious goal and highly unlikely to be achieved, such unions have the capacity for much social and political disruption and a great deal of damage.

Regardless of how the deck is stacked against them, Identity Christians of the racial right are determined to herald in a new American era which is reflective of their concepts of the old American era—an era in which the Constitutional Republic is not one of separation of church from state. In fact, an underpinning tenet of Christian Identity political philosophy is that if a government is to be successful, particularly for a nation of Aryan Israelites, it *must* include the laws of God, and *no* laws of man may supersede these divine sanctions. In no way should the church, the true gospel, be excluded from the state.

"When I was a little kid, we said the pledge of allegiance to the flag," Charles Lee says. "We also prayed in school. Back then, no one raised any objections. By the time I was a man, it wasn't being done anymore. It's almost as if we're ashamed to admit that we are Christians nowadays.

"I don't think that's right and there's a lot of other people who think like I do. In this case, for once, I don't think I'm a minority opinion. I *want* prayer back in school, not some moment of silence, or some generic thing or another to allow for someone else's god. I want our schools to return to moral instruction using the Scriptures as a guide.

"Right from the beginning in this country, a prayer book and the Bible were the fundamental textbooks in American schools. Kids learned to read from it, memorized Scripture, studied the moral meanings of it. For two hundred years that worked just fine. That's not a bad track record. The Klan, as an organization, has always backed this practice and I don't know a single Klansman who doesn't, whether they are Identity or not.

"We've got to get back to it. America was a great country before we turned our backs on religion. And not just any religion, Christianity. We turn our backs on our God so we won't hurt some Buddhist, Moslem or atheist's feelings. But look how they feel about us. In the Gulf War, American soldiers were told not to wear a cross because it was offensive to the Moslems in Saudi Arabia. Don't fly the American flag because it offended the Arabs. And we were there fighting for them. That just doesn't make sense to me."

Lee voices the concern of a number of Americans. He contends that Christianity has never been forced on anyone in this country but up until the early 1960s, it held a revered place in both our society and public education system. Many orthodox Christians argue the same issue. Why is prayer not allowed? Why disallow Nativity scenes at Christmas? Why remove Christian paintings or sculptures from public buildings?

Charles Lee cuts right to the chase. "There is not a doubt in my mind that it's all originating with the Jews and it's all part of Satan's plan to destroy white Christians. Prayer is banned and evolution taught, while creationism—of any kind, much less the true creationism—is simply ignored. Then there is the myth of racial equality being forced down the throats of white kids whose eyes tell them differently. This has to stop. We have to remove the foreign, liberal and the Jewish influences if we, as a people and a nation are to survive."

Lee is quite aware that his vision for America will likely not be realized in his lifetime but he does believe that it will eventually be realized. And when that time comes, the prayers of white Christians will no longer offend anyone because there will be no one in America who is not white Christian. Aryan Israel, in fulfillment of Identity prophecy and once again aware of itself, will assume its rightful place both on this continent and in the world. White Christians, true Israelites, will wait upon the Throne of David, aware of their heritage and of their responsibility to their nation, to their race and to their God, and once again America will be on course.

A portion of the Aryan Nations Oath of Allegiance says "I have a sacred duty to do whatever is necessary to deliver our people from the Jew and bring total victory to the Aryan race. . . . We hereby invoke the blood covenant and declare that we are in a full state of war."

This is the belief and the ultimate goal of the soldier of God who assumes the responsibility for such a struggle and, consistent with the will of Yahweh and the teachings of the Identity movement, does not "hold back his sword from blood" in the service of the cause.

# CHAPTER TWO

# The Uneasy State of the Nation

On the morning of April 19, 1995, a truck-bomb carrying several thousand pounds of ammonium nitrate fertilizer soaked in fuel oil was detonated at the Alfred P. Murrah Federal Building in Oklahoma City, killing 168 Americans and injuring over five hundred others. The force of the explosion was felt not only in Oklahoma City, but throughout the nation. After a futile search for foreign terrorists, the first and favorite suspects in such events, America was shocked yet again to discover the prime suspects to be Americans: Timothy McVeigh and Terry Nichols, two Army buddies who, for reasons of their own, identified their own government as a tyrannical force which must be overcome.

They are not alone in their thinking.

The proliferation of anti-government organizations, separatist groups, tax rebels, out-of-the-mainstream religious sects and all the attendant rhetoric and acts of violence associated with such groups serve to create an unsettling climate of anxiety and despair among many Americans. This anxiety is heightened when government agencies respond in a violent, heavy-handed manner that adds even more disquiet. When one considers such events against the backdrop of our history, it is not difficult to understand how these events are seen as indicative of a decline, even a falling apart, of American society and that ambitious nation created by the framing of the U.S. Constitution. Certainly, the decline of the state is one common denominator that underlies the violence of the radical right, the violence which they believe must be used to preserve any vestiges of the founding fathers' intent. Though it seems a contradiction, they believe that one must actively oppose the government in order to support the nation.

To look at America through the eyes of the radicals—the political and religious dissidents—can be a shocking experience for those who hold more traditional views of our national identity. The United States of America is an amazing nation. It is a mighty nation. Yet it is also a mythical nation, more often than not concealed from its inhabitants behind a veil of self-deception. Our national identity, "the land of the free, the home of the brave," is both fact and fiction. We constantly reinforce this identity through the stories we tell ourselves and essentially become those stories. At least in our own minds. And, though the stories we tell ourselves are marvelous indeed, they are often colored by wishful thinking and a steadfast refusal to look at things realistically. Thus, the self-deception. And self-deception, meticulously created and tenaciously clung to is a belief.

For many—particularly those involved in the white supremacist movements—the deception is not entirely self-inflicted. The white supremacists contend that we have been programmed to see ourselves and our nation in certain ways. They offer, for instance, the "myth" of racial equality presented as fact, maintaining that we believe so strongly in "all men created equal" that we refuse to acknowledge the obvious fact that this is not so.

"Sure, we're equal," Klansman Cadillac John observes sardonically. "That's why we're all segregated into neighborhoods. Any white man who believes this 'equality' bullshit needs to try 'melting' into a black neighborhood after dark sometime. If that doesn't convince him, I don't know what will."

"If we're so equal, then why do we need reverse discrimination?" Klansman Jim Stinson asks. "Why do we need special hiring policies for blacks? Special admissions requirements to schools? Special tests? Quota systems? To me, it doesn't sound as if even the liberals who come up with these ideas believe that blacks are equal."

Equality is not the only identified myth that white racialists point out. The whole idea of liberty and individual freedom is an illusion from this standpoint. Identity Pastor Pete Peters, of Scriptures for America Worldwide and the LaPorte Church of Christ in LaPorte, Colorado, claims in his writings and radio broadcasts that Americans are being enslaved to licenses, permits, taxes, liens, restrictions, ad infinitum, until heretofore-basic freedoms exist only at the whim of government. In this matter, racialists will find any number of patriot organizations willing to concur. John B., a militiaman from Baytown, Texas, claims, "People worry about losing our freedoms. They should be worried because we have so few left. We are living in a dictatorship already. We have been ever since FDR sold us out in the thirties. Americans believe we are free people when, in fact, we are not. The one-worlders have been careful to take our freedoms a little bit at a time because if they tried to do it all at once, there would be war in the streets."

The federal government, from the perspective of those in the movements, is a fearsome foe and a threat to American freedoms of religion, speech, assembly, the right to self-defense and the right to self-determination. There are a number of examples that, from this perspective, speak eloquently of the true state of the nation.

In 1992, federal agent Lon Horiuchi of the FBI's Hostage Rescue Team (HRT), acting in behalf of what those in the movements believe is a government out of control, fired the shot heard round the white supremacist world. At Ruby Creek, Idaho—popularly known as the Ruby Ridge incident—Randy Weaver, his wife Vicki, along with their children, Sara, Sam, Rachel and Elisheba, as well as family friend Kevin Harris, were involved in a stand-off with federal agents. Randy Weaver and his family, separatists and Identity Christians, shared the conviction that the U.S. government is the "Synagogue of Satan." And, as Christians, the Weavers made it clear they wanted no part of such a government.

The Weavers were clearly separatists, something not entirely uncommon in modern Christendom, withdrawn to the wilds of Idaho as commanded according to their interpretation of Scripture. Separatism is not a concept foreign to Christendom, as any number of denominational sects believe in keeping themselves apart from the world. The idea that the Weavers were armed-to-the-teeth rebels spoiling for a fight has pretty well been discounted by information uncovered in the 1995 Senate hearings and other testimony. For the most part, the Weavers wished to be left alone.

Randy Weaver ran afoul of the government when an undercover operative with the Bureau of Alcohol Tobacco and Firearms convinced Weaver to supply him with illegally sawed-off shotguns. A complicated chain of events began with BATF agents confronting Weaver with violation of federal firearms laws and basically attempting to recruit him as an undercover informant to infiltrate the nearby Aryan Nations. Weaver refused. He was arrested sometime later, posted bond, but failed to appear in court.

In late August 1992, federal marshals, attempting to serve a warrant on Weaver, were involved in a gunfight in which fourteen-year-old Sammy Weaver, his dog Striker, and Deputy U.S. Marshal Billy Degan were killed. Randy Weaver and the surviving members of his household retreated to their homestead and refused to surrender. Before the incident was over, Horiuchi—under no duress, without warning or a demand for surrender—fired from his concealed position and wounded Randy Weaver. While Weaver, his daughter Sara, and Harris hurried for the safety of the cabin, Horiuchi fired again, wounding Harris and killing Vicki Weaver who stood behind the open cabin door holding her infant daughter Elisheba.

Weaver, Harris and the surviving children surrendered several days later, and both Weaver and Harris went to trial on a number of charges including murder; conspiracy to commit murder; manufacture, possession and distribution of illegal weapons; failure to appear in court and—according to those in the movements and court records—basically anything else the prosecution could come up with. After three deaths, measureless heartache and millions of taxpayer dollars spent on the siege and the trial, Randy Weaver was eventually convicted of failure to appear in court. The original weapons charge was dismissed as entrapment. In 1996, the federal government, though admitting to no wrongdoing, made a settlement of three million dollars to the surviving Weavers.

Justice?

Hardly, as far as the racial right is concerned. The rules of engagement governing the use of deadly force were altered by the federal agents in charge to the point that they were basically a license to kill anyone the FBI Hostage Rescue Team (HRT) team might get in the crosshairs of their sniper scopes. Vicki Weaver was never charged with a crime. There was no warrant for her arrest. She never brandished a weapon, never threatened or fired at anyone during the whole affair. The only blood she shed at Ruby Ridge was her own. A Senate committee in 1995, conducting an investigation of the siege, determined that fourteen-year-old Sammy Weaver was shot in the back as he ran for home. Ruby Ridge, by any reasonable judgment, is a sordid, tragic event which could have been avoided.

But many among the movements see it as something more, and the common belief is that the government sent federal agents to Ruby Ridge with every intention of killing the Weavers. Yggdrasil, a person or persons contributing frequently to the Internet white nationalist site *Stormfront,* asks, ''Why else would they [federal agents] be carrying silencers?'' Certainly the Weavers expected to be killed. They expected to be killed for their beliefs. Extremely galling to the critics of the government's actions is the fact that the federal marshals involved in the initial shootout were all awarded medals of valor for the roles they played at Ruby Ridge.

''It's almost funny if you think about it,'' Charles Lee says ruefully. ''The way I see it, they get medals to honor the courage they showed by killing a little boy's dog then shooting the little boy in the back as he ran away. Is that valor? If it is, I wonder how much guts it took Horiuchi to hide in the rocks and shoot an unarmed woman holding a baby a hundred yards away?''

Whereas it is true that there are unfortunate mistakes made from time to time in every law enforcement agency, the constituents of the racial right see a clear pattern of abuse of federal power. Ruby Ridge was no unfortunate isolated incident in their minds.

''It was murder, plain and simple,'' says Klansman Jim Stinson. ''Who's going to take responsibility for that? Who's going to be charged with killing Vicki Weaver? What kind of country pins a medal on some son of a bitch for doing something like that?''

At gun shows and preparedness expos throughout the country, anti-government speakers such as Colonel Bo Gritz, former Green Beret who helped negotiate Randy Weaver's surrender, and John Trochmann, founder of the Militia of Montana, speak about the lack of respect for the rights of citizens demonstrated by federal agencies—from the IRS, BATF, DEA, FBI, CIA, and all the various agencies associated with a power-drunk central government. The audience consists of supporters whose attitudes are best summed up by a slogan on T-shirts and bumper-stickers available at such gatherings: ''I love my country but I fear my government.''

For the radical right, a clear and ongoing conspiracy is afoot to deprive the citizens of their rights as citizens. There is a war taking place, and it is a war they did not start. From their perspective, Ruby Ridge is not the only example of unjustifiable federal aggression which compels the patriot revolutionaries to take up arms.

In February 1993, agents of the Bureau of Alcohol, Tobacco and Fire-arms, in an attempt to serve a warrant on Vernon Dean Howell, better known as David Koresh, staged a raid on the Branch Davidian compound at Waco, Texas. The BATF, already under fire from critics and receiving bad press for overflexing its enforcement muscle at Ruby Ridge, came

in with armed SWAT teams in spite of the fact that an inside operative
had informed them that the element of surprise had been lost.

A fierce gun battle ensued and four BATF agents and several Davidians
were killed in the initial shootout. A member of the sheriff's department
in Waco publicly expressed surprise at the raid. "They could have arrested
Howell any time they wanted to," the officer said. "He was in town all
the time. They could have called him and told him to come down here
[sheriff's office] and he would have come. We've done it before."

Jon Mathews, on his Houston talk show, hypothesized that the entire
affair was a funding gimmick. Mathews's basic theory was that BATF
was in hot water and that they hoped to benefit from publicity surrounding
the raid. He had no shortage of callers who agreed with him. And one
caller who offered, "If you have guns and believe in the wrong religion,
the government will kill you."

Regardless of motivation, the agents in the first assault were driven
back and the long stand-off began. As with Ruby Ridge, there was a
small army of federal and local law-enforcement agents at the site as well
as some supporters of the Davidians, including Louis Beam, who was
arrested there, and Timothy McVeigh. The outlay of resources would
seem to point to some major criminal activity taking place at the Davidian
compound. However, the warrants once again addressed firearms and
explosives violations, and there were complaints of ritual child abuse
which were investigated by Waco's Children's Protective Services and
found to be unsubstantiated. Joined by the FBI's Hostage Rescue Team
which was in charge at Ruby Ridge, the BATF kept watch for nearly two
months. United States Attorney General Janet Reno, after a briefing by
the FBI, approved a plan to end the siege.

On April 19, 1993, the HRT and fellow FBI agents launched a second
assault. Using armored vehicles, agents knocked down the walls of the
Davidian main building and somehow, during the confusion, a fire broke
out. The remaining Branch Davidians were killed in the blaze, causing
Dr. William Pierce of National Alliance to comment on his shortwave
radio program, *American Dissident Voices,* "Janet Reno found it necessary
to save the children at the Branch Davidian compound by burning them
to death."

"Does that seem odd to anyone else?" Jim Stinson asks. "Nothing
like a good fire to destroy evidence and cover your tracks."

Stinson is referring to a disturbing pattern of conflagrations where
federal agents are concerned. Robert Mathews, founder of the racialist

revolutionary group, The Order, was killed in a shootout with federal agents at Whidby Island, Washington, in 1983. The house which served as his fortress was burned to the ground. Gordon Kahl, of Posse Comitatus, was killed in a shootout with agents in Arkansas, also in 1983. The farmhouse where he made his stand was burned. The Branch Davidian compound at Waco was burned.

Carl D. Haggard, Commanding General of the United States Special Field Forces Militia, mistrustful of government though he claims no racialist leanings, notes, "I suppose it could just be accidental. You know, just the sort of thing that can happen when battling anti-government terrorists . . . Linda Thompson's films *Waco: The Big Lie* and *Waco II: The Big Lie Continues* tell us everything the government doesn't want us to know about what really happened."

In the years since the event, sources other than the patriot and supremacist movements have also expressed dismay at the way the incident was handled and the eventual outcome. Senate hearings, books, articles, editorials and opinions from experts to the man on the street have decried the loss of life and questioned the "official" version of the Waco tragedy. Charles Richards, in his 23 April 1997 Associated Press report "Film Cites New View of Waco Siege," describes a recent video documentary, a grainy black and white videotape recorded by an FBI surveillance aircraft circling over the Branch Davidian compound at the time of the conflagration. Made with an infrared camera designed to detect heat sources, including weapons fired on the ground, the film, entitled "Waco: The Rules of Engagement," was first premiered at Robert Redford's Sundance Festival in January 1997. While not everyone interprets the government tanks' intermittent white flashes on the ground as bursts of machine-gun fire, a former U.S. Army expert on Forward-Looking Infrared (FLIR), as well as several other people who viewed the film, believes it is evidence that FBI gunfire was directed toward the storage area where the Davidian women and children were told to go during the raid. "I think we need a whole new set of Nuremberg Trials," said an observer from Dallas, after seeing the film. Another viewer said she thought everyone in this country should see the film "and realize how wicked our government is."

If outside observers believe that there was government skullduggery at Waco, at least a few on the other side acknowledge that something was amiss. The FBI's Danny Coulson, although he does not agree that the government is "wicked," says its handling of the Waco situation might have been due to ill-advised tactics.

In March 1993, weeks before the Mount Carmel conflagration, Deputy Assistant FBI Director Danny O. Coulson, founder of the FBI's elite SWAT-type Hostage Rescue Team (HRT), wrote an internal memo voicing his concerns about the tanks and tear gas that on-scene commander Richard Rogers planned to use against the Branch Davidians. Coulson, recognized as the bureau's most experienced tactical expert, had voiced similar concerns a year earlier in 1992 about the plan to use the same tactics against Randy Weaver in Ruby Ridge, Idaho. "At Ruby Ridge," Coulson says, "I turned down [the] plan to use the tanks and tear gas and [the use of] HRT operators to resolve the situation. Two other plans for a tactical resolution were also turned down. Ultimately negotiations succeeded and Weaver and his daughters came out and surrendered." In the Waco situation, Rogers's plans were approved by Attorney General Janet Reno, and it ended in tragedy that Coulson feels could have been averted.

"The more I found out about the ATF raid, the more outraged I was that anyone in authority had signed off on it," Coulson says in his 1999 book *No Heroes: Inside the FBI's Secret Counter-Terror Force*. Coulson is not shy about giving his opinion on controversial issues, including government coverups. "I'm not convinced that we've proven a coverup in the Waco operation yet," Coulson tells the authors in mid-March 2000.

Anti-government cynics, however, gleefully point to recently surfaced documents as proof that there was indeed a coverup in the Waco incident. According to reports such as "No Plan to Fight a Blaze?" (*Houston Chronicle* News Service, 3 March 2000) and "More Holes in FBI's Story About Siege?" (AP, 6 March 2000), not only did the ATF fire more pyrotechnic rounds into the Davidian compound than it previously admitted but, per on-scene commanders Jamar and Rogers, "there would be no plan to fight a fire should one develop."

Ironically, just as right-wing supremacists claim that the media's half-truths add up to outright lies about them, the same reportatorial tactics irk the other side as well. "We have to be fair," Coulson tells us. "There's no way a responsible commander would have allowed the fire trucks to come anywhere near the Davidian compound. Remember the Davidians were shooting at everyone. Their .50 cal rifle has a range of several thousand yards and will penetrate six feet of sand bags. Also, you do not fight a fire from the outside. You have to go into a building to put a fire out. The Davidians would have killed the firemen. Had the Davidians surrendered and set fire to the building on the way out the door, the fire department would have been used."

There is no question among the white nationalists or the right-wing patriot organizations such as the various militia that the government has become the enemy of the people. Yet it is still essentially shocking to witness such events as Waco, Ruby Ridge, and the Oklahoma City bombing. At the same time, even a cursory reading of American history informs that anti-government rhetoric and anti-government violence are as American as Mom's apple pie. And, just as political violence has historically been utilized in this country, we also have a long and established history of violence associated with labor, social issues, race and religion. Even amid seeming periods of peace and rumors of peace, such undercurrents lie at a shallow depth beneath the surface of American life.

When government is perceived as master rather than servant, particularly if one sees conspiracy afoot, does that justify taking up arms? There are any number of anti-government activists, both of the racialist and non-racialist variety, who believe that arms have become necessary. They are not the bloodless revolutionaries of ideas, but those willing to blow the whole thing apart, and they are preparing for war in the streets. Men like Louis Beam, who maintains that "where ballots fail, bullets will prevail" and Jim Stinson, whose cap is adorned with a rifle sight and the admonition to "Vote from the Roof Tops." There are Identity Christians who see the present government as a satanic entity and are so ultra-right they consider Pat Robertson "an apologist for the Jews." There are men who bomb federal buildings in their war against the one-world government that they believe operates against both the Constitution and Scriptural ordinance.

This brings us to the crux of the matter, the issue that drives many of these militant groups. When one believes that government, manipulated by both corporeal and supernatural forces, has evolved into an entity which is antithetical to all one considers right and even holy, does this create the right—perhaps even the duty—of revolution? When one's religious beliefs are discounted and pushed to the fringes of society, when one's rights are trampled by an out-of-control government, when one is forced against one's principles to commingle with other races, other nationalities, other faiths, when one is taxed to support the non-productive and taxed to promote pornography in the guise of art, and taxed to support the murderous and un-Christian practice of abortion, does this create the right to revolution?

These are questions raised by the the soldiers of God. And for them the answers are not difficult. In an elusive network purposely lacking centralized leadership, the constituents of this resistance are activist in a manner that is absolutely unfathomable to those who define themselves as part of the much more moderate religious right. For these activists, revolution is not lingering somewhere out on the horizon. It has already begun and it is most definitely *not* a bloodless revolution. The issues and the enemy are not abstract, but concrete. Most of these white revolutionaries are overtly racist and anti-government and most, although not all, are steeped in the faith of Christian Identity. And there is no doubt in their minds that God is on their side.

Patriots in these movements are aware that the majority of the white race in America is ignorant of their ideology, and most recognize that odds are stacked against them. But many see their mission as divine in origin. They are interacting, they are cooperating, and they have no pretensions toward effecting peaceful change.

As one member states, "This country will be a white Aryan homeland, or it will not be at all."

# CHAPTER THREE

# For God and Country: Grand Dragons, Pulpits, and the Ultimate Right

Most Americans are familiar with the old adage that, unless one wants to get into an argument, it is wise to avoid the topics of politics and religion. This holds true for both religious and political organizations. In a land where the separation of church and state is legislated, it is common among the movements to find religion more often than not married to politics in such a way that a clear distinction between the two is virtually impossible. For a significant portion of the constituents of the white supremacist movements, religion drives racialist politics and anti-federal sentiments.

Along with fellow Klansmen Jim Stinson and Cadillac John Thellin, Charles Lee adheres to Identity doctrine, the racialist theology as preached by Pastor Richard Butler of the Church of Jesus Christ Christian. Other adherents include former Grand Dragon of the Texas Knights Louis R. Beam, Imperial Wizard Darrell Flinn formerly of the Louisiana White Kamellia, and such men as Identity pastors Neumann Britton of California. With varying degrees of militancy and conflicting ideologies, others ministers of the Christian Israel Message include Pete Peters of Colorado; Everett Ramsey of Faith Baptist Church of Houston, Missouri; David Barley of America's Promise, Church and Ministries, Sandpoint, Idaho; and Earl Jones of Christian Crusade for Truth, Deming, New Mexico. Christian Identity, however, is not the only faith of the racialists. White nationalism encompasses many denominations. In fact, those who constitute the anti-federal government far right transcend numerous faiths, political philosophies, and visions for how America should be.

Carl D. Haggard, for instance, avid militia member and commander of several militia organizations, is a Catholic and maintains he holds no beliefs regarding racial superiority. However, he does see a plot to sell the United States out to the dreaded One-World Government. Mark, the leader of the Texas Aryan Nationalist Skinheads, was raised Catholic and recently converted to Identity. Tom Metzger, founder of White Aryan Resistance (WAR) is a former Identity believer and Klansman who now espouses atheism. Regardless of religious affiliations, those of the ultimate right share an intense distrust of government and an equally intense desire to re-form the nation along lines consistent with their own personal beliefs.

Almost to a man, the members of the right-wing organizations are able to speak to the confusion which results from the media's tendency—and the tendencies of so-called experts—to make distinctions between these autonomous organizations and the activities in which such organizations are engaged. Moreover, the racialists maintain that the media fail to take into consideration the religious basis for their beliefs. Without an understanding of faith, there is bound to be a misunderstanding of purpose.

"My racial beliefs are based on Scriptural teachings," Charles Lee states. "Without them, how could I possibly justify supremacy? I was talking to someone a while back—a member of the movement—who wasn't Identity. I asked him how he came to believe whites are superior. He couldn't answer. A lot of people believe that way. There's something inside that tells them they're different but they don't know what it is. Their eyes tell them they're different but they can't explain why. I know why. It's in the Bible.

"For me to just decide that another race is inferior, all of my own accord and with no Scriptural basis for that decision, would probably be sinful. It certainly wouldn't be right. But that's how we're portrayed— mindless, no beliefs, just mean and hateful. But racism is inside us all, we're born with it and it doesn't matter how anyone tries to explain that away. It's real. It's natural. Ignoring the difference is unnatural.

"As for our feelings about the federal government, that's another matter. As a Christian, I cannot set aside the laws of God for any laws of government. But even if I didn't hold those beliefs, I would still be anti-federal government because I can see what they are doing to this country. The media sees it, too. But they can't tell the truth because they're an extension of government. They certainly don't tell the truth wherever the movements are concerned.''

The racialists believe that truth is something that is in short supply in America. Because of the way they are portrayed in mainstream media and what they refer to as ''propaganda,'' many in the movements feel they are easy targets for sanctioned hate crimes and religious persecution.

Jim Stinson, former altar boy and Marine, now Identity Christian and Klansman, is well over six feet tall, lean, with large hands, a firm grip and easy smile. He is certainly not what one might imagine the average racist/terrorist to be. Short-cropped brown hair and a well-trimmed goatee seem to further punctuate his already-intense brown eyes. As he leans forward to speak, he rests his left forearm on the table, inadvertently displaying a complicated tattoo with a swastika, a cross, and other Aryan symbols woven into an intricate visual statement of his identity. Stinson believes that Klansmen and other racialists are convenient scapegoats for everything.

Again displaying the easy grin, he seems amused. ''You know there are all kinds of good Christians out there,'' he says. ''They don't hate anyone, right? That is, they don't hate anyone but us. We believe in our race and our God and we don't back away from that. That makes us the bad guys, the racists. It's open season on us.''

Both men believe they are victims of religious persecution on the part of the government. And, of course, they believe the government is part of a satanic conspiracy to destroy the white race. As far as they—and other members of the movements—are concerned, persecution from the federal government is not something hypothetical or subject to debate. It is real and ongoing.

Lee and Stinson contend that a short time prior to our interview, while on their way to a Klan gathering, they were pulled over by local law enforcement officers. Unlike ''regular'' citizens, they and other believers are considered terrorist elements. As such, they claim their drivers' licenses are tagged by the FBI. When the officer stopped them for a minor traffic violation and entered their identification information into his computer, it spit back reams of allegations and a minor incident became a major ordeal.

As Lee and Stinson point out, for Klansmen, skinheads, members of Aryan Nations and other separatist groups, such harassment is a fact of life.

But is it religious persecution? The Identity Christian knows it is. After all, as Lee says, would a group of Methodists be treated in the same manner? Doesn't the Bible explain that *true* Christians will be persecuted for their beliefs? "In fact, all who want to live devotedly in Christ will be persecuted. Everyone in the country has civil rights but us. And it *is* because of what we believe and *not* for anything we've done."

From the supremacist perspective, everyone is free to believe as they choose to believe *except* Identity Christians. Every other "secret" organization, such as a lodge or religious society other than Identity, is free to operate without federal interference. This further reinforces the "identity" of both the chosen and the satanic. Of course, Aryan Nations, Posse Comitatus and the Ku Klux Klan will never be mistaken for Boy Scout organizations, nor are they as reticent as the Quakers, or as passive as Jehovah's Witnesses. But it is the contention of the adherents to Christian Identity that the federal government, through its heavy-handed and illegal attempts to destroy them, forces them to extreme measures of self-defense.

At a Veteran's Day gathering in Vidor, Texas, on November 11, 1995, members of the Texas White Camelia and the Louisiana White Kamellia rallied at Gould Park to defy both state and federal governments, on the anniversary of the court-mandated desegregation of a federal housing project ordered by federal judge William Wayne Justice, enforced by then-HUD secretary Henry Cisneros, and later appealed to William Hale of the Texas Commission on Human Rights.

"That's exactly it," Charles Lee maintains. "We *defy* the government to tell us how to live, who to associate with, how to think, how to believe. It's not going to happen."

Charles Lee, as leader of White Camelia, was then and is presently involved in a court dispute with the state of Texas because of his refusal to disclose membership records of the organization, records he maintains do not exist. Lee also maintains that membership of White Camelia is not the issue.

"I imagine every law enforcement officer in the state already knows everyone ever associated with our organization for any reason—including you," he says with a grin. "That's not what's bothering them. What bothers them is that when they moved all those black people into the Vidor housing projects a while back [1992], the Klan had something to say about it. They can't do anything about that so they come up with this other thing. That's the way it works, I guess.

"Whenever the government says 'do this' we're expected to roll over for them. After all, they are the government and they know best, right? Well, some of us don't agree with that.''

At the rally, local law enforcement was certainly well represented. Orange County Sheriff's Department officers, Texas Department of Public Safety state troopers, and officers from the City of Vidor were all on the scene. Several officers patrolled the parking lot, apparently collecting license plate numbers from parked vehicles. Occasionally, an officer would ask visitors' names, where they were from, what they were doing. One county officer moved around the outskirts of the crowd with a video camera while several others took still photos. There were a few brief, resentful verbal exchanges between Klansmen and lawmen but, other than the creation of a tense atmosphere, there was no outbreak of trouble.

Klansmen, too, were well-armed with cameras. It presented a ludicrous scene, lawmen filming Klansmen filming lawmen filming Klansmen. Lee was angry about the whole situation. So was his attorney, Rife Scott Kimler, of Port Arthur, Texas, who was also at the rally.

''That's the intimidation,'' Lee said. ''There's no one out here but us—and them. They're the reason no one else is coming around. Look at it, they're taking license plate numbers and running them. You don't call that intimidation? What else can you expect from the KGB?''

Kimler concurred. ''Ask the police why they're taking pictures. Why are they running license numbers of people who haven't done anything? These citizens here haven't broken any laws. But they are having their rights to peaceful assembly compromised.''

David Bailey, the Orange County officer in charge of the operation, responded. ''We're just doing our jobs and no one's rights are being violated. Their people are filming us, too.''

One officer posed for a Klan photographer, pushing back his jacket to clearly expose his badge. Charles Lee walked away in disgust. Even though he has learned to live with such situations, he still does not like them. ''You never get used to having your rights violated,'' he remarked.

Officer Bailey takes all the posturing in stride. ''It's no big deal. They come out here from time to time to do their thing. Sort of reestablish their presence here. My thing is to make sure there's no trouble, and there isn't. Maybe we do scare away some who might have come here but I doubt if we scare away many. This is the way it usually goes, just us and them. I don't expect any trouble.''

But many on the racial right do expect trouble, and cite Gordon Kahl's case as an early example. In the late '70s, Gordon Kahl, the infamous tax rebel and member of Posse Comitatus, in a letter to the IRS, "resigned" from the United States and announced he would no longer "tithe to the Synagogue of Satan." Gordon Kahl refused to pay his taxes. He didn't lie. He didn't cheat. He didn't falsify income reports. He simply refused to pay taxes. Kahl identified the United States government as satanic and the progressive income tax system as the second plank of the Communist Party platform. Gordon Kahl openly avowed to follow the laws of God rather than the laws of man. Because he did this openly, because he challenged the satanic system, Kahl was convinced he would be killed.

The federal government, it seems, was content to allow Kahl to go his own way in this matter. The taxes he owed, a very small portion of a very small income, were perhaps considered not worthy of the effort of collection. But Kahl's seeming immunity from federal prosecution came to an abrupt end when he began to organize and recruit for Posse Comitatus, urging others to also resign from the system and refuse to pay taxes. He even went so far as to appear on television to explain what he was doing and why. Government interest in this Midwestern farmer was suddenly very piqued indeed.

On Sunday, February 13, 1983, in Medina, North Dakota, U.S. Marshals tried to serve an arrest warrant on Kahl for misdemeanor probation violation. Kahl didn't see it as something that simple. He and his companions were convinced the marshals were there to assassinate him. Along with his son Yorie, friend Scott Faul and several others, Kahl defied the marshals' orders to surrender and a bloody shootout ensued. When the smoke cleared, Federal Marshal Ken Muir and Deputy Marshal Robert Cheshire were dead. In a letter written after the shootout (our copy provided by Kingdom Identity Ministries of Arkansas; the letter also included in Ridgeway's *Blood in the Face),* Kahl gives the details of that encounter and, in effect, declares war against the government he had once served valiantly in the Army Air Corps:

> We are a conquered and occupied nation; conquered and occupied by the Jews . . . They have two objectives in their goal of ruling the world. Destroy Christianity and the White race.

> We are engaged in a struggle to the death between the people of the Kingdom of God, and the kingdom of Satan. It started long ago, and is now best described as a struggle between Jacob & Esau.

> . . . Should the hand of Elijah's God continue to be over me and protect me, I shall someday see this once great nation swept clean of Christ's enemies,

and restored to it's former greatness. . . . God has said that there will be a great shaking in the Land of Israel. That started this evening. Let each of you who says that the Lord Jesus Christ, is your personal Savior sell his garment and buy a sword, if you don't already have one . . .

If you've been paying tithes to the Synagogue of Satan, under the 2nd plank of the Communist Manifesto to finance your own destruction, stop right now . . . remove your support from the anti-Christs who rule our nation.

. . . I have no idea where I'm going, but after some more prayer, I will go where the Lord leads me, and either live to carry on the fight, or die if that be the case, and for the present at least, I bid you all good-bye.

Gordon Kahl, Christian Patriot

God led Gordon Kahl to an Arkansas farmhouse near the town of Smithville where a task force of law enforcement officers including FBI and U.S. Marshal SWAT teams brought about the confrontation he had been predicting for years. Less than four months after the deaths of Marshals Muir and Cheshire, on the afternoon of June 3, 1983, Kahl's prophecy was fulfilled. Gordon Kahl and Lawrence County Sheriff Gene Matthews shot and killed one another.

At least that is the official government version. An Identity minister and friend of Kahl's who was close to the incident claims that both Kahl and Matthews were shot in the back. They could not have killed each other, he says, "unless they had arms forty feet long." This is only one of many inaccuracies allegedly represented as facts by government sources. "Death and Taxes," an account of Gordon Kahl's campaign and death, is chronicled on videotape, and Kahl's widow Joan (who later married Identity Pastor Neumann Britton) tells on audiotape a story entirely different from the official account. Louis Beam, a prodigious essayist and frequent contributor to white nationalist web sites, publisher of *The Seditionist,* and frequent contributor to the alternative press *Jubilee,* waxes poetic in his tribute to Kahl with the work "At Last! We Have a Hero," printed in Ridgeway's *Blood in the Face* which contains the verse,

My countrymen led deep into the tunnel of eternal slavery,
I now lead them out with light from the barrel of my Mini-14.

Gordon Kahl is indeed a hero among the anti-government movements. A man can be pushed only so far until striking back is his only recourse. Other Gordon Kahls, other Christian patriots, will take up the fight.

The late Wesley Swift, founder of Church of Jesus Christ Christian, preached the doctrine of race as religion and the necessity of resisting the satanic Zionist Occupational Government. Richard G. Butler, former aircraft executive, carries on that message at Church of Jesus Christ Christian in Hayden Lake, Idaho, where he founded Aryan Nations as the political arm of the church. Butler, James Wickstrom of Michigan, James Bruggeman of North Carolina, Rick Strawcutter and Charles Weisman of Michigan and other Christian Identity ministers and speakers of note believe the government is controlled by Jews who intend destruction for the white race. They also believe the government has gone far beyond any constitutional authority it may have traditionally held and certainly beyond what they feel is the Scriptural underpinning which forms the foundation for that authority.

Although mainstream Christian churches and Identity churches do not necessarily ally themselves with one another, they often do share the same concerns about the role and function of government. Jack Van Impe, Pat Robertson, Jimmy Swaggert, Oral and Richard Roberts and many other televangelists, as well as countless mainstream and fundamentalist ministers throughout the country, rail against the anti-Christian policies of the federal government. Some, such as Van Impe, are positively steeped in conspiracy theory and the apocalyptic visions of Revelation. Yet some of these spiritual politicians also marginalize the Identity Christians while holding, or at least appearing to hold, many of the same beliefs. Charles Lee maintains that it is primarily a lack of courage which keeps many white Americans found in the congregations of such leaders from admitting to innate racial beliefs, even to themselves.

And as for the leaders, they are free to rail as much as they like— within certain limits.

"Many Ko$her con$ervative preachers, talk show hosts, and others who oppose the government are left untouched," writes Michael K. Hallimore of Kingdom Identity Ministries of Harrison, Arkansas, in a personal communication. "There is still freedom to express virtually any viewpoint without pressure being brought to bear, as long as it is not offensive to the Jews. To pretend otherwise is to bury one's head in the sand. A legitimate look into the subject of race, specifically the Jewish problem, is considered taboo."

Is Judeo-Christianity tied into this persecutorial conspiracy? Cadillac John Thellin, an outspoken and passionate member of the Klan, explains in a taped Bible study, *"Judeo* and *Christian* are two words that cannot go together. *Judeo,* in Latin, means 'Jew-God.' How do real Christians worship a Jew God? It can't be done. It's a false religion." And if Judeo-Christianity, which basically refers to *any* Christian faith which recognizes anyone other than Aryans as the chosen—and that pretty well covers all other denominations in Christendom—is a false faith, then what are we to think of its ministers?

This is not a difficult question for an Identity Christian: most ministers other than Christian Identity ministers are false prophets.

Some Identity Christians may conclude that such false prophets are innocently false. That is, they have been taught lies, lies far removed from the truth of the Scriptures and, as a result, continue to perpetuate those lies in the guise of truth. Thus, the ministers are not necessarily intentional liars. However, innocent or not, a false teaching is a false teaching and no matter how it originated, it is still not the Word of God, the Word of Yahweh. Far from leading the flock down the righteous path, mainstream ministers lead their followers down the path to destruction—racial, social and spiritual destruction.

And Identity Christians also believe that the Laws of God cannot be supplanted by the laws of man. These laws, they avow, were the seeds of the American nation which flourished as long as God's Laws were observed.

Stinson, Thellin and Lee are all proponents of American values, the values of our forefathers, and they believe that their interpretation of these values is the correct interpretation. From their perspective, they see themselves as defenders of the American way of life they believe to be presently under attack by those in the government and traditional Judeo-Christian religions. Other white supremacist organizations hold the same beliefs. Richard Butler's Church of Jesus Christ Christian is not merely a gathering place for like-minded believers to gather and worship Yahweh. It is the political, spiritual and social core of Aryan Nations.

Those who meet annually at the Hayden Lake compound are seekers, pilgrims searching for other pilgrims like themselves. They hold beliefs which are often scorned or ridiculed by mainstream society as mean-spirited, hateful, out-of-date, old-fashioned, ignorant. But, even as they embrace the fellowship of other true believers, they are aware that this scorn merely punctuates the truth they already know. Jesus, himself, has told them:

If the world hate you, ye know it hated me before it hated you. If ye were of the world, the world would love his own; but because ye are not of the world, but I have chosen you out of the world, therefore the world hateth you.   (JOHN 15:18–19)

In the early 1980s, from the ranks of Aryan Nations came a violently militant sub-organization known as The Order. Founded by the late Bob Mathews (an Odinist, rather than Identity Christian), who was killed in a shootout with federal agents in 1983, The Order put separatist beliefs into action and engaged in a series of revolutionary acts which included armed robbery, murder and counterfeiting.

In a televised interview on ABC's *Turning Point* on 5 September 1995, Denver Parmenter, former member of The Order imprisoned for these crimes, commented on his own conversion experience: "This Identity doctrine gave me a view of the Bible that I said, 'Wow, this is it. This is the reason things are going wrong.'"

Things are certainly going wrong in the eyes of the Aryan faithful. God's Laws are violated, nature's laws are violated, and race mixing, crime, drugs, and an ever-tightening yoke of tyranny plague the land of the white Israelites. Denver Parmenter, along with the other members of The Order, took direct action in accordance with the faith afforded through such new insight by launching a rebellion against ZOG. The rebellion, in the eyes of the Identity Christian, is obviously sanctioned by Yahweh through the Scriptures:

Put on the whole armour of God, that ye may be able to stand against the wiles of the devil.

For we wrestle not against flesh and blood, but against principalities, against powers, against spiritual wickedness in high places.   (EPHESIANS 6:11–12)

Denver Parmenter, in his television interview, expressed disbelief that the average American could be surprised by such events as Oklahoma City and other acts of domestic terrorism. "Why?" he asked. "That's what we did."

But as a nation, we are surprised. Surprised, fascinated, horrified and confused every time a new plot is uncovered. The series of bomb detonations and bank robberies in Spokane, the bombs set off in Atlanta—at Olympics Park, at a gay night club, at an abortion clinic—the plot by a militia organization to destroy the FBI central records building in Virginia, all these are deeply disturbing events to the general public. However, for the Identity Christian, they have an even deeper significance. The destruction of federal banks and government offices—all part of ZOG— and of buildings dedicated to murder and homosexuality indicate an awakening among the children of Yahweh. These events are merely more evidence that scriptural prophecy is being fulfilled.

If revolution is afoot, and many in the movements believe it is, then we should not too hastily decide that the outcome is a foregone conclusion. After all, as Cadillac John points out, the Boston Massacre was not the most auspicious of omens for the patriots who fought the first American Revolution. The Aryan warriors of the far right—outmanned, outgunned—are firmly committed to their cause. And each knows his God is with him. Lighted crosses call the faithful—the children of Yahweh, true Israel—to the holy unity of the Servant Nation, the Anointed of God.

In his taped Bible study, Cadillac John observes, "The other day I was watching a film on one of those idiotic Jews and they said, 'you can't win.' Ladies and Gentlemen, I've got a little book here. That book is the *Holy Bible*. That book says I can't lose."

# CHAPTER FOUR

# White Israel

If one is to understand the political and social positions of the Identity racialist organizations, it is necessary to first understand the religious faith around which such world views are constructed.

Christian Identity holds that the Aryan race, not the Jews, is true Israel. The term *Aryan,* used to describe a racial type, is a common though technically incorrect usage. *Aryan* originates from the Sanskrit "arya" or "noble" and is more properly used to describe an ethnic type descended from early speakers of Indo-European language. In a modern sense, the term is broadened to include more than linguistic stock, and is used to describe the Caucasoid racial type as well. To frame the term more specifically, for those in the movements—like the Nazis of the Hitler era—it refers only to those who are of Anglo-Saxon, Scandinavian, Celtic or Teutonic descent. For Identity Christians, it also refers to a race of people who are special to God and superior because of His favor, a race bound by the Laws of God and charged with enforcing those Laws throughout the earth. This is the "identity" of the Identity Christians and the key factor defining white supremacists.

White supremacy, in America, is a very old concept. The sentiments of anti-Semitism were unpacked in the New World, along with much other European baggage, by the very first settlers on this continent. British Israelism was carried by Puritans into the New World, Pilgrim colonists who sang "Ye chosen seed of Israel's race" and read from *The Book of*

*Common Prayer,* "Now we, brethren, as Isaac was, are the children of promise" (The Fourth Sunday in Lent), who favored the Geneva transla-tion of the Bible and preached the Doctrine of the Elect. While Protestant denominations in the developing colonies did not always clearly label their Anglo-Israelite teachings as "White Israel," tensions as a result of slavery heightened the awareness of racism as slave-owners viewed blacks as inferior "beasts of the field" and white superiority became a prominent element in Anglo-Israelism. Thus racism, as expressed in the movements, is rooted not only in religious belief but in history as well.

Manifest Destiny, the belief in the pre-ordained and divine destiny of white Americans to rule the continent of North America, led to wars of attrition and genocide and forced Native Americans to live on reservations. The "white man's burden" was carried throughout the world through colonization in Africa, North America, South America, the Hawaiian Islands, Asia, and the Middle East throughout the nineteenth and twentieth centuries.

In the United States, the official policy of Manifest Destiny was one governmental program that met with success. As noted on one of the posters of WAR (White Aryan Resistance) *White Men Built This Country; White Men* **Are** *This Country.* From an Identity perspective, it is not just the white race, but white Christians in particular who are responsible for the building of America. Hence, it is clear that the present beliefs of the white separatists are very much in tune with those of the Christian founding fathers. Were these pioneer builders early Identity Christians?

"Of course." Charles Lee smiles as he answers. "Identity is simply Christianity before the Jews got hold of it. *Judeo-Christianity* is the strange religion. My religion is simply old-time religion, straight from the Scriptures, straight from God." Lee believes Identity to be the true Christianity encompassing the laws of both the Old and the New Testa-ments. He argues that this is the body of beliefs professed by Jesus of Nazareth, and the beliefs that true Christians still profess. "If I weren't a Christian," he says, ". . . well, I don't know what I'd be if I weren't a Christian."

Cadillac John concurs: "Make no mistake about it, white racists built this country. White Christian slave-owners. I'm a Christian and a racist and I'm not about to apologize to anyone for that."

For those who adhere to segregationist or supremacist beliefs, the bloodline and the faith must be kept pure. Since the settlers of the original thirteen colonies were primarily white Protestant and many were slave-owners, this led to some rather radical ideas by present standards, ideas which were and still are commonly accepted as fact by many in the movements. On the issue of race, it was not uncommon prior to and after the Civil War to hear even mainstream Christians speak of the black race as the "Simionadae," the highest order of ape, the only apes capable of language.

Identity Christians, such as Cadillac John, do not back off from such beliefs in the name of political correctness. Some white supremacists refer to non-whites as "mud-people" or the "muds." This is based on the Dualist (another Identity variation) belief that Satan, trying to usurp the role and function of God, formed the dark races from mud in a parody of the creation. Some Identity ministers maintain that the correct term is "pre-Adamite." Both terms carry the same significance.

In pre-Civil War America, the idea of Christianizing slaves and Indians was one which was held as somewhat blasphemous by many white Americans. Or, if not blasphemous, the idea was seen as something of a quaint amusement occasionally equated with Samuel Johnson's observation about women preachers as "like a dog walking on its hind legs. It is not done well, but you are surprised to find it done at all."

Charles Lee notes that most Identity Christians, himself included, view the notion of sending missionaries to Africa or other non-white countries as a bit ridiculous. "They may be around in the afterlife, probably will be," he says, "but it will be through natural birth and death. They aren't Israel and they can't become Israel. It's not their fault, it's just the way it is." Cadillac John is a bit more candid as he tells the audience that "niggers don't have souls."

Mike Hallimore, an Identity theologian from Arkansas, explains a Seed-line Identity principle that qualifies this contention. Adamic man, the white race, the descendants of Adam, he says, "are trichotomous, composed of body and soul and spirit. Only Adamic man has the potential for eternal life." Pre-Adamites (the dark races) have only body and soul. The spirit has no relation to intellect. There are intelligent blacks and intelligent Jews, but IQ doesn't matter. "It isn't the mental difference, but the spiritual difference," he says. "All races have a type of salvation, but not eternal life."

Whereas more traditional Dispensational theology revolves around salvation through faith and faith alone to enter the family of God, White Israelism revolves around the idea of the chosenness of a specific people as the children of God. This does not mean, however, that the darker races cannot benefit from true Israel. Aryans have exported the Christian way of life all over the globe so that everyone could live a more productive and stable way of life. But Lee observes, "Somewhere along the way, we fell into a trap of lies and deceit and our people have lost their way. Our people will never know where we are going and who we are until we get back our true identity of God's chosen people—Israel."

R. B. Thieme, Jr., pastor of Berachah Church in Houston, Texas, has examined this issue of chosenness for over fifty years. A veteran of World War II, Thieme studied at Dallas Theological Seminary and claims extensive academic training in Greek, Hebrew, theology, history and textual criticism. He translates Scripture from the original languages in the course of his sermons, which have the flavor of a theological lecture class. Thieme is the prolific author of theological/historical books and tracts (which he gives away or accepts donations for) through his R. B. Thieme, Jr., Bible Ministries.

Although Thieme's views on the Scriptures are not universally accepted among the members of the various Christian denominations (and given the often wide diversities of belief, this should not be surprising), he is still one of the few mainstream ministers to openly address the faith of Christian Identity. In his 1991 book *Anti-Semitism,* he articulates the basic orthodox Christian belief that the Jews are the "chosen" and therefore are bound to a separate relationship with God which encompasses Old Testament rules and covenants that do not bind non-Jewish peoples. In this perspective, Thieme does make a distinction between the historical British Israelite movement and the American brand that calls itself Christian Identity. British Israelites, he says, are "mixed up Gentiles" that have usurped the title *Israel* and deny the Jews their rightful place in God's plan. Only a few scattered groups of historic British Israelites remain in the United States, by his estimate, but "an even more sinister group, a pseudo-Christian movement called 'Identity churches,' has incorporated these false teachings into an even more virile guise." Thieme calls Identity "so-called churches" that are essentially hate-mongers that promote the superiority of the white race and says that "Relentless vilification of the Jews and racial bigotry are the cornerstones of their blasphemous 'theology.' "

Identity Christians are accustomed to hearing such judgments, as well as being called hate groups. However, it must be noted that it is not uncommon among religious factions to hear one group speak of the beliefs of the other as "heresy," and such labels may be expected to be leveled against any group that holds itself apart.

One cannot overlook the separatism that defines "the Chosen." This holds true in any serious examination of the Scriptures. The inherent overtones in the Christian Bible or the Jewish holy books—the Pentateuch (the first five books of the Old Testament), the Talmud, the Mishnah (a collection of oral laws compiled by Rabbi Judah in the second century A.D.)—and the implications of separatist instructions contained therein are obvious. But if one substitutes the players, Aryans for Jews, then one is beginning to understand the underpinning beliefs of separatism that define Christian Identity.

The point here is not that one group is innately superior to the other, but that each group claims a "specialness," a divine distinction that separates it from the others. The Jewish people, in this sense, use the same criteria as other groups in regard to defining their ethnocentric identity. There is no denying that the Talmudic writings compiled over the centuries bear witness to the extent to which Jews, as an autonomous group, are commanded to hold themselves above, or at least apart from, Gentile peoples. However, the presence of this phenomenon in their beliefs does not make them unique among the peoples of the world. In fact, it merely illustrates this odd commonality of the "us" superiority and—as some of our subjects have pointed out—few dare to hang the term "Jewish Supremacist" on adherents to this particular system of belief.

Identity Christians point out that other groups do this as well. Catholics, historically, have denied the idea that any non-Catholic can enter the Kingdom of Heaven. Jehovah's Witnesses refuse to serve in the military or swear allegiance to the flag or, as a rule, pray with non-Jehovah's Witnesses. Therefore, the same faith which serves to unify a people also serves to separate them from other peoples, and the desire for a separate nation of like-believers is not uncommon. Jews, after all, established a separate homeland for themselves in 1948. Israel *is* a Jewish homeland— although there are many non-Jewish citizens living there—and, in order for that homeland to exist, quite a few Palestinians were given their walking papers. Christian Identity white separatists whose goal is to establish an Aryan homeland plan to issue similar walking papers to non-whites who might be living in the territory at the moment.

Christian Identity, it seems, is a rather well-kept secret in America. Those who do note its existence often have a visceral and profound reaction to its tenets. The usual response is to discount the movement as an attempt by racists to cover hateful and perhaps illegal activities with the cloak of religion. This may, however, be too simplistic an explanation. Perhaps, considering the traditional tenets of more mainstream faiths, such a position might be equivalent to saying Judeo-Christians believe in forgiveness and tolerance to cover their natural tendencies toward weakness and cowardice.

Charles Lee believes Identity to be the true Christianity, which entails the laws of both the Old and the New Testaments. He argues that Identity *is* the Christianity professed by Jesus of Nazareth. The Old Testament prophesies the coming of the Messiah, and the New Testament records the coming of the Messiah who fulfills the prophecy.

R. B. Thieme's assertions of blasphemy notwithstanding, Charles Lee is a true believer. So are thousands of other Identity Christians. The fact that they are attacked, marginalized, discounted and denigrated by other faiths does not deter them in their beliefs or the intensity with which they believe. Because they see themselves as God's chosen, they expect such resistance since they are engaged in mortal combat with the forces of Satan. And, like many other Christian sects, they believe they are blessed through the persecution they may experience at the hands of unbelievers.

Christian Identity is the philosophical basis of both White Camelia and Aryan Nations. It is the belief that drives numerous racialist entities. It is both an organizational principle and a link between many otherwise autonomous groups. To understand how these particular white suprema-cists interact, one must first understand the tenets of Christian Identity and specific interpretation of Scriptures as outlined in their Bible study.

However, it must also be noted that there are variations in the Identity doctrine. "Identity" is every bit as broad a term as "Protestant" or "Jewish" and certainly does not explain the full range of beliefs that may be lumped under this generalized umbrella. British Israelism, Christian Identity, Covenant theology, and "Seedline" Doctrine all refer to some of the same basic concepts and beliefs, yet there are also vast doctrinal gulfs which are not easily bridged. One Covenant Identity theologian from the West Coast notes that whereas "Identity" certainly covers the idea that the white race is the true Israel of the Bible, some Covenant Christians are now prone to shy away from the term because of its association with violent racialist movements and "hot-heads who have taken one concept and run with it." He goes on to state, "I believe the whole thing is part of the concentrated attack on Christianity and an attempt to discredit everyone through the actions of a few."

E. Raymond Capt, biblical archeologist and adherent to Covenant theology, says, "For every one of the militants who profess Identity beliefs, there are a thousand other believers who do not prescribe to their particular doctrine." Capt has written a number of scholarly books and booklets, as well as producing documentary films through his Covenant Media Productions, to address the migration of the tribes of Israel to Europe and other Biblical topics. Though he, too, believes in the concept of White Israel, Capt's perception of the role of the chosen is much different from the militant perception held by such racialist entities as Aryan Nations.

"The Chosen are to be a blessing to all mankind," Capt says. "I'll teach Christ to anyone—black, brown, white, yellow—it doesn't matter, anyone. *All* of God's creations are good." Capt maintains that the idea of White Israel is not a declaration of war on other races and notes that the concept has a long and established history in all Christian faiths. "Identity" then, for most Covenant Christians, is not a denomination such as Baptist or Methodist, but rather an article of belief that transcends doctrinal differences. As for the mission of the racial right and the question of the Jews, Capt explains, "The Bible says to leave them alone, don't touch them. Even if the whole notion of demon-seed were true, God does not command us to do anything about it. Tares grow among the wheat and God and His angels will take care of that—*God and His angels*. I don't see how it can be much clearer than that."

"Seedline" Identity Christians draw an altogether different conclusion and they do not see how their view can be much clearer, either. The "Seedline" doctrine holds that just as the white race is chosen of God, Jews are the demon-seed, literal descendants of Satan. Seedline is the racial branch of Identity that defines the origin of the struggle between good and evil, the faith that is embraced by the racial right. Interpretation of some points might vary among the believers, but to Seedline adherents there is no question that the basic truths are in the Bible if people will take the trouble to study correctly.

Christian Identity, whether the militant Seedline or the milder Covenant variety, hinges on Bible study and the concept that mainstream orthodox Christendom is misled through both unintentional and intentional mistranslation of Scripture. Thus, they reason, if the Word of God is changed, it is no longer the Word of God. And if a faith is built around false Scripture, it is a false faith. The truth can be determined, but it requires a careful study of existing biblical translations. To accept each or any particular translation as an unquestionable document would be to presume that every

Bible in Christendom is a verbatim duplication of the original manuscript. Identity holds that nothing is further from the truth and that every Bible translation has errors. Once the errors have been ferreted out, the truth will remain. And the truth is unquestionable, direct from God, and the authority from which all civilized law is derived.

The ancient texts which constitute the Old Testament were initially written in Hebrew (with portions in Aramaic), and the New Testament with its earliest translations in Greek. In the full-scale English translation of the entire Bible, commissioned by King James and completed in 1611— now called the King James Version—scholars translated directly from Hebrew (the Old Testament) and Greek (the New Testament). Together these two volumes constitute the *Holy Bible*. Christian Identity theology maintains that *only* the Testaments as originally written by the prophets can be accepted as the Word of God. The rub is that most people cannot read them in their original languages and must depend on translations, thereby creating the possibility of distortion in the intended message. No matter how meticulous the translations are, errors, however unintentional, can occur when words or phrases in an idiomatic context do not translate well into another language, much less across several translations. In some cases, literal word-for-word translation cannot be made at all. Therefore, constant referencing and cross-referencing of the texts must be made to discern true meaning.

Identity theologians maintain that truth is in woefully short supply in so-called "Christian" denominational churches across America and that Christians in general are indeed ignorant of the very faith they claim, mainly because of the narrowness of their study. Christians must believe in the entire Bible—*both* books—and *both* must be studied to discover meaning. Churchgoers who disregard the Old Testament might be skeptical of its history or its miracles, or be confused by its prophecies, or reject the laws set forth in it because they believe the laws are repudiated by the New Testament. From the Identity perspective, these are New Testament Christians and, through their false beliefs, they are in grave error.

New Testament Christians, as Identity adherents reason, may well be ignorant of scriptural truth. Though they speak confidently of the doctrines of their faith, they have difficulty locating the source of these doctrines in the New Testament when called upon to do so. They believe, not because they have discovered these principles in the Bible, but because they have been taught them from the pulpit, swallowed them whole at Sunday School, been firmly convinced by false prophets and teachers.

And many Identity Christians hold that a number of these false doctrines are so blatant that they cannot possibly have resulted from accidental misinterpretation of Scripture. This, then, leads the Seedline Identity Christian to pose some important questions.

Is God actually so incompetent that He had to repeal all of His old laws, cancel all promises, ignore all prophecies and start over again with a project He could handle? Is the Old Testament a chronicle of God's mistakes? Is it possible for a valid religion to be organized around a bungling deity who made so many mistakes without even knowing He was wrong? Around a deity so weak, He cannot even enforce His own will once He recognizes it?

Charles Lee does not think so. "I am a messenger," he says. "I spread the Gospel. Some people call it the Gospel of Hatred. I call it the Gospel of Jesus Christ. Christianity is not just in the New Testament, it is in the Old Testament, too. Proof of the New is found in the Old." And it is a Gospel intended for White Israel.

It is Lee's contention that "Judeo-Christians" are blinded by misunderstanding and unable to defend the faith against atheism, agnosticism, Communism, non-Christian faiths and other entities which seek to destroy it. Because of the tenuous nature of their understanding, due to the efforts of those who deliberately mislead them, they can offer only their faith's denominational attitude in defense. And they may well receive the judgment that awaits the ignorant as well as the un-Godly:

> My people are destroyed for lack of knowledge: because thou hast rejected knowledge, I will also reject thee, that thou shalt be no priest to Me: seeing thou hast forgotten the Law of thy God, I will also forget thy children. (HOSEA 4:6)

The message of the Identity Christians is that the Bible is actually *one* book, though presented in two parts. And no one can fully understand one part without the other. Christianity, they maintain, is as prevalent in the Old Testament as in the New but more difficult to recognize because Old Testament Christianity is in the form of symbols, prophecies and rituals. Once this linkage is ascertained, the recognition of the totality of the faith, the truth, according to God and the prophets, becomes apparent. This, in actuality, is not a radical departure from more conventional forms of Christianity.

However, the Identity interpretation of what this truth establishes *is* a radical departure and is the underpinning element of Christian Identity, both its milder Covenant Theology branch and its militant Seedline branch: the truth of God, as revealed in the Scriptures and the fulfillment of God's promises to *His* people, establishes the true identity of the Israelites, which has been for so long concealed from them.

For Identity Christians it establishes the white race as Israel just as Christ used the Old Testament to establish his own identity: "Search the Scriptures; for in them ye think ye have eternal life: and they are they which testify of me" (John 5:39).

Christian Identity holds that Aryans are the true Israel people, the true heirs of the Covenants, the true guardians of God's law, in essence, the agents of God on earth.

Essential to the faith is the belief that Old Testament laws have *not* been repealed or revoked. As Christ himself states, "Think not that I am come to destroy the Law or the Prophets: I am not come to destroy, but to fulfill" (Matthew 5:17). The reasoning then is that the only Laws of God which have changed are the ones called "ordinances" which are those relating to the rules of feast days, sacrifices and offerings. Ordinances, in the Old Testament, illustrate the faith of the ancient Christians that Christ is *to come*. Modern Christianity hinges on the belief that Christ has *already come*. Therefore, the ordinances no longer apply.

All other biblical law is still in effect. Charles Lee explains, "If God's laws are known, kept, and enforced, then we, as a nation, will not experience all the troubles we're experiencing now. Economic laws ensure prosperity, agricultural and dietary laws ensure health, moral laws ensure tranquility, justice, and decency—the kind of things we used to both have and expect in this country. The political laws of the Scriptures ensure authority and respect. The Bible has laws governing immigration and naturalization to protect the integrity of the various races and nations, to ensure the purity of blood that is necessary to preserve all the various peoples Yahweh has created. Laws that command racial separation of His people ensure their survival. In short, Old Testament law provides the basis necessary to bring forth and maintain a high civilization."

Identity Christians believe that if one is to understand God's message in the Scriptures, one must not only be aware of accurate translation but must also understand the players in the divine drama. The identity of true Israel is then revealed through prophecy, and fulfillment of the covenants is revealed in the two books. This endeavor links Israel to the true God and Ruler of all.

How such connections are made can be discerned by examining the tenets of the Christian Identity movement and how they hinge upon particular covenants: God has a name and it is Yahweh. Yahweh is the God of the Israelites, His chosen people, and an active agent in the lives of His people. Satan is also a real and active agent on earth. Also known by his angelic name Lucifer "the Light Bearer," he is a component of the "Angelic Conflict" doctrine which declares that the enmity between God and Satan is not metaphoric, but is instead an actual and ongoing conflict which will last until the return of Christ. At this time, or at the end of the thousand-year reign, the defeated Satan will be "cast into the pit" as Christ sets up His reign on earth.

The origin of this conflict was begun before the Old Testament. Satan, originally an archangel charged by Yahweh to be a "governor" of the earth, had his own agenda and that agenda included usurping the "identity" of God. For his audacity, his rebellion, Satan was cast from Heaven, along with his minions who joined him in rebellion, and was doomed to be "reserved in everlasting chains under darkness" (Jude 1:6). It is the intention of this evil Prince of the World to destroy the white race—the Adamites who are descended from the first white man—to make wars upon them and to wipe them from the face of the earth, and this enmity is still expressed today. Seedline Identity holds that just as there is a people of God, there is also a direct lineage of Satan, and these two lineages are set against one another now and forever. For Seedline Identity Christians, Jews are the children of Satan.

The proof that Seedline adherents have of the anti-Christ nature of racial Jews, of Judaism in general, is evident in the rejection of Christ and His crucifixion at the hands of the Jews (even though the physical act of crucifixion was carried out by the Romans). However, the redemptive nature of Christ's first mission was completed with his corporeal death as a man at Calvary when he stated, "It is finished." Christ's next coming will *not* be as savior of the individual, and the Identity Christian knows that it will not do to greet His next arrival with doubt and a cross.

But the salient issue of Christian Identity is the matter of deception. Even as the Pharisees of old rejected Jesus as the Christ, He is still being rejected by the Pharisees of modern Christendom and their Jewish cohorts. Their efforts serve to keep true Israel blind to its own identity, unaware of its disconnection from Yashua, Christ the Messiah, and from the promise of Yahweh.

Thus, the greatest act of deception in all of history is the Jews' usurpation of the title "Israelite." This crime against the true Israelites—the Aryans—has been abetted by orthodox Christendom and can be ascertained through biblical understanding. However, those who adhere to the Seedline branch of Identity maintain that exposing the deception is a tall order.

Seedline theologian Mike Hallimore of Kingdom Identity Ministries based in Harrison, Arkansas, notes that many churches in Christendom have traditionally taught the concept of Anglo-Israel, including the Mormons, Baptists, Methodists and Pentecostals. He also contends that this is not conjecture, that the books are out there for anyone to see. At the same time, the idea of Anglo-Israel is very much in disfavor today and he holds that resistance to the truth is demonstrated most vociferously by the Jews. "The enmity comes not because we identify with Israel, the 'seed of the woman,'" he says, "but because we expose the other side of the equation, the 'seed of the serpent.'"

Seedline beliefs notwithstanding, British Israelism, Covenant theology and variations within Christian Identity all point to the biblical covenants as the "fingerprints" by which true Israel may be identified. And Identity doctrine maintains that these fingerprints belong to Anglo-Israel, the heirs to the covenants.

# CHAPTER FIVE

# Heirs to the Covenants

**A**dam was not the first man.

The *American Institute of Theology* (AIT) Bible study guide, which reflects Seedline interpretation, discusses in detail this pivotal issue. God would make His covenants with His chosen people and, as the AIT explains, they were *not* the first of His creations. In Genesis 1:25–28, the Bible tells of the sixth day when God created beasts of the earth, and He created *men,* in the plural: "Male and female created He THEM. . . . The Bible makes it unmistakably clear that we are not all descended from Adam and Eve, for there were other races on earth, already old, already numerous, when Adam was formed."

Not until after the seventh day when God had rested did He create Adam— the first *white man*—and, unlike the nameless beasts, Adam's name is the clue to his identity. The AIT's Chapter 9 "Adam and Eve" explains:

> In the next chapter, Genesis 2, we find THE ADAM (in the singular) formed. The Hebrew word, "aw-dawm" (rendered "Adam" in English) is from a root word meaning "To show blood in the face" or "of a ruddy complexion" . . . a word obviously not applicable to the dark races, which we know from scientific evidence to be much older than the White Race.

> . . . It follows that Eve (which means "life-giver"), being Adamic, could not have mothered the earlier Yellow or Black races; an idea which is only a popular misconception engendered by fallacious Christian Education.

Identity points to the order of creation to demonstrate that beasts of the earth, male and female, were created in God's image—that is, with God's shape—but lacking a complexion light enough to allow a blush. Therefore, the darker races existed upon the earth prior to the creation of Adam and Eve in the Garden of Eden. The Adamic race, the light-skinned peoples, begin *their* Genesis in the Garden and it is with this race *only* that Yahweh makes his Holy Covenants.

In the first Covenant, Adam and Eve are created for eternity and given dominion by God over all, the garden, the earth, and the beasts of the field. This first Covenant, made with Adam in the Garden of Eden, is also called the Edenic Covenant.

Before the creation of Eve, Yahweh brings before Adam "every beast of the field," but among them is found no suitable wife, no "help meet" for him (Genesis 2:20). Obviously the "beasts" had at least a human shape or a union would have been ludicrous. Would God have expected Adam to marry a scorpion? An eagle? Identity doctrine teaches that this passage refers to the older, darker, human-like races that existed on earth prior to the divine creation of Adam (the term "beasts of the field" is reserved for the Negro race). The AIT's Chapter 95, "Anthropology Confirms the Bible," describes the darker races as beings created "as nearly as possible like man to take from Adam's shoulders many of the tasks of subduing the earth, maintaining the Garden of Eden and other duties of the earth and the field."

From the beginning, the "beasts of the field" and other pre-Adamic races are deemed unsuitable for the intermingling of blood through procreation with the light-skinned Adam, forever establishing their status in relation to the progeny of Adam. Yahweh Himself adjudges that such unions between Adamites and pre-Adamites are improper, and Eve is created from the rib of Adam.

Yahweh creates Eve for the sole purpose of establishing a white race, a noble race, sons of Yahweh, dearer to Him than all the pre-Adamite races on the face of the earth. It is unto Adam that Yahweh breathes "the breath of life," divine Spirit with the potential of life eternal. Adam is "Spirit Man." Eve, created from Adam, is rejoined with Adam to establish a divine and eternal union of purity.

For the student of Christian Identity, the trees of the Garden are metaphors for races. Ezekiel 31 illustrates the meaning of the trees:

Behold, the Assyrian was a cedar in Lebanon, with fair branches and a shadowing brow, and of a high stature ... Therefore his height was exalted above all the trees of the field, and his boughs were multiplied, and his branches became long ... All the fowls of heaven made their nests in his boughs, and under his branches did all the beasts of the field bring forth their young and under his shadow dwelt all great nations ... nor any tree in the garden of God was like unto him in his beauty. I have made him fair by the multitude of the branches: so that all the trees of Eden that were in the Garden of God envied him.   (EZEKIEL 31:3, 5–9)

The trees then are "racial" trees and Eve's sin is both racial and sexual, as is Adam's. And the consequence of such sin constitutes the fall from Grace.

The Seedline faction of Identity holds that Eve is tempted by Satan in human-like form. Satan has been misrepresented as a serpent because of the mistranslation of a Hebrew word *nachash*, which actually means "enchanter or magician." "It is certain," says the AIT, "that the one who seduced Eve was no mere scaly snake wriggling along the ground." Eve "partakes" of the fruit of the tree of "knowledge of good and evil." Again, the tree of knowledge of good and evil is a racial tree and Eve's sin is of a sexual nature. When she states that she was beguiled, she is actually saying she has been physically seduced by Satan. Again, according to Chapter 9 of the AIT, misunderstanding arises around the mistranslation, rendering the Hebrew *nasha* as "to beguile" rather than its more accurate meaning "to lead astray, to seduce." Thus Eve, then Adam, who previously had no physical/sexual component to their relationship, "partook" of the fruit which was "pleasant to the eyes" and capable of making men wise. Their partaking of the sexual fruit did indeed result in earthly wisdom, but the price was high and the knowing painful.

According to Seedline theory, the seed of Satan has been planted at this point but does not become evident until the second Covenant is in effect.

A second Covenant, the Adamic Covenant made with Adam after the Fall, is established for the now-mortal condition of fallen humanity. As discussed at length in the AIT's Chapter 10 "Cain and Abel," again Adam and Eve are under the restorative dispensation of God, still embued with their spiritual conception but their physical being now humanly vulnerable. But part of this new Covenant is grounded in a curse. The curse of mortality, the curse of toil, pain in birth, death, and sorrow. The curse of enmity. Of the other races on earth before Adam, says the AIT, "among these other races there are those who are simply pre-Adamic; and one, at least, which is Satanic."

The strict "Seedline Doctrine" of Identity teaches that in the original act of sin, this Satanic race was born. Eve conceives a child of Satan as well as a child of Adam—Cain and Abel, born twins but by different fathers. With the birth of Cain, a direct lineage of Satan is established on earth. Abel is the true son of Adam. The enmity between the righteous seed of Adam and the evil seed of Satan is expressed in the first great act of violence in the Old Testament, the murder of Abel by his "half-twin-brother" Cain.

Cain, born first and of satanic origin, can find no favor with Yahweh, and his offerings, the fruit of the earth, are scorned by Yahweh. Yahweh, however, takes much satisfaction from the offerings of Abel, who brings the first-born of the flock, which foreshadows the coming of the "Lamb of God" in a symbolic representation of Christ. In jealousy, and consistent with his brutal origin, Cain spills the blood of Abel. Banished from the Garden, Cain fears for his life because outside the Garden, "every one that findeth me shall slay me" (Genesis 4:14). Cain himself offers proof that there are other peoples in the world at this time. God "set a mark upon Cain, lest any finding him should kill him" (Genesis 4:15), this *mark of Cain* apparently an identifiable physical characteristic. Cain journeys to another country, mixes his seed with other-race pre-Adamites to further mongrelize his bloodline, and spreads the seedline of Satan on earth.

It is at this point that Identity theory splinters somewhat. According to a variant faction of Identity belief, Cain is a son of Adam who succumbs to Satan's evil influence. In jealousy, Cain kills his brother Abel and is banished from the Garden by God. Marked by God and swearing revenge, Cain travels to an other-race country and procreates, and it is this contamination of the original bloodline of Adam that marks the beginning of an evil race dedicated to the destruction of the pure bloodline of Adam. Cain's race, bearing God's identifying mark which is both a protection and a curse, settle in Edom and his mixed-race progeny of "Esau-ites," or Edomites—Cainites, Canaanites, Kenites, and other names through the ages—are dedicated to the destruction of the pure bloodline of Adam. (This topic, using Hebrew classifications to define the various types of beings, is explored at length in the AIT's Chapter 11, "Man and Beast.")

This conflict between the seed of Yahweh's earthly family and the seed of Satan is a consistent theme throughout the Bible—the eternal conflict between Good and Evil—and the progeny of Cain are mentioned from time to time in various contexts:

> Certain men, the children of Belial, are gone out from among you, and have withdrawn the inhabitants of their city, saying, 'Let us go and serve other gods, which ye have not known. (DEUTERONOMY 13:13)

"The term 'Sons of Belial,' " says Seedline minister Mike Hallimore, "is used both in a literal sense to designate the children of Satan, and in a figurative sense when referring to evil Adamites, much like 'S.O.B.' is used today." If these certain men, these "children of Belial," are the descendants of Cain, the descendants of Satan, the liars, the deceivers, the seducers, Yahweh is not shy about stating how they should be dealt with. He instructs the Israelites:

> Then shalt thou inquire, and make search, and ask diligently; and behold, if it be truth, and the thing certain, that such abomination is wrought among you;

> Thou shalt surely smite the inhabitants of that city with the edge of the sword, destroying it utterly, and all that is therein, and the cattle thereof, with the edge of the sword.

> And thou shalt gather all the spoil of it into the midst of the street thereof, and shalt burn with fire the city, and all the spoil thereof, every whit, for the Lord thy God: and it shall be an heap forever; it shall not be built again.   (DEUTERONOMY 13:14–16)

The Seedline doctrine of Christian Identity provides the basis for tracking and identifying this "seedline of Satan" through all the generations. The answer to the question of who they are is provided by Christ Himself. Ages later, in the New Testament, Jesus tells the Pharisees, "Ye are of your father the devil. . . . He was a murderer from the beginning, and abode not in the truth, because there is no truth in him. When he speaketh a lie, he speaketh of his own: for he is a liar, and the father of it" (John 8:44). As illustrated in the taped sermon "The Viper Connection" by Identity Pastor Ray Barker of Christian Israel Covenant Church of Colville, Washington, the family resemblance is unmistakable. Christ identifies the Jews as the pretenders and the offspring of Satan, vipers, generation of vipers, demon-seed who cannot hear His voice because He speaks the truth and, as children of Satan, the truth is not in them.

The third Covenant, the Noahic Covenant made with Noah after the Flood (Genesis 7), illustrates the divine commandment of racial segregation. Identity Christians believe in the Flood. However, they do not believe the floodwaters covered the entire earth, nor was there need to flood the entire earth. As explained in the AIT's Chapter 15, "Noah's Flood Was Not World-wide," Yahweh is concerned primarily with the Adamic peoples, and it is the Adamic peoples who violate his laws. Noah and his family are the last of the line of Adam who still practice Yahweh's commandment of separatism. "These are the generations of Noah: Noah was a just man and perfect in his generations [family descent, racially pure], and Noah walked with God" (Genesis 6:9).

It seems that the Israelites have been committing the sin of Eve, and "mongrelization" is rampant. This really is not surprising if one accepts the idea that Adam is not the first man, only the first white Spirit Man and, when he and Eve are driven from the Garden, they eventually settle where other, darker races are already established. Therefore, the inevitable happens. Where there is racial integration, there is commingling of the blood and Adamic purity is lost in the pollution of the bloodline. From this perspective, it is reasoned that if Yahweh had not had a purpose for the white race, He would not have gone to the trouble of creating it. Since Yahweh did create the white race, did he create it to be swallowed up and destroyed through intermarriage with the darker races? The answer, from this line of reasoning, is obviously no.

Thus, the commandment to build the Ark was Yahweh's intervention to protect the bloodline of Adam. Noah took his family inside while the deluge purified the land of mongrelized Adamites. But Yahweh flooded only that part of the earth which was necessary to eradicate the erring Adamites and their mongrelized offspring. After the flood, God told Noah and his family to "be fruitful and multiply," that is, multiply the restored purity of the white-Adamic bloodline. Thus true Israel, today's Israel nations and peoples of the world, are descendants of Noah who descended from Adam and Eve and kept the commandments of Yahweh to maintain the integrity of their race and their status as "an holy people unto Yahweh, thy God . . . Yahweh hath chosen thee to be a peculiar people unto Himself, above all the nations that are upon the earth" (Deuteronomy 14:2).

The fourth Covenant, the Abrahamic Covenant, also concerns itself with race and nation but is of great import to the Israel people in other aspects as well. As Identity Pastor Ray Barker points out in his taped sermon, "The Pillar of Destiny," the first eleven chapters of the Bible describe the Creation. Chapter 12 of Genesis introduces Abram, later named Abraham, and from that point until the end of Revelation, the rest of the Bible is about the descendants of Abraham. "One man's family," says Barker, and that man was Abraham, progenitor of the Israel nation.

God's covenant to Abraham was "I will make of thee a great nation, and I will bless thee, and make thy name great; and thou shalt be a blessing: And I will bless them that bless thee, and curse him that curseth thee, and in thee shall all families of the earth be blessed. . . . I will make thee exceeding fruitful, and I will make nations of thee, and kings shall come out of thee" (Genesis 12:2–3, 17:6).

Abraham fathers Isaac, and Yahweh promises Isaac: "I will perform the oath which I swear to thy father Abraham. I will make thy seed to multiply as the stars of heaven, and will give unto thy seed all these countries; and in thy seed shall all the nations of the earth be blessed" (Genesis 26:3–4).

Isaac fathers Jacob, whom Yahweh renames Israel, and from Jacob come the twelve tribes who comprise the nation of Israel, one tribe for each of Jacob/Israel's twelve sons. The tribe of Jacob's son Joseph will later be divided between Joseph's sons Ephraim and Manassah, both of whom receive special blessings from their grandfather Jacob—the promise to become a great nation and a company, or commonwealth, of nations—and cause the tribes of Israel to be numbered thirteen. Thus Israel becomes the great Anglo-Aryan cultures of the world, fulfillment of Yahweh's promises that through Abraham a great nation and a company of nations would spread throughout the earth.

The seedline of Satan, however, has hardly been idle throughout this process. Israel, the Aryan racial nation, deceived again by the children of Belial, turns from Yahweh and suffers for it during their period of enslavement.

In the covenant made with Abraham, before their rise as a great nation, Israel suffers four hundred years of servitude in a foreign land. In this land, Egypt, another descendent of Abraham, Moses, enters into a fifth covenant with Yahweh.

The fifth Covenant, the Mosaic Covenant containing the Ten Commandments, is delivered to Moses on Mt. Sinai, after the Israelites' flight from Egypt. At this time Yahweh presents to Moses the codified version of His divine laws. Of apparent interest and validation to Identity Christians is the proposition advanced that these Laws of God are the laws of the Anglo-Saxon peoples and of no other nation on earth. Identity Christians claim that even the Jews, who are usurpers of the legacy of the covenants, govern themselves by other laws, primarily the Talmud whose teachings are referred to in the Bible as "the tradition of the elders." However, the ancient Israelites violate the Mosaic Covenant while wandering in the wilderness, and yet another covenant is established by a patient Yahweh before the next generation can enter the promised "land of Canaan," the land of Palestine.

The sixth Covenant, the Palestinian Covenant, expresses the will of Yahweh through the condition that the blessings of the land will be Israel's only if Israel keeps the Laws of the Mosaic Covenant. Inevitable punishment and the loss of the land is to follow widespread transgressions. The Israelites, by this time, are apparently stubborn and willful because they soon depart from this covenant as well, worshiping idols and doing evil until the nation is so weakened that it falls to foreign aggressors and they are taken from their lands as captives.

When the prophet Samuel reunites the remnants of Israel into a whole nation again, he also heralds the era of the Kings. Israel, heretofore, has had only Yahweh as a spiritual King, with anointed judges. But Israel wants to be like "other nations," and rejects its God YHWH in favor of an earthly ruler. This marks a clear declension in both spiritual and earthly power. Samuel, the chosen prophet of God, anoints Saul the first King of Israel. But Saul, being somewhat willful himself, does not please Yahweh. Saul is arrogant, disobedient and jealous, and Samuel is sent by Yahweh, still faithfully guiding his people, to tell Saul that because he has not kept faith with God, he is to be supplanted.

Samuel then comes to anoint King David, the second king of Israel. David, too, has his faults but still is beloved of Yahweh. Through David, God establishes the seventh Covenant. More than any other scriptural passage of the Old Testament, this covenant supplies the fingerprints by which true Israel may be identified.

The seventh Covenant, the Davidic Covenant, proclaims, "David shall never want a man to sit upon the throne of the House of Israel. . . . As the host of heaven cannot be numbered, neither the sand of the sea measured: so will I multiply the seed of David" (Jeremiah 33:17, 22). The Israel people are to have a new language and a new name, they will move into new lands and lose trace of their heritage for a time, but they will regather in a new land, conquer the wilderness, multiply into great numbers, and settle into the land promised them, a land of great agriculture and mineral wealth. Yahweh promises David that his throne and his royal line will continue forever, and adds this promise:

> I have been with thee whithersoever thou hast walked, and have cut off all thine enemies from before thee, and have made thee a name like the name of the great men that are in the earth. Also I will ordain a place for my people Israel, and will plant them, and they shall dwell in that place, and shall be moved no more; neither shall the children of wickedness waste them any more, as at the beginning. (1 CHRONICLES 17:8–9)

This Davidic Covenant alone, in Identity theology, is enough to establish the true identity of the chosen although the various branches can offer many other scriptural passages which support it.

That the white race is heir to God's Covenants is not a new idea, states Covenant pastor George Southwick of The Bible Educator Ministry of Santa Maria, California. It is, instead, a centuries-old belief verified by both scripture and history. "I was ordained in the Glad Tidings Temple in San Francisco almost half a century ago," he says, "and I preached for several years before I learned what people the Bible is *really* talking about.

"The revelation came to me almost fifty years ago is nothing more than the old paths that are mentioned in the Word of God. Our Plymouth brethren knew it and brought the message to the New World. But modern people like new-fangled interpretations, and so we add them even if they're wrong. People of today have been led far, far astray.

"I have a copy of a magazine dated 1922," Southwick says, "from the Apostolic Faith Church of Wales and Great Britain. The first message is entitled 'The Joseph Who Cannot be Destroyed.' Even back then, shortly after World War I, it talks about a New Age and a New World. The author talks about the Covenant People and states, 'It will be seen that the Covenant blessings given to our fathers Abraham, Isaac and Jacob rest not upon the Jews as a separate people but on Ephraim and Joseph who carry the birthright blessing for the whole House of Israel. The Word of God cannot die, and in the promises given to Joseph and his seed, we see foreshadowing of the New Age which is upon us.' I have books and magazines even older that speak of the Covenant People, and they aren't speaking of Jews."

Identity maintains that *no* Jewish lineage can be traced, unbroken, back to the throne of David. The dissemination of the Israelites notwithstanding, where is the throne which has endured through all this history? And there *must* be one since Yahweh has proclaimed there would be. Who sits upon it? Not a Jew, because Jews do not fit the description of the Israel of the Davidic Covenant. Where is the land of the Israelites? The land cannot be Palestine (Israel) because the Jews have already been driven from it and have had to reconquer and hold it with the assistance of a number of non-Jewish allies. And just who are "the children of wickedness" who afflict Aryan Israel? They are the usurpers of the title Israel, the false pretenders to the Throne of David and the children of Belial. As G. R. Hawtin states in his book *The Abrahamic Covenant,*

> none of the blessings of greatness and nationhood, given to the sons of Joseph, fit the Jews in any sense of the word. . . . Any thinking person must surely know that the Saxon nations have been and still are the recipients of all these blessings of heaven and earth and the wealth that lies under the earth. God's word declares that His covenant people are to be the leading nations of the world. . . . Ephraim England has become a world wide commonwealth [and] Manasseh, his brother [the United States], has become the greatest nation on earth.

Thus, Seedline Doctrine, Covenant theological theory, British Israelism and American Christian Identity basically maintain that if one identifies the recipients of God's promises to his chosen people, then he will have identified the chosen people. If the promises are false, then the Bible is false; but if they have been fulfilled, then the people to whom they are fulfilled are identified as Israel. So, from the Identity Christian's standpoint, the following may be deduced:

- Adamic peoples are Christian and have been since early times.

- The Adamic race constitutes great nations and companies of nations.

- Adamites are a numerous people throughout the earth.

- The Adamic race has expanded in colonies throughout the world.

- Adamites have improved the lot of colonized lands, bringing technological and cultural advances.

- Adamic civilizations are the only truly great civilizations.

- Adamites have maintained the continuity of the throne of David. All the thrones of Scotland, England and Ireland have been occupied by descendants of the House of David. And, of course, it is Adamic Israelite stock, including the House of David, which initially colonized America.

- Of the prophecies and promises made by Yahweh to Israel, all have been fulfilled among the Anglo-Saxon, Teutonic and Scandinavian races.

The biblical basis for identification of true Israel is certainly a cornerstone of all Covenant Identity beliefs. The Anglo-Saxon Federation of America publishes and distributes Covenant-based literature through Destiny Publishers in Merrimac, Massachusetts. In one undated brochure, *The Servant People: Anglo-Saxon Identity and Responsibility,* Anglo-Israel is addressed in familiar terms. The significant question is, the brochure states, "Do our beliefs conform with this declaration and are we prepared to accept the Scriptural identification of this specially-selected people, even if the weight of proof designates them to be other than the Jews?"

The same brochure, which lists no author or copyright date, discusses the specific concepts of Covenant theology. These concepts negate the status of the Jews as chosen people, claim the identity of Israel for the white race and explore the scattering and re-formation of the tribes, among other things.

It is important here to expose a fallacy, long taught by the Christian Church, that the Jews gave us Christianity. This is called the Judeo-Christian concept, embraced by Protestants and Roman Catholics, as well as Jewry, and it is a grotesque misnomer. It is motivated by the spurious Jewish claim to be the "chosen people" and the false contention that Jesus Christ was a Jew.

If Jesus Christ is of the House of David, then from a Covenant perspective, He could not have possibly been Jewish. The article goes on to claim:

These theological allegations, while highly suitable for propaganda purposes, have no Scriptural foundations, for the Jews not only opposed their Messiah and King, but they crucified Him. Then they persecuted his followers, among them the Benjamites living in Galilee. It was from this tribe that Jesus chose his disciples, except for one, Judas, who betrayed him.

Judas Iscariot, it is noted in some Identity teachings, was the only Jew among the twelve. For the fundamentalist Seedline Identity Christian, the persecution and crucifixion of Yashua the Messiah provides further evidence of the true nature of the Jewish people.

Charles Lee remarks sardonically, "Look, if you're arrested, tried, and sentenced to death, does it make it any difference who actually executes you? Yes, the Roman soldiers took Christ to Calvary and nailed him to a cross. But who clamored for his death? Who actually brought it about? All throughout the history of Christianity, Christians have known who was responsible for the murder of Christ and it was not the Romans. Make no mistake about it. If Jesus Christ were to begin his ministry today, the Jews would crucify him again. The ADL would lead the charge."

However, as E. Raymond Capt has noted, to Covenant Identity Christians the concept of Anglo-Israel as the chosen people does not necessarily entail antagonistic relationships with non-Anglo peoples, rather a responsibility. In the undated booklet *The Covenant People,* also published by Destiny Publishers, W. J. Cameron agrees. People might ask, he says, by what right God chooses one race above the other.

> I like that form of the question. It is much better than asking by what right God degrades one people beneath another, although that is implied. God's grading is always upward. If He raises up a nation, it is that other nations may be raised up through its ministry. . . . raise a degraded people to a better condition.

Divine selection is not simply a prize, Cameron says, or a mere compliment paid to a man or a race, but a burden imposed. It is certainly not "pandering to the racial vanity of a 'superior people': it is a yoke bound upon the necks of those who are chosen for a special service."

This idea is something that most Americans, most people in the world for that matter, should find familiar. It is an integral component of the theory of the "White Man's Burden" which was generally held as fact, at least by white Europeans, all throughout the period of European colonization of large parts of the non-white world. And, for most Covenant Identiy Christians, such beliefs are not denominationally attached to any particular theological orientation but indeed transcend doctrinal differences. The Anglo-Saxon Federation of America, in an undated pamphlet entitled "Statement of Belief" makes the claim:

We do not constitute a new sect or a new religion. We are Christians of many denominations who have banded together to proclaim the national message of the Bible, upholding the authenticity and accuracy of the whole Scriptures from Genesis to Revelation. We stress particularly the neglected fact of the modern identity of the Israel of God and the necessity to restore in our nation the administration of the commandments, statutes and judgements of the Law of the Lord, which must ultimately become the law of the land.

The burden then of the covenants to Anglo-Israel is not to accept a passive role in world events. Instead, it is a call for action. The implications of restoring the Laws of God to the laws of the land involve educational, political and social activism, and above all spreading the message of God and preparing for the Kingdom which is yet to come. The Anglo-Saxon Federation's "Statement of Belief" also states clearly the responsibility of Anglo-Israel: "Now, in these stirring age-ending days, it devolves upon us who know these great truths to be faithful and diligent in our witnessing as we await the coming of our triumphant Lord."

To the traditional seven covenants commonly accepted, according to the AIT Bible study guide, Identity Christians add an eighth Covenant, the "New Covenant in Jesus Christ"—the New Testament. Before Jesus' birth, He was destined to fulfill the Old Testament prophecy. As the angel said to Mary, "And behold, thou shalt conceive in thy womb, and bring forth a son, and shalt call his name JESUS. . . . and the Lord God shall give unto him the throne of his father David: And he shall reign over the house of Jacob for ever" (Luke 1:31–33). That the prophecy and the New Testament are intended for Israel is not disputed, but as G. R. Hawtin points out in *The Abrahamic Covenant:*

The Jew cannot possibly fulfill the world wide promises given to the house of Israel. The Jew himself would be the first to admit that from the manger of Bethlehem until now, his whole attitude has been anti-Christ. How then could the promise made of Jesus, "He shall be the glory of Thy people Israel," be made applicable to them?

For many, no further proof is needed to explain the identity of Anglo-Israel and the yoke of the chosen. Certainly, no further proof is needed for those who believe their birthright has been usurped by a Satanic race known as Jews. This concept of usurpation explains the "radical" and "anti-Semitic" (Identity redefines this term as "anti-Jewish") doctrines embraced in varying degrees of intensity by branches of the Christian Identity tree, as well as defines the mission of the Israel people. As the author of AIT's Chapter 88 "The Destiny of Our Race" says:

> As Yahveh's Covenant People, we must rediscover, as a nation, the faith in divine guidance that led our forefathers to face every hardship and danger with courage dependent on Yahveh, who prospered their undertakings. Today, as in Biblical times, a spirit of fear and defeatism prevails in the face of threats by our enemies. This gross disability will continue to weaken the Israel peoples until they realize there is a national purpose in the plan of Yahveh that made Israelite nations great.
>
> . . . The answer lies in the acknowledgment of our origin and destiny. . . . The destiny of the nations, which are to be the nucleous of the Kingdom of God upon the earth, is still Divinely controlled.

A cornerstone of Identity theology is rooted in the origin of the Israel peoples as the regathering of the "lost" tribes of Israel. Proofs of identity are offered by theological, historical and archeological spokesmen such as E. Raymond Capt of Covenant Media Productions, Ray Barker of Christian Israel Covenant Church, Earl Jones of Christian Crusade for Truth, Everett Ramsey of Faith Baptist Church and others whose ministry is based on evidence that solves the riddle of the "lost" tribes.

Whereas the fingerprints of white Israel may be found through a study of the covenants, their footprints are imprinted upon the soil of modern Europe.

# CHAPTER SIX

# The Chosen People: The Stone and the Throne

[Jacob] dreamed, and behold a ladder set up on the earth, and the top of it reached to heaven: and behold the angels of God ascending and descending on it. And behold, the Lord stood above it, and said, I am the Lord God of Abraham thy father, and the God of Isaac ... And Jacob awaked out of his sleep, and he said, Surely the Lord is in this place ... and [he] took the stone that he had put for his pillow, and set it up for a pillar, and poured oil upon the top of it. And he called the name of that place Bethel ... [and said] this stone, which I have set for a pillar, shall be God's house.   (GENESIS 28:12–13, 16, 18–19, 22)

[The second time Jacob visited Bethel, God] said unto him, what is thy name? And he said, Jacob. And [God] said, Thy name shall be called no more Jacob, but Israel: for as a prince hast thou power with God and with men, and hast prevailed.   (GENESIS 32:27–28)

Identity Christians—the Israel people, Anglo-Saxons, the Celtic peoples and latter-day inheritors of the Abrahamic Covenant—believe they know where the Kingdom of God will be. It will be on earth, and it may well be in Britain.

*Brith-ain.* "The covenant land."

Isaac's sons. I-*saac's* sons. Saxons.

*Cellt* or *kellt:* ancient stone knife used to circumcise Aryan babies; therefore, *Celtic* refers to "the circumcised people."

The stone that Jacob anointed at Bethel (*Beth-el* "House of God"), also called the Stone of Destiny, Jacob's Pillow, Jacob's Pillar, the Bethel Stone, later the Stone of Scone, embodies the prophecy that wherever the Stone lies, "the race of Erc" (Fergus Mor McErc, first Scottish king) shall reign. Since the sixth century B.C., the stone has lain in the British Isles.

Since the sixth century B.C., the Stone of Scone, also called the Coronation Stone, has been used successively by Dalriadic, Irish, Scottish, English and British monarchs as an important part of their enthronement ceremonies.

Anglo-Israel, the Stone of Destiny and the British throne are links in a chain of prophecies, from Jacob's anointing the stone at Bethel, to Irish kings being crowned upon the same stone at Tara before the time of Christ, to the present Queen Elizabeth II's being crowned upon the same stone in London's Westminster Abbey in 1953. The bloodline of the British royal family is of the House of David, and on the way to coronation, every British monarch passes under the west window of Westminster Abbey with its figures of Abraham, Isaac, Jacob, the twelve patriarchs, and Moses. Another significant factor, says G. R. Hawtin in *The Abrahamic Covenant,* is that British monarchs at their coronation are anointed with oil compounded from the same properties as the oil that was used to anoint the kings of Israel.

"It's hard to imagine how people can be ignorant of this connection to Israel," says Dr. E. Raymond Capt, Biblical archeologist, author and Covenant Christian. "The lineage has been common knowledge for centuries and taught from the pulpit for centuries. The Caucasian peoples of Europe are the descendants of the Israel of the Bible. British Israelism is not the proper term for it . . . you might as well call it Canadian Israelism or New Zealand Israelism. Actually it's just Christianity. The fact remains that it is fact."

Whether these events are principally of secular or religious significance to the world, to the fiery Seedline Identity Christian and the milder Covenant Identity Christian alike they are an indication that God's plan is being fulfilled. In 1996 the Stone of Destiny was moved from London back to Scotland. Perhaps it is already in the final location that marks the kingdom that God promised to his chosen people. Or perhaps not. Dr. Everett Ramsey, in an America Today newsletter of the Faith Baptist Church and Ministries, interprets this move as a sign that England is not the center of the Kingdom of Israel.

"God's kingdom will be on earth, the Bible says so," says an Identity minister from the Southwest. "It says 'Thy kingdom *come,*' not that we will go to the kingdom. God's kingdom will be an earthly kingdom. It might be in Britain, but I don't think so. I think it will be in the United States. We're a 'company of nations,' like the Bible says, and if our ancestors came from Britain, that's the same thing."

Jacob's Stone, the Stone of Destiny, might have to come to America for such a kingdom to be established. The stone pillow of Jacob is not a relic to be worshiped, but it is a visual sign of God's covenant, a holy object that has been in the presence of God. Its presence among God's people has been important since the days of Jacob/Israel, inasmuch as the Israelites carried it with them on their forty-year migration in the wilderness, and its location is still a matter of importance. Today's Identity Christians understand the significance of the anointed stone of Bethel and its symbolic link to the Throne of David.

"The Anglo-Saxon Israel belief is not based on theory but archeological facts," says Capt, referring to portions of his 1985 book *Missing Links Discovered in Assyrian Tablets.* "The Assyrian cuneiform tablets, unearthed in the excavations at Nineveh and translated by Professor Waterman of the University of Michigan, not only record the captivity but also record their escape and migrations west through Europe as Cimerians and Scythians into Western Europe. . . . It was these so-called 'Lost Tribes of Israel' that founded the Anglo-Saxon-Scandinavian-Lombard-Germanic-Celtic nations of today, the homelands of White Americans."

If Jacob's Pillow/Pillar stone was in Bethel in the Middle East during Old Testament times, how did it get to twentieth-century Britain, first through Spain, then to Ireland's Tara "seat of Irish kings," then to Scone in Scotland, then to Westminster Abbey in London? And how does each stage of its journey strengthen modern Anglo-Israelites' belief that its ultimate destination was foretold in the Old Testament and is the "appointed place" Jesus spoke of in the New Testament?

Neither biblical nor secular history gives an unbroken sequence to show where Jacob's Stone was at all times through the centuries. But in some places where both types of account are silent, reasonable assumptions can be allowed. For example, if Jacob was alone at Bethel, he most likely would not have carried the stone away with him at the time. The stone measures 26 inches long, 16 inches wide and 11 inches high, and it weighs 152 kg, or 336 pounds. Regardless of who may have carried it away or who later retrieved it, or where it was during specific periods of time, silences of this type are either incidental in the scheme of the prophecy or, according to one authority, are an integral element in the prophecy to ensure the stone's safety through troubled times. Events that are recorded in history, both biblical and secular, have given enough information for scholars to trace the route of both the stone and those who transported it from its place of consecration in Bethel to the covenant land of Britain.

"From Bethel to Westminster is a long distance in both time and space," says Capt. "Any attempt to connect the two involves the necessity of reconstructing a consecutive, feasible story." The first step is to establish the true identity of the stone. The tradition that has subsisted from time immemorial, Capt says, is that the Stone of Scone is none other than that on which the head of Jacob rested when he dreamed of the ladder with angels ascending and descending upon it.

In his *Jacob's Pillar: A Biblical Historical Study,* a 96-page, fine-print, fact-packed volume, Capt traces in painstaking detail the route of the stone and the peoples that carried it. He supplies geographic and linguistic analysis, archeological evidence, local customs and folklore, and provides peripheral support in the form of maps and illustrations, genealogical charts, quotes from ancient authorities, and scriptural references. The arrival in Ireland of the Bethel Stone, he says, rests upon the authority of and records of Ireland and the traditions that still abound there. Ancient Irish poets and historians and storytellers were honored because of the tremendous value which the people set upon recording and preserving their history. It is an examination of these records that gives credence to the basic truth of the traditions.

A portion of Capt's book *Jacob's Pillar,* severely abbreviated here, begins by making these points: the divine significance of the stone called Jacob's Pillar was known to the ancient Hebrews as they carried it with them in their wanderings. In many instances, Scriptures speak of *"the* rock" instead of *"a* rock," such as God's telling Moses to "smite the rock" (Exodus 17:6) with no apparent need to identify which rock He was speaking about, and Joash's coronation in which he stood by "a pillar" (II Kings 11:14), mistranslated in the King James Version but subsequently translated *"the* pillar" in later versions. Capt also cites the *Encyclopedia of Freemasonry* (1921), which shows that Jacob's Stone was the cornerstone first rejected in the building of Solomon's temple. Not only was the stone "in the rough," the tradition says, but it contained a crack which could have split at any minute, and it was left lying for years. This was the stone Jesus called "the stone that the builders rejected, the same is become the head of the corner'' (Matthew 21:42). When the stone's identity was at last recognized, it became the cornerstone of the House of Israel, the Coronation Stone of kings.

Migration is the heart of the Israelites' story, and Capt concentrates on identifying the location of Jacob's Stone on these migrations, as well as pointing out the intervals in which the stone is not mentioned at all. During those times, he says, it is logical to assume that it was in the hands of some part of the people of Israel, inasmuch as it does reappear. Between 745–721 B.C., the Ten-Tribed Kingdom of Israel (the House of Israel) and a large portion of the southern Kingdom of Judah were taken into captivity (II Kings 17:3-6). Archeological tablets found in the excavations of the Assyrian Royal Library at Nineveh have indicated that many of the Israelites escaped and traveled by way of the Caucasus Mountains— hence the name ''Caucasians''—into the Steppes of Southern Russia. The narrow passage by which they entered, called ''the gate'' (Micah 2:12–13) in ancient writings, is still called the ''Pass of Israel,'' and the ''standing pillar'' or pillar-stone mentioned by Hosea is presumed to be Jacob's Stone. After a sojourn in Iberia—ancient Latin for ''Hebrew'' and an early name for Spain—eventually these Israelite peoples ended up in Hibernia—Gaelic for ''Hebrew,'' an early name for Ireland—thus setting the stage for the appearance of Irish kings and an Aryan kingdom.

Charles S. Braeden, in *These Also Believe,* says that the whereabouts of these ten ''lost'' tribes has been one of the perennially interesting questions raised by the Bible. But ''Anglo-Israel has the answer. These tribes were not lost. They could not be, if prophecy was to be fulfilled, and God's promises made good.'' The western movement was composed of members from tribes of Judah and Dan. From Judah came the old Scottish kings of Ireland, and from these tribes is traced the lineage of the royal house of England.

Linguistic evidence of the tribe of Dan's migration remains in place names they left behind them, as Braeden points out. Dan broke away from the others while they were still in Egypt and sailed away to Greece, where he settled near Argos, became king and renamed the people *Danai.* The tribe of Dan settled on the sea coast and became a maritime, migrating people who, following the custom of giving places and rivers their own name, made it easy to follow them through Europe: along the *Dan*ube, the *Dan*ieper (Dneiper), the *Don*, the Rho*dan*us (ancient name of the Rhone,) the Rhine (ancient name Eri*dan*us), until they arrived in *Den*mark and Scan*din*avia. These were the northern Danites, the tribes that would become the Danes, the Vikings, the fierce Norsemen of Scandinavia, the Celts and Gaels, the Normans, the Goths, the Angles, Saxons and Jutes, the Picts and Scots—which in turn would become, in the eyes of Christian Identity doctrine, the great white cultures of the world.

Hawtin, in his tracing the tribe of Dan in its migration across Europe, makes the point that in the Hebrew language, there are no vowels. Hence the name Dan, in its original Hebrew, was spelled DN and, when incorporated into a place name, could have been spelled Dan, Den, Don, Din, etc. Hawtin adds to the list the Dar*dan*elles, Mace*don*ia, *Dn*eister, the rivers Jor*dan* and *Dn*eister, the *Dan*au and the *Dan*inn, the *Dan*ast and *Dan*dari and *Dan*ez, the U*don* and Eri*don,* and titles such as the Spanish *don.* "There is no grander theme upon the scrolls of history," he says, "than the struggle of the Anglo-Saxons westward." Once they settled in Ireland and England and Scotland, the tribe of Dan continued to leave place names such as *Dan*slough, *Don*egal, *Dun*glow, Lon*don*derry, *Dun*dee, *Dun*kirk, *Dun*stable and E*din*burgh.

This same period of time is covered with emphasis on different details in the AIT Bible study guide. Chapter 40, "Historic Proof of Israel's Migrations," gives alternate etymology of *Saxon* as having derived from "Sakke" or "Sacae" or "Scythians" and throughout this study, the authors of the AIT cite references to "blond Scythians." It was the forerunners of these early blue-eyed, blond Scythians who, according to Professor George Rawlinson, settled in Armenia, or Southern Russia, and developed the Indo-European language. [Linguistic historians identify Southern Russia, Lithuania or Armenia as the birthplace of the Indo-European parent language that evolved into Germanic languages, English, the Nordic and other Aryan languages.] The authors of the AIT also cite Sharon Turner's *History of the Anglo-Saxons,* "one of the most thoroughly documented historical studies ever produced whose reliability is beyond question," in which the Anglo-Saxons of Britain are traced back to these blond Scythians, "as the people of Israel became known in the land to which they were deported." Although Turner's book is silent on the location of the Stone of Destiny at this point, it clearly says that the blond, blue-eyed people of Israel became known as Scythians, and then as Anglo-Saxons.

Two events, centuries apart but both with biblical and historical evidence, figure prominently into Christian Identity's identification of Anglo-Saxon/Aryan peoples as direct descendants of King David and inheritors of the Throne of David. In addition, both events lay the groundwork for the Stone of Destiny's relocation into Ireland to become the Coronation Stone for the British royal line.

In *Jacob's Pillar,* Capt devotes several detailed chapters to the prophet Jeremiah and the probability that it was Jeremiah who carried the Stone of Destiny to Ireland. But the foundation for this act was laid more than twenty-six generations earlier at the time when an odd event happened as twin sons were born to Judah, son of Jacob/Israel. Because the eldest son of Judah would be the rightful heir, the midwife had ready a scarlet thread to mark the firstborn baby as soon as the mother Tamar started into labor:

> And it came to pass, when she travailed, that the one put out his hand: and the midwife took and bound upon his hand a scarlet thread, saying, This came out first. And it came to pass, as he drew back his hand, that, behold, his brother came out: and she therefore said, How hast thou broken forth? This breach be upon thee: therefore his name was called Pharez. And afterward came out his brother that had the scarlet thread upon his hand: and his name was called Zerah. (GENESIS 38:28–30)

Clearly, both would be inheritors of the birthright somewhere along the line, Capt says, and the midwife's "You have created a breach for yourself" would indicate that at some point in descent of the Pharez line there would be a break in the sequence. The lines of both brothers Zerah and Pharez played a major part in establishing Anglo-as-Israel and relocating the Stone of Destiny onto British soil.

The scarlet thread of the line of Zerah can be followed more through secular history than Biblical: the son of Zerah, Darda "the Egyptian," was Dardanus the Egyptian founder of Troy. The descendants of Dardanus ruled in Troy until the city was destroyed in the famous "siege of Troy" in about 1200 B.C. and the last of the royal Trojans, Aeneas, escaped to Italy and subsequently founded the great Roman Empire. In about 1103 B.C., Aeneas's son (or grandson) Brutus migrated and reestablished his group in "the Great White Island" (an early name for Britain due to its chalk cliffs), and built a capital city he named "New Troy," now called London. So the descendants of Jacob/Israel through his grandson Zerah migrated through Spain and Italy into Britain, then spread to Ireland.

Secular history at the time, as Capt shows in the ancient "Leabha Gabhala," or "Book of Conquests of Ireland," identifies the inhabitants of Ireland as the "Tuatha De Danann," or the "Tribe of Dan." The

Tuatha De Danann were a seafaring people, the chronicles say, and are credited with bringing Jeremiah and Jacob's Pillar to Ireland. Another ancient book of Irish chronicles, the "Planatation of Ulster," has a section of genealogy that includes William the Conqueror, and there are several Irish names mentioned as belonging to the "Red" or "Scarlet" branch of Judah. It was probably their ancestor Zerah's hand bound with a scarlet thread at birth that accounts for the origin of the "heraldic sign employed today in Ulster, northern Ireland, consisting of a Red Hand coupled at the wrist with a scarlet thread."

Secular historical evidence at this point places Anglo-Israelite peoples on Irish soil, not yet including the Stone of Destiny, but biblical history involving descendants of Zerah's twin brother Pharez starts to fill in another part of the prophecy.

The descendants of Jacob/Israel through his grandson Pharez are believed to have also migrated to Ireland and to have facilitated Jeremiah's taking the Stone of Destiny to Ireland, but the circumstances were more complex as well as subject to interpretation, and dependent to a large part on inference based on ancient Irish chronicles.

The ninth king down the line from Pharez was King David. The royal line of Pharez, established in David, was unbroken until the twenty-sixth king, the wicked King Zedekiah, when God commanded "Take off the crown; exalt him that is low, and abase him that is high" (Ezekiel 21:26). Zedekiah was dethroned and all his sons were slain, a breach in the Pharez line that made Zedekiah the last king to reign over Judah.

However—and this is where Identity Christians sit up and come to attention—there is more to God's command concerning the line of Zedekiah: "I will overturn, overturn, overturn, it: and it shall be no more, until he come whose right it is; and I will give it to him" (Ezekiel 21:27).

Identity Christians also understand the significance of how many "overturns," or cataclysmic moves Jacob's Stone has undergone—what Identity Pastor Ray Barker calls "moving the Throne of David"—and since the autumn of 1996, they believe that the end times are near.

Interpretation of God's "overturn" in the King James Version, translated as "ruin" in other versions, is of paramount importance in the tenets of Christian Identity beliefs, as is the threefold repetition of the word. God said this in reference to the "ruin" of Jerusalem by the Babylonians in 588 B.C. and to King Zedekiah, who was contemporary with both Ezekiel and the prophet Jeremiah, and with Jeremiah's scribe Baruch. With this connection, Ezekiel's allegory of the cropped cedar tree (leaderless nation) and the "tender twig" (young woman) that replants it with new life in a new land makes eminent sense. Ordinarily, with Zedekiah's sons slain, that would be the end of Zedekiah's bloodline. But Zedekiah had daughters who carried the same blood.

At this time of Jerusalem's destruction in 588 B.C., God said to Jeremiah, "I will make thee to pass with thine enemies into a land which thou knowest not," the word *pass* implying "passage by boat or by sea." Jeremiah knew the land of Egypt and its environs, Capt points out, therefore the assumption that Jeremiah went by sea to a land he had never visited before. With Jerusalem in shambles, its holy objects would have been in danger. When Jeremiah left Egypt for this new land, for safekeeping he would doubtless have had in his possession the Stone of Bethel, the symbolic Throne of David. For the same reason Jeremiah would have taken with him the daughters of Zedekiah, "tender twigs" who carried Zedekiah's blood, the bloodline of Israel.

Skip to ancient Irish chronicles written at about this time, the sixth century B.C., to historical records such as "The Chronicles of Eri" and "The Annals of Clonmacnoise" and others from which Capt quotes. Ancient records of Ireland refer to the arrival of an "eastern king's daughter" and an old man, "a patriarch, a saint, a prophet called 'Ollam Fodhla'" (Hebrew for "revealer" or "prophet") and his scribe-companion called Simon Brug, Brach, Breack, Barech, Berach, as it is variously spelled. Reportedly, they brought with them ancient holy relics. Among these were a harp, an ark or chest, and a stone called in Gaelic "Lia-Fail," meaning "Stone of Fate" or "Stone of Destiny."

Irish tradition asserts that the "eastern king's daughter" was the daughter and heir of Zedekiah, the last king of Judah, possibly a daughter named Scota, and that Ollam Fodhla was the prophet Jeremiah. That Simon Brug was Baruch, Jeremiah's scribe that figures prominently in biblical history, that the harp was King David's harp, and that the ark or chest was the Ark of the Covenant. And that the stone "Lia-Fail" was Jacob's Pillar, the stone that Jacob had anointed with oil, the stone at Bethel that had been in the presence of God.

Further Irish tradition says that the place in which they settled was named after a princess "Tea Tephi" or "Teah" who requested a choice hill as her dower, and that the Stone Lia Fail became associated with that place where Teah Tephi married and where kings gathered. Through variant spellings of Teah's name (or from "Tamar" or "Tamhra"), the hill became known as Tara, the seat of Irish kings. "Tradition has it," says Pastor Ray Barker, ''that it was the prophet of Israel Jeremiah himself that performed the coronation ceremony upon King Eochaidh and Queen Teah Tephi. When Eochaidh was crowned high king, he was crowned upon this sacred stone, the Stone of Destiny, or Jacob's Pillar Stone, just as all the other kings of Judah/Israel had been crowned before him.''

This was Tara, the place where every king in ''Eireann'' for about 1040 years was crowned, where Celtic kings' coronation ceremonies took place *on* or *upon* the Stone Lia Fail. The ''harp that once through Tara's halls did play'' might or might not have been the harp of David but, as Capt points out, ''the royal arms of Ireland is a representation of the Harp of David and has been for 2500 years.'' Biblical tradition has it that Jeremiah died in Egypt, but Irish tradition points to one of two places in Ireland, both near Tara, where Jeremiah is said to have been buried. In addition, the mystery of Teah Tephi's burial is yet to be uncovered, both the actual burial site and the significance of a stone at Tara with markings that identify Ireland's first Queen of the Davidic line and hint that important relics are also buried in the grave-vault.

According to Capt, regardless of who may have carried Jacob's Stone from Egypt through Spain to Britain, the historical fact remains that it *did* end up in Ireland. It *did* end up in Tara, coronation place of Irish kings. It bore, then as now, two carrying rings embedded in the ends with a trench worn between them, as friction from a sturdy carrying pole would have made. It had and still has a crack, as the one mentioned in the Freemasons' description. Whether it was the prophet Jeremiah or another person who carried the Stone of Destiny to the British Isles, its arrival fulfilled a part of the prophecy that Identity Christians know is still not complete.

When the Stone arrived in Ireland during the sixth century B.C., this completed one ''overturn'' of the three-part prophecy as the Stone of Destiny joined the Anglo-Israelites on British soil.

''I will overturn, overturn, overturn, it: and it shall be no more, until he come whose right it is, and I will give it to him.'' The verse from Ezekiel indicates that there will be three ''overturns'' before the end times begin.

''The 'end times' means the coming of Christ,'' says Charles Lee. ''Like the change of seasons, you look for the signs, and this is one of them.''

The first ''overturn'' saw the Stone moved from Bethel to Ireland. The second "overturn" took place a thousand years later, about A.D. 500, when the stone was moved from Ireland to Scotland.

As accounted in Capt's *Jacob's Pillar,* at that time Fergus Mor McErc (Erc the Great), from the Irish Gaelic Kingdom of Dalriada, successfully invaded the Western coasts of Scotland, the land of the Picts. Fergus knew of the prophecy given by St. Patrick that "wherever the Stone is found the Scottish race will reign," and in declaring himself King of Scotland, Fergus desired that he be crowned upon the stone. He sent that information to his brother Muircheartach, King of Ireland, and his brother sent the stone to Fergus in Scotland. Thus in about A.D. 500 in Dunadd, Scotland, Fergus Mor McErc became the first King of Scotland, crowned as he sat upon the Stone Lia Fail, the Stone of Destiny. In the British Isles, Irish kings had been crowned while sitting on the stone, now Scottish kings.

The stone remained in Dunadd until A.D. 575 when it was taken to Iona, a tiny island of the Inner Hebrides, for the crowning of Aidan, another Irish Gael from Dalriada. (It was carried by St. Columba, the missionary grandson of Fergus Erc the Great.) After one more move to Dunstaffnage, on the mainland of Scotland, in A.D. 843, Kenneth Mac Alpin was crowned sitting upon the Stone Lia Fail as the first King of the United Kingdom of the Picts and the Scots. One of Kenneth I's first acts as king was to found a church at Scone, near Perth in Scotland, and bring the stone to Scone. It was placed in the monastery where it became known as the Stone of Scone, and it remained in Scone for almost five centuries.

During these five centuries in which the Stone of Scone was the coronation seat for Scottish kings, King Kenneth II had an inscription engraved on one side of the stone:

> Ni fallat fatum, Scoti quocunque
> Invenient lapidum regnare tenentur ibidem.

In English:

> If fate go right, where'er this Stone is found
> The Scots shall monarchs of that realm be crowned.

Internecine political rivalry had not yet become bothersome at this time, but by A.D. 1296, King Edward I of England, called "Longshanks," had the power to withstand the forces of Scots nationalist William Wallace, supersede the wishes of Robert the Bruce, king of Scotland, and forcibly remove the Stone of Scone from Scotland and install it in London's Westminster Abbey. Robert the Bruce's letter of protest, the "Declaration of Arbroath," called Scotland's Declaration of Independence, addressed to the Pope and signed by thirty-eight Scottish lords, contains this passage:

> Most Holy Father and Lord, we know and from the chronicles and books of the ancients we find that among other famous nations our own, the Scots . . . journeyed from Greater Scythia by way of the Tyrrhenian Sea and the Pillars of Hercules, and dwelt for a long course of time in Spain. . . . Thence they came, twelve hundred years after the people of Israel crossed the Red Sea, to their home in the west where they still live today . . .
> ("Declaration of Arbroath," second paragraph)

Thus in thirteenth-century Scotland, not only was the Scots' Israelite identity known, but also the purity of their bloodline. In the Scottish kingdom, as Robert the Bruce says in the same document, "there have reigned one hundred and thirteen kings of their own royal stock, the line unbroken [by] a single foreigner."

This move from Scotland to England was the third of the three "over-turns" mentioned in Ezekiel, until the coming of "he whose right it is," to whom *it* will be given.

In 1296 when King Edward I of England carried the Stone of Scone out of Scotland and into England, he had a special hardwood chair built in Westminster Abbey to hold it. Known as "Saint Edward's Chair," or the "Coronation Chair," this six-foot-seven-inch-tall throne-chair held the stone on a sturdy ledge just under the seat, so that when an English king sat, he was sitting upon the Stone of Scone. This chair is still in the chapel named for him.

King Edward I was aware of the Scots' reverence for the stone when he installed it in Westminster Abbey in 1296 and he was aware of the prophecy, as engraved on it by Scottish King Kenneth II, that a *Scot* would occupy the throne wherever the Stone of Destiny was located. This prophecy took on added significance three hundred years later when Queen Elizabeth I of England died childless in 1603. Ironically, or perhaps prophetically, her kinsman James VI of Scotland became James I of England, left Scotland and journeyed to London to sit upon the Stone of

Destiny for his coronation as King of England. The prophecy was again fulfilled, even if a Scot had to change countries in order to be crowned sitting upon the Stone of Jacob. With the exception of James I's daughter Mary Queen of Scots, every British monarch since King Edward I's time, including the present Queen Elizabeth II, has been crowned in King Edward's Coronation Chair, sitting upon Jacob's Stone.

"Comparatively few Bible scholars are aware of the fact," says Capt, "that the Monarchy of Britain as well as most of the other monarchies of Europe are descendant from Judah." In the Scottish National Library there is a Gaelic manuscript by Dugald the Scot, son of McPhail, in A.D. 1467, containing the complete genealogies of the Scottish kings showing their descent through the Irish kings by way of Judah, Jacob, and Isaac back to Abraham. In Windsor Castle there is also a genealogical table showing the descent of the British kings from David through the Irish and Scottish lines. "Thus," says Capt, "the Monarchy existed long before there was a British Nation." He adds,

> Whatever may be said of the story of Jacob's Pillar, as we have traced it, all will agree that it hangs together. While evidence for some links may not be strong, others are quite clear. God said plainly that He would "overturn, overturn, overturn"—"until He (Shiloh, the Messiah) come whose right it is; and I will give it to Him." (EZEK. 21:27). The Throne was "overturned" three times—from Jerusalem to Ireland; from Ireland to Scotland, and then from Scotland to England. This completed the three "overturnings." God's commission to the prophet Jeremiah "to pull down" the Throne of David and "to replant" it was accomplished.
>
> (Capt, *Jacob's Pillar*)

Since 1977 when the above was written, a fourth relocation of Jacob's Stone—from England back to Scotland in 1996, the 700th anniversary of its removal—has more than completed the prophecy given to Jeremiah. While this move may or may not be considered an "overturn," it is at least what Capt in 1997 calls "a change of address."

On November 15, 1996, on orders from England's Prime Minister John Major, the stone was driven across the River Tweed in the back of an army jeep. Escorted by the Coldstream Guards, piped home by soldiers of the King's Own Scottish Borderers skirling a jubilant new tune "The Return of the Stone," Lia Fail, the Stone of Destiny, was returned to the Scottish nation.

Preserving centuries of tradition, as well as biblical prophecy, the stone will be taken back to London temporarily for the coronations of all future British monarchs. The Israel people see proof of Anglo-Israel in the books of history and in the fulfillment of the prophecy of Joseph/Israel to the sons of Joseph: "David shall never want a man to sit upon the throne of the House of Israel . . . a great nation and a company of nations will be of thee . . . and kings shall come out of thy loins." Capt, after describing the English coronation ceremony with its symbolism, concludes:

> Today Britain has the honor and blessing of being custodians of Jacob's Pillar and maintaining the continuity of David's Throne. In this way, they fulfill God's covenant with David. . . . "For thus saith the Lord; David shall never want a man to sit upon the throne of the house of Israel" (Jer. 33:17). . . . One need not worry too much about the geographical location of the Stone. Through the ages, Jacob's Pillar seems to have fulfilled its Divine purpose and the prophecy of Israel. Perhaps we are reaching the time when the "Old Order" passeth, and a Divine "New Order" shall be established.   (Capt, *Jacob's Pillar*)

The promised kingdom might not come without a struggle. A militant element among the soldiers of God feel that, if they must dispossess the non-Israel peoples now occupying the territory appointed for the new kingdom, God's chosen will be victorious. This assurance is based on a promise from Yahweh given long ago: "If the Lord delight in us, then he will bring us into this land, and give it us; a land which floweth with milk and honey. . . . neither fear ye the people of the land; for they are bread for us: their defence is departed from them, and the Lord is with us" (Numbers 14:8–9).

For the believers, the location of this great nation and company of nations is another part of the prophecy that is yet to be revealed, but when the time is right, God's people will assemble in the appointed place.

They may have already begun. As Hawtin observes in *The Abrahamic Covenant,* the rapidly growing United States of America is "a separate Israel nation that at the present time represents the greatest single concentration of Anglo-Saxon, Israelitish people on earth."

# CHAPTER SEVEN

# Seedline, Identity, and the War of Eden

The "Seedline" branch of Christian Identity is a stringent system of beliefs, Scripturally based, literally interpreted, active in application. *Seed* and *line* are understood to denote race and lineage, the seed of Adam pitted against the seed of Satan in a war that began in Eden.

"It's also called Two-Seedline Identity from Genesis 3:15," says Seedline minister Mike Hallimore of Kingdom Identity Ministries, "since all Christians believe in at least one seedline. But Seedline isn't a 'branch' of Christian Identity. It's the root and trunk of the tree! It's the non-Seedliners that are a later 'branch,' actually a hybrid between Identity and their churchianity background. . . . People who want to 'play church' would lead us into another denomination rather than God's Heavenly Kingdom on earth, and this will not be honored by our God who determines the destiny of nations."

While it is not accurate to say that Covenant Identity Christians are thinkers and Seedline Identity Christians are doers, the media would do well to learn the difference. Not all soldiers have the same commission, and on the battlefield a soldier has no obligation to defend his actions. "Most activists are Seedline," says Hallimore, "but most Seedliners are not activists and certainly shouldn't be equated with violence. Likewise, many non-Seedliners are wimps, but not all non-Seedliners are wimps. . . . In some cases, so-called 'leaders' who lack the spiritual capacity to understand the full message, some of them racially mixed themselves, would want to 'water-down' the racial aspects of biblical teaching. God said 'Because thou art lukewarm, and neither cold nor hot, I will spue thee out of my mouth' Revelation 3:16. Men who call themselves soldiers and are led by their own mind instead of the Holy Spirit fall into the same category. . . . Non-Seedline ministries use a variety of terms [to describe themselves], including 'Identity' until the heat is on, then they run from every word the press wants to use in a bad light.''

Covenant Pastor George Southwick is a believer in the Christian Israel message, although he avoids the term ''Identity'' and rankles at the idea of being lumped into the same category with Seedliners. Southwick rejects Seedline doctrine and argues that it is based on a misunderstanding of scripture and is logically flawed from the beginning. His contention is that if Adam and Eve both partook of ''sexual fruit,'' then God's chosen are descendent of a homosexual and a harlot. ''The way these Seedliners talk about Mother Eve,'' Southwick says, ''it's a wonder righteous women in the congregation don't take a frying pan to them.'' Where Southwick does agree with Hallimore, however, is that the press uses terms such as ''seedline'' and ''identity'' to present both systems of belief in a bad light.

Terminology notwithstanding, actions violent enough to make the national news can be justified biblically within this righteously defiant faction of Identity—what one person calls ''deadly Seedline'' and Seedliners call ''a stronger calling''—with its Christian soldiers who do not fear the enemy or the press.

Kingdom Identity Ministries in Harrison, Arkansas, is a Seedline ministry that announces on its web site: ''Kingdom Identity Ministries is a Politically Incorrect Christian Identity outreach ministry to God's chosen race (true Israel, the White, European peoples).''

''Some of you will be disturbed by what you see on our web site and in the material we distribute,'' says Hallimore. ''You are not interested in truth, and will use overworn clichés such as 'You can make the Bible say anything' to justify your ignorance and unwillingness to take an honest look at what the Scriptures teach. You would rather parrot the politically-correct lies told by the media and Judeo-Christian churches of today. . . . We are careful to support what we say with verifiable facts. . . . True Bible, true history, true science, and common sense do not contradict one another.''

Kingdom Identity Ministries utilizes a variety of outlets to spread its message, states Hallimore. In addition to its active prison ministry, its

*Herald of Truth* radio broadcasts air seven days a week from shortwave stations in Miami, New Orleans, and McCaysville, Georgia, over satellite and micro-rebroadcasters, and can be heard live on the Internet. With this world-wide coverage, Hallimore believes that *Herald of Truth* fulfills the prophecy "And this gospel of the kingdom shall be preached in all the world for witness unto all nations; and then shall the end come." Another outlet is KIM's web site, where users can read its statement of beliefs, keep abreast of Identity activities, and access KIM's mail-order outreach, which offers books, audio and video tapes, and other materials by noted Identity pastors, theologians, and scholars such as E. Raymond Capt, the late Sheldon Emry, Dan Gayman, Howard B. Rand, and others. Of special interest are works by the late Wesley Smith and Bertrand L. Comparet, whose Seedling teachings comprise a cornerstone of Kingdom Identity Ministries's theological platform. KIM's *Doctrinal Statement of Beliefs* is, according to Hallimore, "*the* definitive explanation of what Christian Identity is all about."

In 1998 Hallimore was "highly honored" to have *Your Heritage,* the ministry founded in the 1950s by Bertrand Comparet, become a part of Kingdom Identity Ministries. Included in the collection are Comparet's extensive library of rare books, original sermon tapes, photographs, personal files and study notes. These materials will be made available for research, along with KIM's own collection of rare books and materials, Hallimore says, when sufficient funds have been raised to house and catalog them. In addition to *Your Heritage,* another exclusive aspect of Kingdom Identity Ministries is management of the AIT, a quite special responsibility.

*The American Institute of Theology* Correspondence Bible Course (AIT) is the only comprehensive Bible study program that expounds Seedline principles, or any other detailed aspect of Identity teaching, for that matter. Originally founded by Bertrand Comparet in 1965 as a correspondence school based in Newhall, California, the AIT is now administered by Kingdom Identity Ministries in Harrison, Arkansas. According to information provided by Hallimore, the original purpose for this impressive 300-page volume was to provide a course of Bible study for "those who desire an accurate, non-denominational understanding of the Christian Israel Holy Scriptures."

Eight theologians worked for two and a half years, completing this course in 1970, and access to the copyrighted volume is limited. Printed by Kingdom Identity Ministries on multicolored paper according to lessons, it is bound in an attractive binder and provided through Kingdom Identity Ministries and Saxon University to students for testing and a diploma. The AIT was "written in great part by Bertrand Comparet" and portions were written by the late Dr. Wesley Swift, but those portions are not identified, and no authors' names appear on the title page. Hallimore calls the late Bible scholar and attorney Bertrand L. Comparet "the greatest Identity scholar of the twentieth century. Virtually every Identity minister of any prominence has either taken the AIT course or purchased it as a Reference Manual."

In addition to Biblical exegesis with a chapter devoted to each book of both Old and New Testament, the 95-chapter AIT volume contains political commentary and related scientific studies, historical references, portions of the Apocrypha, maps, charts and tables. With its lesson-style format, it is used as a text in a Basic Theology Course as part of the curriculum of Saxon University, established in 1995 in Houston, Missouri, by Faith Baptist Church and Ministries and Senior Pastor Dr. Everett Ramsey. The volume is also among the written material available to state and federal prisoners through the prison ministry of both Kingdom Identity Ministries and Aryan Nations, but not without distribution problems. Hallimore says that although there are sometimes difficulties with prison officials who deny access by Identity pastors or unfairly screen inmates' mail, prisoners who cannot relate to mainstream "Christian*dumb*" churches easily grasp the concepts of Identity. Prisoners with access to teachings in the AIT are overwhelmingly Seedline. (Some states, such as Texas, do not pay prison inmates and their money is limited. Prisoners who do not have cash may substitute stamps.) As of March 2000, the AIT is being revised and is to be retitled *The Millennium Edition,* but its basic teachings are unchanged.

The core beliefs of the Kingdom Identity "Seedline" Doctrine, as listed in its "Doctrinal Statement of Beliefs" (also posted on the Kingdom Identity Ministries web site), include 23 multi-part tenets with more than 300 Scripture sources as support. These beliefs are the theological base upon which Identity is built, Seedline being only one portion of the Doctrine. Tenets in the "Doctrinal Statement of Beliefs," greatly condensed and omitting the Scripture sources for brevity, include the following:

WE BELIEVE in YHVH [Yahweh] the one and only true and living eternal God.

WE BELIEVE the entire Bible, both Old and New Testaments . . . the history, covenants, and prophecy . . . about a specific elect family of people who are children of YHVH God through the seedline of Adam.

WE BELIEVE Yahshua the Messiah (Jesus the Christ) to be the incarnate begotten son of God . . . born of the Virgin Mary . . . who died for our sins . . . arose from the grave on the third day . . . and ascended into Heaven where He is now reigning at the right hand of God.

WE BELIEVE membership in the church of Yahshua . . . is by Divine election. Only the called children of God can come to the Savior to hear His words and believe; those who are not of God, cannot hear His voice.

WE BELIEVE in water baptism by immersion . . . Baptism being ordained of God as testimony to the New Covenant as circumcision was under the Old Covenant.

WE BELIEVE God chose unto Himself a special race of people that are above all people upon the face of the earth. These children of Abraham through the called-out seedline of Isaac and Jacob . . . are the ones to whom the Messiah came, electing out of all twelve tribes those who inherit the Kingdom of God.

WE BELIEVE the White, Anglo-Saxon, Germanic and kindred people to be God's true, literal Children of Israel.

WE BELIEVE in an existing being known as the Devil or Satan and called the Serpent, who has a literal "seed" . . . commonly called Jews today.

WE BELIEVE that the Man Adam . . . is father of the White Race only. [Only] Adam and his descendants can know YHVH God as their Father, not merely as their creator. Adamic man is made trichotomous, that is, not only of body and soul, but having an implanted spirit . . . distinguishing him from all other races of the earth.

WE BELIEVE that as a chosen race, we are not to be partakers of the wickedness of this world system, but . . . be a separated people. This includes segregation from all non-white races . . . Race-mixing is an abomination in the sight of Almighty God, a satanic attempt meant to destroy the chosen seedline, and is strictly forbidden by His command-ments.

WE BELIEVE that . . . Theocracy being the only perfect form of government, and God's divine Law for governing a nation being far superior to man's laws, we are not to add to or diminish from His commandments. All present world problems are a result of disobedience to the Laws of God.

WE BELIEVE men and women should conduct themselves according to the role of their gender in the traditional Christian sense that God intended. . . . Homosexuality is an abomination before God and should be punished by death.

WE BELIEVE [in] the establishment of the Kingdom of God upon this earth.

The final tenet ends with the belief that Yashua the Messiah (Jesus Christ) will return to restore righteous government on the earth, and all evil shall be destroyed. This belief is shared by Identity Christians across the board, but those of the pugnacious Seedline persuasion would prefer to destroy as much of the present evil on earth as is in their power, before Jesus returns. "While I believe in administering the Laws of God (including the 21 capital offenses) as the Law of the land," says Hallimore, "I do not believe in ex post facto laws and would not punish someone for crimes committed prior to their implementation." The AIT's Chapter 86 "There is No Pacifism in the Bible" does not say that there is never a place for pacifism, but it does say that "Jesus Christ Himself recognizes that there can never be 'peaceful coexistence' between good and evil."

Identity Christians do not find it contradictory to revere Jesus and condemn Jews. Quite the opposite, since Yashua was not a Jew, and He Himself condemned Jews. A key point is that the Son of Man did not come from "a generation of vipers."

According to Identity Pastor Curtis Clair Ewing's tract "A Study Into the Meaning of the Word Gentile as Used in the Bible," a great deal of confusion and misunderstanding has been caused by the use of the word *gentile* in English translations of the Bible. The word *gentile* or *gentiles* [uncapitalized by Ewing] that is translated variously as "heathen," "people," "another" or "others," as well as "nation"—a word akin to the Hebrew *goyim* and the Greek *ethne*—is a word with plural concept that applies to a group rather than to an individual. Like the Latin word *gentilis,* the connotation refers more to a "non-something" than to a "something," and its meaning derives from its speaker. Used by a Roman it means non-Roman, used by a Jew it means non-Jew, and used by an Israelite it means non-Israelite.

The AIT's Chapter 33 "Who Are the Gentiles?" says that everywhere you find the word "Gentile" used in the Old Testament, it is a mistranslation of the Hebrew word *goy* or *goyim* which means "nation." So why didn't they translate it correctly? Because they—the English translators—translated it to fit the official doctrines of the church of their day (1611 if referring to King James, for example), no matter what that did to the true meaning of the word. The word *gentilis,* or Gentile, from Latin simply means "one who is not a Roman citizen." "The church hierarchy of the English translators determined what its doctrines should be," the author of the AIT says:

> . . . and if the Bible didn't agree with them, so much the worse for the Bible. Men were still being burned at the stake for heresy in those days: and "heresy" meant any religious ideas which differed from the official doctrines proclaimed by the Bishops. So the translators did the best the Church would allow them to. . . . In the King James' Version, you will see that it is never used in the correct sense. . . . Therefore, it has no authority at all.

> In short, wherever you see the word "Gentile" in the Bible, remember that the correct word is "nation", "race", or "people". Sometimes it is used when speaking of ISRAEL nations or the ISRAELITE race . . . In other instances, the context will show that it is being used of a nation which is non-Israelite. Only the context in which it is used will show you which meaning to give it.

And if Christ Himself offers condemnation to the Jews, calling them *you* "vipers" and forbidding them entry into the Kingdom of God, can the Servant Nation do less?

*Crosstalk,* an occasional, non-copyrighted, undated publication of the White Camelia Knights, devotes two pages of one issue to this topic which reads, in part:

> One of the most destructive ideas ever advanced in human history is the false and unscriptural notion that Jesus was a Jew. Many, many people are in bondage to this false notion. They are not aware of the Satanic practices of Jews. They are not aware of their vicious, Christ-hating behavior. . . .

> . . . the word "Jew" is not mentioned in the Old Testament until after the deaths of Abraham, Isaac, Jacob, Joseph, Moses, King David and Solomon. The translators incorrectly substituted this sickening word for "Judean" which merely meant they were residents of Judea. In Judea, at that time, there were members of the black, yellow and white races, plus many mongrels such as the Jews. Then, as now, they confused nationality with race, unfortunate but true.

> . . . But today thousands of preachers and teachers within these organizations [orthodox denominations] boldly and flagrantly deny the Deity of Jesus Christ

and the authority of the Bible, and are encouraged and frequently financed by the modern apostate Jews. These traitors while remaining inside these denominations and taking the names involved in their rich tradition have denied and betrayed every basic principle, not only of the denomination, but of the Christian religion as such.

The *Crosstalk* article claims it was the Sadducees, a group composed entirely of Jews, who led and controlled the infiltration of Jerusalem, as well as the appropriation of the title "Israel." Identity Christians hold that it was this group addressed by Jesus when He stated, "Ye serpents, ye generation of vipers, how can ye escape the damnation of hell?" (Matthew 23:33). John the Baptist, himself a harbinger of the Lamb of God, refused to baptize the imposters—the Jews in Israelite clothing— and echoed the words of Christ as he turned them away. "O generation of vipers, who hath warned you to flee from the wrath to come?" (Matthew 3:7).

It must be noted that, for the faithful, terms such as "generation," "nation," and "people" are used to denote race and *race only,* despite the inconsistency of English translation from words in Hebrew and Greek. Seedline Identity holds that it is a mistake to translate these terms in any other way and certainly they should not be confused with nationality in the sense of citizenship. But as an individual can be evil, so can a race through its lineage.

Given the tenets of Seedline belief, which hinges upon the Angelic Conflict, everything that happens upon the earth is seen as a component of a supernatural struggle and weighed on the scale of good and evil. The racialist believers see conspiracy in the government, racial destruction in integration, AIDS as a curse—more precisely a blessing—from Yahweh which can be eradicated with the simple eradication of homosexuals and drug users, tolerance for non-Christian religions as a slap in the face of the true God, and the Jews as the evil entity behind every other evil on the planet.

As a devout believer, Cadillac John Thellin looks forward to the end times, to the fulfillment of the prophecies of Revelation, to the millennium, to the reign of Christ and the end of these evils. He doesn't think we have far to go. "Look around you, man," he says. "You just take a look around and tell me that you don't see how screwed up things are in this country . . . in the world."

The Judeo-Christian idea of Jesus Christ as the "Prince of Peace" only is an erroneous conception as far as Seedline Identity is concerned. Cadillac John states, "He will come with fire and sword, and I'll be right there with him, in a body that cannot be killed . . . that will never die. It says right there in the Bible, Luke 22:36, let him who doesn't have a sword, sell his coat and buy him one."

John Thellin is not alone in his militant vision of the Second Coming or in his preparations for the return of Christ, which is far removed from the Rapture embraced by many in Christendom. Readiness for the end times, the reign of Christ, eternity, has long been a part of orthodox Christianity although there are many denominational variances on how such end-times beliefs are understood. One conventional perspective is that the prophecies of Revelation are given to Christians that they may understand the portents of the Second Coming and prepare themselves for the tribulation. In fact, there are any number of believers who welcome the end times because they signal the return of the Savior. Such is the case for most Identity Christians, both Seedline and non-Seedline.

There has never been, in the entire history of Christianity, a shortage of apocalyptic visionaries—those who see the tribulations foreshadowed in the most common of events and omens at every turn. Even the apostle Paul seems to have expected Christ to return in his lifetime. The implications of the coming fulfillment of the prophecies are often interpreted in ways which are widely varied. However, almost all of these interpretations include the idea of persecution directed toward the followers of Christ. And many include the ideas of separation, of withdrawal into the relative safety of enclaves of like-minded believers. Such was the case with David Koresh and the Waco Branch Davidians.

Koresh and company, not Identity Christians but sharing some of the same beliefs, were anything but passively contemplating the mysteries of faith as they stockpiled arms against the persecution they knew would be coming from the Satanic federal government. They believed in the chosen few, the small handful of the righteous, standing firm and resolute against both corporeal and supernatural forces arrayed against them. Both prophet and Messiah to his followers, Koresh constantly warned of the need for vigilance, preparedness, the will to resist evil. It was, he told them, better they should all perish together rather than yield to the Beast—the federal government of the United States. The government, it would seem, was willing to bring on the Armageddon that Koresh spoke of, and several Identity Christians were among those in Waco observing from the sidelines.

Charles Lee notes that ''Armageddon happens every day. What day isn't the end of the world for someone? David Koresh was wrong in his religious beliefs, in my opinion, but I don't hold that against him. What he was *right* about was the need for people to be able to protect themselves when they have to. And he was right again when he identified who they needed to protect themselves against. The federal government fully intends to strip us of our freedoms. Whatever else he may have been wrong about, Koresh was right to preach that Christians need to defend themselves and their faith. If they don't, there won't be a faith . . . there won't be any Christians.''

In a sermon delivered at Aryan Nations, Pastor Richard Butler reiterates the idea, ''You have to kill the thing that is killing you.'' As far as the racial right is concerned, the policies of the federal government—affirmative action, welfare, special privileges for special interest (racial) groups, unfair taxation, abandonment of sovereignty to one-worlders, sanctioned abortion, forced integration and race mixing, intrusive and unfair laws interfering with the individual's rights to freedom and self-determination—are all killing the Aryan race.

The Statement of Beliefs of Aryan Nations/Church of Jesus Christ Christian provided by Aryan Nations (which differs in thoroughness from the abbreviated version posted on the Internet and differs in wording from the Kingdom Identity Doctrinal Statement), among its twelve major tenets announces its stand and addresses the areas in which White Israel is most often attacked. Portions of the Aryan Nations tenets (again condensing and omitting the Scripture sources for brevity) state:

WE BELIEVE the Bible is the true Word of God (Yahweh) written for and about specific people. The Bible is the family history of the White Race, the children of Yahweh placed on earth through the seedline of Adam.

WE BELIEVE that Adam-man of Genesis was the placing of the White Race upon this earth. Not all races descend from Adam. Adam is the father of the White Race only.

WE BELIEVE that the true, literal children of the Bible are the Twelve Tribes of Israel, now scattered throughout the world and now known as the Anglo-Saxon, Teutonic, Scandinavian, Celtic, Basque, Lombard, Slavic, and kindred peoples of the earth. . . . Yahweh blessed Abraham and promised that he would be the ''father of nations.'' This same promise continued through the seedline of Abraham . . .

WE BELIEVE that there are literal children of Satan in the world today. These children are the descendants of Cain . . . a result of Eve's original sin, her physical seduction by Satan. . . . there is a battle and a natural enmity between the children of Satan and the children of Yahweh.

WE BELIEVE that the Canaanite Jew is the natural enemy of our white Christian Race . . . The Jew is like a destroying virus that attacks our racial body to destroy our white culture and purity of our race.

WE BELIEVE that there is a battle being fought this day between the children of darkness (today known as Jews) and the children of Light (Yahweh, the Everliving God), the White Race (the true Israel of the Bible).

WE BELIEVE that Yahweh created pure seedlines (Races) and that each have a specific place in His order on this earth under the administration of His Life Law . . . *[There is no race hatred in this statement; it was and is the plan of Yahweh to bless all through the seed of Abraham.]* [preceding brackets and italics in the original. Eds.]

WE BELIEVE in the preservation of our Race, individually and collectively, as a people, as demanded and directed by Yahweh. We believe our Racial nation has a right and is under obligation to preserve itself and its members.

WE BELIEVE that the present world problems are a result of our disobedience to His Divine Law. His intended purpose is that His racial kinsmen are to have dominion over this earth. Our Race, within itself, holds divine power; and when we abrogate and violate Divine Law, we give power to our enemies. Evil is the result to all.

WE BELIEVE that the redemptive work of Jesus was finished on the Cross. As His divine Race, we have been commissioned to fulfill His Divine purpose and plan: the restitution of all things.

WE BELIEVE the words of Jesus Christ: "For nothing is secret that shall not be made manifest; neither anything hid, that shall not be known and come abroad."

WE BELIEVE that there is a day of reckoning. The usurper will be thrown out by the terrible might of Yahweh's people as they return to their roots and their special destiny. We know there is soon to be a day of judgment and a day when Christ's Kingdom (government) will be established on earth, as it is in heaven. . . .

The codification of beliefs into a statement of faith is a major foundation of other Identity churches, as well, and while the wording and thoroughness vary, the basic tenets of the statements indicate a unified stand against the forces that they have identified as their enemies.

For Identity Christians, not only the government is involved in killing the white race, but mainstream Christian churches as well. As one Identity theologian says in a newsletter, referring to Southern Baptists, "Pastors teach false doctrine so openly that they make fools of themselves." The denominational teachings of mainstream Christianity, many Identity pastors claim, are actively leading people astray from the path of true Christianity—Anglo-Saxons, Aryan peoples who should recognize their identity as true Israel—in both doctrine and practice. For Seedline Identity Christians, this is directly attributable to the influence of the "seed of the serpent," the Jews, who have insinuated themselves into every aspect of American life including the Christian faith and particularly into the workings of the federal government.

For anyone reared in Western Christian civilization, such anti-Jewish concepts should not be foreign. For centuries Jews were the evil "Christ-killers" of orthodox Christendom, but in modern Christian denominations, it is generally accepted that Jews can gain redemption and salvation by conversion to Christianity. However, for the more unorthodox segments of Christendom, such as Seedline Identity, this is not the case. "You don't change fathers with a so-called conversion," says Mike Hallimore. "When you baptize a Jew, all you get is a wet Jew. Martin Luther said 'If I were to baptize a Jew I should conduct him to the Bridge leading over the River Elbe, I should fasten a stone to his neck and should thrust him into the waters.' . . . Christ was speaking to 'believing Jews' when He told them they were of their father the devil."

"I have spent my whole life fighting against the Jew and against the nigger," J. B. Stoner announces by way of introduction to a gathering of white supremacists in 1993. Stoner, a long-time Klansman, is a former attorney disbarred following his eventual conviction for the bombing of Bethel Baptist Church (a black church) in Montgomery, Alabama, in 1958. Three years after his 1977 indictment, Stoner was convicted of this crime and began serving a ten-year sentence in 1983. He is now a free man. Stoner was at one time the defense attorney for James Earl Ray, convicted assassin of Dr. Martin Luther King.

"I am not going to tell you to go to one church or another . . . Methodist, Baptist, whatever . . . one is about as rotten as the other," he remarks, later in the same speech. Stoner maintains that the "rottenness" of contemporary Christian teachings and practices is due to Jewish influence and urges his listeners to get involved in an Identity church which, as he points out, is the only appropriate faith for a white man. It is the only faith which promotes the white racial right to self-protection, to the concepts of racial continuance and identity.

In the beliefs of Christian Identity, it is not just the right to self-protection—indeed, that is a given sanctioned by Christ himself—but it is also the mission of the Servant Nation which is at issue, a mission recognized by both Seedline and Covenant Christians. Identity Pastor Ray Barker explains in a sermon, ''God has chosen Israel to be a Servant Race, and God has chosen his people Israel to be a witness of Him to the rest of the world. God has blessed this nation so that we could be a blessing.'' Belief in this special calling is a given in Identity, but the zealous faithful often have to contend with conflicting loyalties. White Israel is the earthly agent of Yahweh, and for those who recognize that divine calling, fealty to God and the mission of God outweigh adherence to any other guidelines or sanctions formulated by man—or the agents of Satan. This includes the various interpretations of rights and blessings given to the Israel people in the Laws of God which cross swords with U.S. law. And in this conflict, the faithful know which must supersede.

Seedline adherents—given their doctrinal beliefs—consider such alienation to be anything but an accidental occurrence. In fact, it is simply further proof that the War of Eden still rages. Thus, all the ills of modern American society and indeed all the ills which plague the world today are seen as components of the Angelic conflict, a physical manifestation of a supernatural struggle begun in the days of the Creation.

As always, being one of the chosen is not an easy task. The Father of Lies and his children are every bit as committed to the destruction of the Aryan race as the Identity Christians are to its preservation. Yet, from the perspective of the Identity Christian, the struggle is on behalf of Yahweh and therefore cannot be lost. The Seedline Christian is quick to point out that the signs of this conflict are all around us—in government, arts, the media, the quasi-religion of ''Judeo-Christianity,'' and the dying communities of the working class.

Identity Christians know the white race must suffer to come to a full realization of who they are. When times become hard enough, the sleeping giant of the Aryan will waken to claim his true heritage; when enough white businesses are closed, when enough white people are clogging the unemployment lines while non-whites are working at the jobs that whites once held, when enough dark faces invade his neighborhoods with drugs, perversions and alien ways, then true revolution will occur. Though certainly seen as something looming on the horizon, that time has not yet come.

And because most Christians, and most whites in general, simply do not understand the significance of what is happening around them, the necessity for such organizations as the Aryan Nations, the various skinhead groups, the Klan and all the other Aryan supremacist groups is manifestly evident for Identity Christians. As far as Seedliners are concerned, the movement is both a crusade and a self-defense measure. All the people interviewed for this work, regardless of their affiliation in terms of specific organizations, are consistent in one overriding belief: the white Christian is targeted for destruction.

The perpetrators of this genocidal plot are, of course, the Jews. Identity Christians of the White Camelia support this claim with scriptural interpretations and quotes, as do countless other Seedline-based ministries whose beliefs reflect the teachings of the AIT. "The whole history of the world can be explained by the enmity YHVH put between the two seeds as recorded in Genesis 3:15," says Mike Hallimore.

It is this gamut of evils historically perpetrated against YHVH's people that the AIT addresses with Scriptures, explanations, and exhortations. Combating God's enemies—the seed of Satan—is a major commission for the Israel people, but only separation from other unwholesome influences in the world will ensure continuation of the purity of the Adamic bloodline.

The AIT's Chapter 21, "Does God Command Racial Segregation?," traces the ways in which interbreeding and mongrelization have caused the downfall of individuals and potentially of nations, and the righteous elimination of race-mixers purified them.

Chapter 29, "God's Immigration Laws," gives scriptural evidence that "the world's overflow from pagan lands who hate our god [sic]" is unacceptable to Yahweh, "Lest strangers be filled with thy wealth; and thy labours be in the house of a stranger . . . Let them be only thine own, and not strangers' with thee" (Proverbs 5:10, 17). When greedy non-Christian aliens are allowed into our country, they "either remain a hostile enemy bloc within our borders or else mongrelize and destroy our own race by mixing the seed."

Chapter 32, "Job: An Allegory of the Adamic Race," says of the victimization of the white race by "unclean spirits," the Jews: "We are rapidly approaching a one-world monetary system, a one-world government and a one-world religion. None of these systems can help the Adamic man know the will of God, because they are man made and oriented to things physical, not spiritual.'' When Job defied his ''friends'' the nay-sayers and realized his true relation to God, ''the Lord blessed his latter end more than his beginning. Here is the resounding victory of the Adamic race over Satan.''

Chapter 56, ''Can Anything be 'Judaeo-Christian'?,'' says: ''Seven different times, Jesus begins His denunciation of the Jews with the words, 'Woe unto you, scribes and Pharisees, hypocrites!' . . . Without one single exception, Jesus utterly rejected and condemned Judaism, in language as strong as He ever used against complete idolatry. . . . Christianity and Judaism are completely and irreconcilably inconsistent.''

God's chosen still fight the war that began in Eden, the seedline of Adam in combat with the seedline of Satan, a war in which His people are guaranteed victory but not without determination, struggle and a dogged obedience to the Laws of Yahweh. ''God wrote it, through His Prophets, and His commandments are always right,'' the AIT says emphatically: ''FOR OUR OWN GOOD, FOR THE VERY SURVIVAL OF OUR WHITE RACE UPON THE EARTH, AND THAT WE MAY FACE OUR GOD WITH A BETTER CONSCIENCE, WE HAD BETTER OBEY THESE LAWS OF HIS.''

Chapter 86, ''There Is No Pacifism in the Bible,'' is even more emphatic, particularly dealing with those who sin openly. If you see someone committing a wrong, it says, don't ''merely stand around murmuring pious platitudes about the desirability of good conduct! Your duty—and we do mean DUTY—as a good Christian is to stop him, if you have to kill him to do it.''

# CHAPTER EIGHT

# Ministry of the Warrior Christ

Branson, Missouri, is a small town nestled into the rolling green mountains of the Ozark range. Ablaze in neon, the Branson Strip features rows of show clubs lining both sides of the four-lane road and bearing the names of entertainers such as Anita Bryant, Jakov Smirnoff, Mickey Gilley and other performers who are quickly building Branson's status as a tourist Mecca. In fact, Branson promises to soon give Nashville a run for its money as the country music capital of the world. The Branson Strip ends at the edge of town, becoming a winding mountain road. A large billboard on the right advises that just ahead is The Shepherd of the Hills Homestead and Outdoor Theatre. On the billboard, two armed and mounted Klan night riders, in nineteenth-century regalia, are on the move. Branson, Missouri—modern, industrious, thriving—is hardly unaware of its history and its roots.

In late April 1997, the Fourth Annual Super Conference of Christian Israel Churches—hosted by Pastor Everett Ramsey of Faith Baptist Church in Houston, Missouri—was held at Branson's Lodge of the Ozarks. The parking lot outside the Lodge is jammed with cars and motor homes bearing license plates from Texas, Pennsylvania, Ohio, Oregon, Louisiana, Minnesota, Idaho, Georgia, and other states. Rarely do two adjacent vehicles display the same state's plates. Charter tour buses are a steady stream along the heavily traveled Strip, depositing vacationers, tourists and conventioneers from across the country at the various motels, lodges, restaurants and clubs. Moving among the sightseers and tourists, there are other pilgrims, pilgrims whose purpose in Branson has nothing to do with the clubs, the scenery, the family-oriented entertainment industry which is the pride of Branson.

Identity Christians and those interested in investigating the faith have gathered from all over America to hear such speakers as Pastor Pete Peters of the LaPorte Church of Christ in Colorado; Biblical archeologist E. Raymond Capt of California; historian and author Richard Hoskins of Virginia; Charles Weisman of Michigan, lecturer and prolific author of Identity books and tracts; Col. Gordon (Jack) Mohr, Baptist minister and author who is known for having been the first American prisoner of the Korean War; Pastor James Bruggemann of North Carolina, Director of Stone Kingdom Ministries; Pastor David Barley of America's Promise Church and Ministries in Sandpoint, Idaho; Pastor Earl Jones of the Christian Crusade for Truth, Deming, New Mexico; and the host Dr. Everett Ramsey of Missouri. Above the stage stretches the blue and gold banner of Saxon University, setting for the awarding of theology degrees Friday evening.

Among the crowd in the Crystal room are neophytes and long-time believers, Mennonites, Baptists, Pentecostals and Christians of other faiths—the majority also believers in the message of Christian Israel, others simply curious—as well as a couple of slightly nervous writers. A number of the men are bearded, sporting bushy and angular styles reminiscent of the Amish and reflecting a passage in the Bible admonishing men not to trim the corners of their beards. The women are modestly dressed and children roam about the halls and outside by the fountains, finding the gurgling water much more fascinating than any of the activities in which their parents might be engaged. One man, a Midwestern pastor of a mainstream Christian church, attends because he wants to see for himself "what this Identity thing" is all about.

The Branson Conference draws a considerable number of attendees, an announced figure of six-hundred-fifty. First on the program is E. Raymond Capt, who shows his latest video-documentary, "Faith of Our Fathers," followed by a variety of speakers. There is, of course, Christian entertainment featuring singers and music, both nonprofessionals and professionals, which might surprise someone accustomed to more conventional religious gatherings. Among them is the Boatright family with their handcrafted dulcimers and harps. Jonathan Brown, a composer and musician from Springfield, Missouri, sings his original compositions which include such lyrics as "take the law into your own hands and read it into the night," and titles with historical allusions such as "Sinners in the Hands of an Angry God." Tonya Brown, a young woman from Illinois, sings of the evils of abortion. Jonathan Brown is one of the few long-haired men attending the conference, his thick, dark hair tied back into a ponytail and reaching the middle of his back. "Jonathan is a Nazarite," one of the men in the crowd explains. "He doesn't believe in cutting his hair."

There is an easy familiarity among many in attendance. Acquaintances who perhaps have not been in touch for a while greet one another warmly with handshakes and hugs while new friendships are forged among others. However, if the music provokes the idea among the uninitiated that this is no conventional Christian group, then all doubt is removed as the conference proper gets under way. Speaker after speaker delivers the message of Christian Israel to the receptive audience and the choruses of "amens" so long a part of the Southern revival experience.

It should not be surprising to find members of more mainstream denominations in attendance. The message of Christian Israel has met with some success among Christians whose faiths do not traditionally include this particular doctrine of the Elect or Seedline beliefs as tenets. However, Identity Christians are also missionaries to other Christians, with an eye toward promoting those specific tenets that *are* Identity. It would not be erroneous to consider some missions as stealth. Suppose, for instance, that adherents to Christian Identity infiltrated local churches. Suppose they were to feel out the congregation, seeking potential converts. As Charles Lee has pointed out, "There are people sitting in pews across the country who feel the same way we do." Might not such pews prove fertile ground to sow the seeds of Anglo-Israel?

If such soil were fertile enough, it would not be a particularly strenuous stretch of the imagination to envision an absolute ideological takeover of an entire congregation. In the more right-wing and fundamentalist congregations, where there is already a strong distrust of government as well as a pre-existing and equally strong belief that Armageddon is due around the turn of the century or soon thereafter, this is not a quantum leap in logic. Even if such mass conversion does not take place, it is still likely that the occasional convert will be picked up from time to time.

Evangelism has always been an element of Christianity. The obligation of the faithful to spread the word of God exists in every Christian faith. For some believers it is a more integral component of faith than for others, but all must bear witness of Christ. Such ministry is also an obligation of the Christian Identity faith. This is the purpose of Kingdom Identity Ministries in Harrison, Arkansas; of the Church of Jesus Christ Christian, in Hayden Lake, Idaho; of the Christian Israel Covenant Church in Colville, Washington, as well as other outreach ministries both national and international. Among these is Scriptures for America Worldwide, directed by Pastor Pete Peters of LaPorte, Colorado.

Pastor Peter J. Peters of the LaPorte Church of Christ, a prominent Identity author and speaker whose candor often triggers profound emotional responses among those exposed to it, attacks controversial issues with single-minded intensity, and peppery essays and sermons. In the best tradition of old-time evangelism, he alternately elevates the faithful at the Branson conference by speaking to their courage, commitment and faith and excoriates them for their gullibility, frailness, and spiritual shortcomings. "I love you all," he says to the crowd. And they love him back.

The Branson conference, like most other religious conferences and conventions, primarily consists of "preaching to the choir" of like-minded believers, rather than seeking converts at these particular meetings. But the lifeblood of any religious movement is in converts for, without converts, such movements go the way of the Shakers. And Identity Christians insist their message will be carried to potential converts in spite of all the barriers erected by ZOG and the ministers of "Churchianity." An idea, particularly of divine origin, cannot be killed with bullets, stopped at borders, censored or censured out of existence, or otherwise held at bay by men. For the Identity Christian, it is the message of power, of victory, of the will of God and there is no way to effectively resist it.

As a minister of Yahweh, Pastor Peters's ministry extends far beyond his public lectures and sermons. Peters also spreads the Word through Scriptures for America Worldwide web site, shortwave radio programs and mail ministries. In his tract *The Bible: Handbook for Survivalists, Racists, Tax Protestors, Militants and Right-Wing Extremists,* Peters makes the point that America's problems are a result of the distortion or abandonment of the biblical principles which made the country great to begin with. Peters maintains that Jewish conspirators, corrupting the Scriptures with the doctrines of Karl Marx, are intentionally changing the Christian religion in order to bring about global enslavement. The "robust faith" of the founding fathers, he claims, found in pure and undiluted readings of the Scriptures, has been rendered into a "passive pablum," a conglomeration of foreign ideas and doctrine for a people totally alienated from their Creator.

Prayer, penance and the hope of the rapture are the weak-sister tactics of Judeo-Christians, as far as the Identity Christians of the racial right are concerned. The war with the Jew is a war to the death. It is holy war, an ongoing war that has been fought by every Adamic generation since the Creation. Many Identity believers and ministers, such as Pete Peters, see in the Bible a chronicle of that war and the heroes of Yahweh who have fought it.

In his *The Bible: Handbook* essay, Peters holds up examples of the type of men God honors and blesses. He lists the "survivalist" Noah, the "militant" Samson, the "tax protestor" Gideon, the "right-wing extremists" Shadrach, Meshach and Abednego, the "racist" Phinehas and the "paramilitarist" Christ Himself.

Noah, for instance, is a survivalist in the sense that he is designated by Yahweh, as a righteous man, to be the instrument by which the lineage of God's chosen will be ensured. As Noah builds his ark of gopherwood, he endures the questions and taunts of the sinful who do not understand, who do not believe. Yet the floods come and the "crackpot" Noah and his family survive while those who doubted drown. Preparation—unpopular, misunderstood, made light of—is the key to survival, and survival itself is a key element of the responsibility of the Servant Nation.

Thus, those Christians who take steps to guarantee their continuing existence through whatever tribulations may occur are acting within the will of God. But Identity Christians are also quick to point out that it is not through mere physical preparation that survival is assured. On the contrary, survival is best assured through *spiritual* preparation. Only through careful reading and interpretation of Scripture can such spiritual preparation be accomplished.

Yet, beyond preparation for the strife that is sure to come, Peters notes in his *Handbook* essay, that resistance to un-Godly government policies is also Scripturally sanctioned. Gideon, a "tax-protestor," is another hero of the Scriptures (Judges 6) lauded by Pastor Peters and held up as an example for twentieth-century Americans. When the children of Israel were besieged by the Midianites who "came as thick as grasshoppers" (and perhaps arrived, Peters suggests, every April 15th), the Midianites plundered the Israelites' crops, stole their possessions, and kept them impoverished. Gideon cleverly threshed his family's wheat in a winepress to hide it from the Midianites, and for this action was visited by an angel who called Gideon "a mighty man of valor." Selected by God to overthrow the Midianites, Gideon is regarded as a hero in both the Old and New Testaments, despite modern distortions of New Testament admonitions to Christians to submit to rulers and authority.

Peters, like most of the faithful, sees little if any legitimacy in the current policies of the federal government. One believer at the Branson conference notes that "any government law which is in conflict with the law of God is void as far as I'm concerned. I'll have nothing to do with it and absolutely don't feel bound to obey it." Yet, the "churchianity" ministers of Judeo-Christianity, it is argued, regularly and consistently twist God's Law in favor of man's law, distorting the Scriptures to suit their own purposes.

These "distorted" Scriptures, as Peters explains, mislead Christians into following a government no longer operating on the principles of God. This government, from Christian Identity perspectives, has long since become the Synagogue of Satan, the Evil Empire, and is no longer a force for good. Thus Romans 13, which speaks to the righteous subjecting themselves to the rule of "higher powers" (leaders) as agents of God and therefore agents of good, is no longer applicable. Nor are verses like I Peter 2:13 which states in part, "Submit yourselves to every ordinance of man for the Lord's sake" nor Titus 3:1 which reminds God's people "to be subject to principalities and powers, to obey magistrates, to be ready to every good work."

Pastor Peters maintains in *Handbook* that passive submission to oppressive government is certainly *not* what these passages speak to. In fact, the founding fathers and the ministers of the Revolutionary War era took up arms rather than submit, as obedient Christians are bound by God to do. Peters offers, instead, Jeremiah 48:10: "Cursed be he that doeth the work of the Lord deceitfully, and cursed be he that keepeth back his sword from blood."

As for militants, in the same essay Peters addresses the idea that all the heroes of the Bible were militant, and righteously so. Warriors trained in military proficiency, men such as Samson, were blessed by Yahweh and honored for their militant feats and loyalty to God. Peters does note that Christ was patient and taught patience, that it is better to turn the other cheek and endure wrongs rather than to react hastily. He draws a parallel with the Christian forefathers and their patience with King George prior to the American Revolution, which was fought as a last resort. Samson, too, was patient, becoming militant only after the death of his family at the hands of the authorities of his day. Then he became militant indeed, eventually slaying thousands of Philistines with the jawbone of an ass and pulling the temple of their false god down around the ears of thousands more. Peters calls modern Christianity "passive" and "state-approved," a Gospel whose message has become so distorted that Christians no longer react with the righteous anger that inspired our ancestors.

There are also role models for righteous extremism. In the book of Daniel, the three young men Shadrach, Meshach, and Abednego are given as examples of "right-wing extremists." By defying the orders of King Nebuchadnezzar to bow down and worship his idol—in essence, a "law" duly passed by an evil government—they became resistors, rebels, outlaws. They refused to bow down and were cast into a fiery furnace. But Shadrach, Meshach, and Abednego did not perish in the flames, as the king intended. Their faith and the hand of God protected them.

And there are role models for racialism. The racist Phinehas of Moses' day, consistent with the will of Yahweh, slew the race mixers Zimri of the Simeonites and the woman Cozbi of the Midianites, thereby averting a plague upon the tribes of Israel. Phinehas, angered when Zimri boldly brought a foreign woman into the Israelite camp, took his javelin into the man's tent and ran it through both with one thrust. For this heroic act in putting the race mixers to death, a priesthood was established by Divine edict in Phinehas' name: "Phinehas . . . hath turned my wrath away from the children of Israel while he was zealous for my sake, that I consumed not the children of Israel . . . Wherefore say, Behold I give unto him my covenant of peace: And he shall have it, and his seed after him, even the covenant of an everlasting priesthood" (Numbers 25:11–13).

The "paramilitarist" Jesus presented His battle plans in parable form. Identity Christians accept the promise that Christ the Aryan warrior, with the immortal soldiers of the Angelic Host, will eventually remove the blight of the unholy from His kingdom, purging the tares from the divine garden. As Jesus explained the parable to His disciples:

> He answered and said unto them, He that soweth the good seed is the Son of man; The field is the world; the good seed are the children of the kingdom; but the tares are the children of the wicked one; The enemy that sowed them is the devil; the harvest is the end of the world; and the reapers are the angels.

> As therefore the tares are gathered and burned in the fire; so shall it be in the end of this world. The Son of man shall send forth his angels, and they shall gather out of his kingdom all things that offend, and them which do iniquity; And shall cast them into a furnace of fire: there shall be wailing and gnashing of teeth.

Then shall the righteous shine forth as the sun in the kingdom of their Father. Who hath ears to hear, let him hear. (Matthew 13:37–43)

Cadillac John, speaking of the end times, remarks, "It doesn't sound all that peaceful to me." Jim Stinson concurs. "When Christ returns, the blood will flow in the valleys to the depth of a horse's neck. It's going to be anything but pleasant. Nothing at all like the 'rapture' people speak of. People will pray for the mountains to tumble down and cover them."

Even if this prophecy is correct and the outcome is a foregone conclusion—that is, the defeat of Satan and the forces of darkness—that does not absolve the Servant Nation from spreading the gospel of Christ or from making war on the enemies of God at the present moment. The responsibility of Christian Israel to fulfill both prophecy and destiny is often spoken of among Identity Christians as a heavy burden to bear—and Christians of all persuasions have noted over time the burden of faith. But the Identity Christians, Aryan Israel, believe their burden to be particularly difficult to bear because it is generally misunderstood and often vilified. It is one, they maintain, which must be shouldered with courage, with resolve, with conviction and, if necessary, willingness to die.

In the final years of the twentieth century, groups of modern-day white Israelites claim the title and responsibilities of the Phineas Priesthood (spelling changed from King James' Phinehas). Today's Phineas priests believe that modern plagues are still a result of disobedience to God's laws, specifically the commandments that Yahweh relayed through Moses, laws which are still in effect. If the children of Israel refuse to obey God's commandments, Moses said, "all these curses shall come. . . . The Lord shall make the pestilence cleave unto thee, until he have consumed thee from off the land, whither thou goest to possess it. The Lord shall smite thee with a consumption, and with a fever, and with an inflammation, and with an extreme burning, and with the sword, and with blasting . . . and they shall pursue thee until thou perish" (Deuteronomy 28:15–22).

Clearly these commandments involve broader remedies than merely ridding the world of race mixers. Modern day Phineas priests, says Identity speaker and author Richard Hoskins, are men who know the Holy Scriptures, who respect all the Laws of God and only the Laws of God, who defy threats of government and federal prisons—and who must be taken very seriously. This premise is examined in Hoskins's 1990 book *Vigilantes of Christendom: The Story of the Phineas Priesthood.*

Hoskins, a financial analyst, stockbroker and historian from Lynchburg, Virginia, is an imposing figure at the Branson conference. With his shock of white hair and soft Southern accent, he explains to the rapt congregation the lineage of those in the room, traced through the bloodlines of kings, to the prophets of the Old Testaments. As a long-time follower of Identity, Hoskins has studied the "unique Western priesthood" of Phineas for more than twenty-five years to determine what triggers their often violent actions. These men, he maintains, act not for personal gain or position, but for principles. "It makes little difference whether you agree or disagree with the Phineas Priesthood," Hoskins says in the foreword of his book. "It is important that you know that it exists, is active, and in the near future may become a central fact in your life." Action, rather than formal affiliation, defines the Phineas priest.

If the American public was unaware of the existence of the Phineas Priesthood in 1990 when this was written, it was about to learn.

The prophetic nature of Hoskins's foreword hit the national news less than two years later, along with the killings of an anti-Christian radio announcer, a homosexual porn-shop owner and an interracial couple. Four years later, in October of 1996, members of the Phineas Priesthood left an apocalyptic message with their distinctive signature—an old variation of the Christian cross with a semi-circular arch forming a "P" at the top of the vertical bar—at the scene of a bomb detonation and bank robbery in Spokane, Washington. The existence of the Phineas priests was not new, but the world's awareness of them was.

Since the biblical days of Phinehas, for whom the Priesthood was named, many men throughout history have been willing to be branded outlaws in their struggle to correct injustices of government and punish violaters of God's law. Robin Hood, writes Hoskins, was a Phineas priest who sired a host of imitators. Whether Robin Hood was an actual person or an ideal, his name is synonymous with stealing from wealthy government officials and tax collectors and sharing his gains with the poor. Much like twentieth-century Jesse James, Hoskins says, who, legend holds, robbed banks and railroads built by foreigners and gave much of the money to the needy. Twelfth-century Crusaders were Phineas priests, the Templars, Hospitalers, and Teutonic Knights who pledged to follow a life of poverty in their aim to drive the infidel from the Holy Land.

The influence of aliens has played a major part in corrupting Christian society, Hoskins notes, both in biblical days and now. The plague is God's curse, but aliens and strangers are the "disease factories" by whom the plague is spread. The mixing of blood with aliens causes the ultimate plague—death of the bloodline—and it was for Phinehas' killing to avert this plague that he was praised by God. Modern Phineas priests who for the same reason carry out the identical biblical commandment to kill for a holy reason must, instead, contend with a government that views it as murder.

Might this ancient commandment be misconstrued as a license to murder? Possibly in some cases, concedes one Identity minister. Not everyone who claims to be a Phineas priest is a true Phineas priest. Killing race mixers "can be Biblical or not, depending on whether the person is led by the Holy Spirit. A true Phineas priest is only doing a righteous act commanded by God." Bombs and bank robberies, while technically not within the priestly sphere, may be justified under certain conditions. If the Phineas priest is Spirit-led and sincere about his mission, then stealing from a Jewish banker can be considered "the spoils of war."

While most Identity Christians do not subscribe to the violence entailed in the more stringent beliefs, Christian warriors see the Laws of God as most definitely in conflict with the laws enacted by the Zionist Occupational Government. Subverting and perverting the ideals of the American republic—a nation forged in revolution and blessed by Yahweh—ZOG now, as always, works for the destruction of the white Christian. The righteous, unlike Israel of old, clearly see through the deception and recognize the face of the Evil One behind the benign mask of modern American government.

Once awakened to the truth, they argue, it is incumbent upon the Identity Christian to carry the message of White Israel to others of the flock. That is, after all, the stated purpose of messengers like Charles Lee and, as Lee himself has noted, it is not within his power to determine how the message will be received. It is only his responsibility to carry it. "It's clear to me," he says. "Sometimes I can't imagine how anyone who has read the Bible can miss it. Maybe after all this time I shouldn't be surprised."

And, indeed, the message is not always well received. One young woman from the Southwest, attending the conference in Branson, her first, is taken aback. "I was raised in the Assembly of God church. I've probably been to hundreds of revivals," she says, "and they're one long continuous prayer. I've only heard one prayer since I've been here. I've heard a lot about who the enemy is and how he's out to get us and how we should defend ourselves but I haven't heard anything about salvation, about the love of Christ." After the first day, she does not return.

For the faithful, such responses are expected. Charles Lee observes that many white Christians have been too indoctrinated with the false teachings of Judeo-Christianity to ever be reached. Though he expresses regret, he also knows such rejection of the Word is unavoidable and does not let that deter him from his mission. As far as Identity activists are concerned, one cannot sit back passively and wait for the return of Yashua. Even if the defeat of Satan is a foregone conclusion, there is still much footwork for the soldiers of the warrior Christ. And it does not fit in well with the philosophy of the Identity faithful to abstain from the fray.

For the Identity soldier, there are many battlefields. "How can any Christian justify sitting back and waiting for some 'rapture' or another to save them from the world?" asks one Identity believer. "I mean, if something's right, you fight for it. If it's right, you should fight for it even if you lose. Preserving the white race is right. We've managed this far haven't we?"

Louis Beam, in a speech at the 1992 Aryan Nations Conference, is more to the point. "We've been conquering for seven thousand years. Why should we stop now?"

Pastor Richard Butler, on the same program, notes, "The worst thing people like Jim Bakker and Jimmy Swaggert could ever teach people is that somehow or another you can withdraw into the corner and say a prayer and that somehow God is going to clean up your house for you."

Ministers of Yahweh, like modern Phineas priests, are not afraid to clean house. They know they will be misunderstood by the world, their motives distorted, their devoutness questioned and, whenever possible, their actions punished by the unrighteous in power. But as agents of Yahweh—wearing the yoke of the Elect—and warriors of the Servant Nation, they live by the commandments of the Holy Scriptures and fear no earthly consequences, even though consequences are sure to follow at this stage in history at the hands of ZOG.

# CHAPTER NINE

# ZOG: The Nature of the Beast

As Identity Pastor Neumann Britton is prone to state in his sermons, "Jews *are* the Beast." For Seedline Christians, Jews embody the anti-Christ. In their eyes, Jews are the one clear explanation for the troubles of the world in general and America in particular. Jews constitute the one overriding threat to the integrity, prosperity and very existence of the Aryan race. Jews are the one entity completely devoted to establishing the reign of the Beast through the New World Order.

Historically the Jews, the "nation within nations," have not fared well when a society undergoing any type of difficulty has turned a jaundiced eye in their direction. The generations of the chosen people are rife with examples of expulsions, pogroms, and other attempts by non-Jewish nations and societies throughout the Middle East and Europe to drive out or exterminate the Jews. Hitler himself, in *Mein Kampf,* explains how he undergoes a transition from viewing the Jews as simply another religious faith to seeing them as the root of all Germany's problems.

There is no question that Jews were and are the objects of much hatred. Though such ill will toward them is generally attributed to racial or religious intolerance, some of their persecutors insist there is something more. Certainly Seedline Identity Christians insist there is something more and that *something* seems to elude the rest of the world.

The racial right asks white people to consider Jewish identity by asking the question Hitler posed to himself in *Mein Kampf:* "Is this a Jew?"

Certainly there is no denying that many non-Jewish Americans hold stereotypical and often prejudicial attitudes toward members of the Judaic faith, a group Pete Peters calls the "Kosher Nostra." The idea that Jews are international financiers who control the banks, usurers, slumlords, and opportunistic businessmen is held by any number of people who might not otherwise align themselves with the racial right or adhere to racialist philosophy. Any number of Americans believe that Jews control all media and entertainment including television, newspapers, magazines, films, and radio. It is a relatively simple step for the white supremacist to play on such attitudes as they point to Jews as propagandists and shapers of culture and values contrary to the interest of the sons of Adam.

It is, however, a bit surprising to hear black voices added to the anti-Semitic rhetoric decrying the evils found in "Jew York City" which no less a personage than Reverend Jesse Jackson has publicly referred to as "Hymie Town." Black separatists such as Louis Farrakhan of the Nation of Islam, as well as his predecessor Malcolm X, espouse the same critical views of the Jews as those found in such white separatist organizations as Aryan Nations, the KKK and WAR.

Richard Butler of Aryan Nations notes, "Mr. Farrakhan is a black patriot who hates jews and Whites. Mr. Quadaffy is a patriot who hates jews. Nelson Mandela is a black who has accepted jews and their communist tyranny as a means to get the Whites whom he hates above all others." (Personal correspondence, 2 February 1996.)

"Nation of Islam is right in a lot of their beliefs," Charles Lee states. "Of course they're wrong in a lot of their beliefs, too. They believe in separatism and that's right. They also see the Jews for what they really are. Nation of Islam knows as well as we do that the Jews are the root of most of the world's problems."

This line of reasoning, from the perspective of the racial right, demands reframing Hitler's second question: Is this a German (American)?

Cadillac John Thellin is blunt in his assessment of the matter. "Jews are contrary to every American value we've held dear since this country was formed. Liberalism is Jewish and it's destructive. Race-mixing is Jewish and it's destructive. His religion is destructive; his politics are destructive; his way of life is destructive. Hell, Jews can't get along with each other, much less anyone else. Jews are killing America in slow doses and every bit of it is intentional. Communism is Jewish and so is every loss of freedom and perversion of our Constitution in this country."

"America is a white Christian nation," Charles Lee says. "And Jews hate white Christians. As an American, my loyalty is to my God and my country. There is no inconsistency in that. I consider myself an American. Jews don't. They may have been born here, but when it comes right down to it, a Jew always aligns himself with Israel.''

This view is also held by Identity Christians of the younger generation. Mark, of the Texas Aryan Nationalist Skinheads, observes, ''Where do their loyalties lie? With America? I think they may lean a little more toward Israel.''

The conclusion among modern white separatists then is the same that Hitler drew. Jews constitute their own nation, and loyalty to that nation supersedes every other nationalist concern, no matter what ''host'' country they may be living in. Just as Hitler answered the question ''Is this a German?'' with an emphatic no, the members of the racial right are just as emphatic that whatever else Jews are, they are certainly not Americans.

For the Seedline Christian, yet another question must be answered: ''Is this *not* the seed of Satan?''

The very word ''Jew'' might mean any number of things to those individuals on the racial right. As noted, there can be any number of variations of belief among the white supremacists. The same holds true on how the Jew is perceived. R. B. Thieme points out in his book *Anti-Semitism* that there are three types of Jews which can be understood from the basis of Christian Scripture: . . . [Rom. 9:6–7] distinguishes between racial Israel, those who are Jews by birth; religious Israel, those who are Jews by religious tradition; and regenerate Israel, those Jews who have believed in Christ.

Thieme describes the notion of racial purity as ''a myth'' and notes that among the Jewish people, who are generally accepted as Israelites, interracial marriages existed in the lines of Joseph, Moses, and David, and all progeny were considered Israelites. Today, it is not uncommon to find Jews whose visage describes a Middle Eastern origin or a face that is a map of Ireland. Black Jews, Oriental Jews, Hispanic Jews are also found among the chosen and they are not necessarily Jews merely through conversion to or acceptance of Judaism. Indeed, the intermarriage of peoples throughout the centuries has resulted in Jews of different races.

Religion, on the other hand, is also descriptive of Jews, and Thieme addresses the historical antagonism between Judaism and Christianity which has long been a part of both faiths: ''The Bible condemns religion (Jer. 8:8–12, Matt. 23) and rightly so. In the name of religion and alleged Christianity horrible crimes have been committed.''

Thus, it is clear that there is a bit of difficulty defining *the* religious Jew. The regenerate Jew is perhaps the easiest for the mainstream Christian to pin down. In effect a Jew, racial or religious or both, becomes regenerate through a process of conversion to Christianity.

These are not necessarily the means by which followers of Judaism describe themselves. The intricacies of the Jewish faith and Jewish identity are much more complex than the treatment offered by Thieme who, after all, is presenting a brief description for Christian readers from a mainstream Christian perspective. And certainly these descriptions of the Jew are not embraced by the Seedline Identity Christian.

Seedline Christians of the racial right maintain that the Jews—demonic in origin—are in a constant state of war with Yahweh and all followers of Yahweh. Anti-Christ and anti-Christian, they are beyond redemption, beyond salvation and—no matter what they believe or how they believe it—will under no circumstances be included in the Kingdom of God. They are the destroyers of races and the perverters of souls. They are the power beyond the "Synagogue of Satan." They are the "Shadow Government." They are the "Zionist Occupational Government," or ZOG.

"Every time you turn around, people are raising all kinds of hell about who *we* hate, how much *we* hate," Jim Stinson maintains. "What about the Jews? The blacks? Do you think they're capable of a little hate? If you don't think the Jews hate Christians, then take a look at some of the things in the Talmud. We're cattle to them. If you don't believe it, read some of their teachings. They hate us."

Stinson's arguments are based on doctrinal interpretations and hinge upon two basic concepts. First, the Holy texts of Judaism constitute basically the same books of the Christian Old Testament. Therefore, the concept of "chosen people" is the same, only the players have changed. The covenants bind Israel, obstinate and disobedient as ever, to a special set of rules and a special relationship with Yahweh. Arguments can be and are raised as to who exactly constitutes Israel. Likewise, arguments can be and are made regarding the true meaning of the scriptural commandments toward the separation of the chosen. It is not surprising that the racial right argues these commandments in terms of race and segregation. Certainly these aspects of division are incorporated into Seedline doctrine along with the special designation of the chosen.

Second, there are additional expressions of the Hebrew faith found in the teachings of the Talmud. Like the Scriptures which constitute the Old

Testament, most of the Talmudic writings are very old and they are still included in religious training. These teachings are something the Identity Christians are quick to point out as subjects the Jews are unwilling to discuss with the non-Jewish "Goyim" world. Identity Pastor Ray Barker, in his taped sermon "The Viper Connection," calls the Babylonian Talmud "sixty-three books of the most Satanic filth that you can imagine." Pete Peters, in his tract *The Real Hate Group*, claims that the true teachings of the Talmud are carefully kept Jewish secrets and his tract contains quotes attributed to the Rabbinical writings which sanction death for any non-Jew who studies the Talmud and any Jew who helps him. Peters quotes passages which claim Jewish teachings instruct Jews to lie to Gentiles to conceal the truth of the Talmud, passages which identify non-Jews as "cattle" fit only for servitude, passages which allow sexual violation of Gentile girls over the age of three, passages which allow Jews to lie, cheat and steal as long as they are discreet so "Israel may not suffer." The point of all this, Peters says, is that Christians who advocate religious tolerance for the Jews should take a look at how intolerant Jesus was of the Pharisees:

"Woe to you, scribes and Pharisees, hypocrites! For you are like white-washed tombs which on the outside appear beautiful, but inside they are full of dead men's bones and all uncleanness. Even so you too outwardly appear righteous to men, but inwardly you are full of hypocrisy and lawlessness." (MATTHEW 23:27–28)

It is beyond argument that certain passages in the Bible speak to both racism and hatred. Christian Identity, as noted, is not prone to glossing over these passages or ignoring them. Mistranslation of Scriptures, of course, confuses things and the true identity of the seed of Satan is masked in Judeo-Christianity just as is the identity of true Israel. Due to this confusion, as explained in *Crosstalk,* the undated White Camelia news-letter, most separatists hold erroneous views on who the Jews are. The untitled article reads in part:

... Jews are evil, anti-Christian, un-Christian, and in control of most of the organized evil of the world, such as prostitution, international slavery, international money-changing, profiteering on wars, racketeering in labor, corruption in politics, modernism in religion, atheism in the school system, promotion of lewd propaganda through theaters and picture shows etc. Even though many good people are aware of these evil practices, they are frustrated and disturbed in their appraisal of the Jew because, by error, they believe Jesus was a Jew.

Seedline believers harbor no such misconceptions. As far as they are concerned, Yashua has identified the Jews, and common sense and one's eyes should bear out the truth of the matter.

But the Jews are powerful and very worthy opponents as far as the racialists are concerned. The truth does not get to the American public because Jewish-controlled newspapers and television and movies do not want it to get out. From the racialists' perspective, white America has been so thoroughly brainwashed that even the most obvious truths are beyond them. For instance, there is a certain fatalism attached to Charles Lee's faith and his mission as he sees it. He accepts the responsibility of advancing his religion, spreading its gospel, and when confronted with the reality of massive rejection of such tenets on the part of the American people, his response is one of acceptance. "This is only for white people," he says. "I don't care what the Jews think. I don't care what anybody else thinks. When the race war comes, then those whites who belong will align themselves with us. The others are a part of the anti-Christ and don't belong anyway."

And the race war must come because it is part of the conflict begun at creation. Lee's fatalism—or perhaps his conviction of belief—is again apparent as he states, "People can say whatever they want. They can shout 'equality' all they like, but when armed blacks are roaming the streets raping, killing and burning and the Jews are egging it all on, I won't need to tell anyone anything. The military used to have this philosophy that they couldn't make anyone fight but they could take them to where the fighting was taking place. Once there, with bullets whizzing around your ears, you usually make the right decision."

"No one yells 'equality' louder than the Jews," Stinson adds. "And no one believes in it less. As far as their relations with non-Jews are concerned they have a lousy track record. Look at Palestine. They're counting on a race war in America and doing everything they can to promote it. Whites and non-whites mixing it up and the Jews coming out as the winner. They've been setting this up for centuries."

For the racial right, the conspiracy of the Zionist Occupational Government is an expression of the anti-Christ nature of the Jews. Stinson articulates a common belief among the racialists that Jews are trouble-makers, causing discord, unrest and war among any and all non-Jewish peoples throughout time. Not only are they seen as purveyors of political discord but also of spiritual poison. Jews are seen as the originators of communism, socialism, integrationism, pluralism, multiculturalism, atheism, and an absolute plethora of "isms" antithetical to the traditions of white America and Aryan Israel. Jewish control of the media and of financial and other institutions, from this line of reasoning, has led to the control of governments worldwide, including the United States government. This is not a national issue only, but a worldwide issue. ZOG, the Synagogue of Satan, One-Worlders, One-World Government and New World Order all refer to the Jews and the plot to enslave the entire planet and every non-Jew on it.

In one edition of *Posse Noose Report,* distributed in 1983 by Identity Pastor James Wickstrom's Posse Comitatus group in Evansville, Wisconsin, Americans were warned that State police were storing food and distributing disposable body bags throughout the states, that the government was building concentration camps within the borders of the United States, and that a "cashless" society was being implemented in America that virtually enslaved citizens to the Zionist bankers. Wickstrom noted:

> The "Cashless Society" (bank computers) is now interlocked from East to West Coast. Each business can be connected with their electric cash register through a telephone hookup to their local bank computer . . . Isn't it nice how Rockefeller and his Jewish cohorts have made it so easy. Only one thing wrong—many people are waking up to the scheme and also to the constitution-ality of **LAWFUL MONEY** versus **PHONEY MONEY** and the **LAWS** and **RIGHTS** of "We the People". "Hangin tree, oh Hangin Tree . . ." (Ridgeway, *Blood in the Face)*

Wickstrom, in the same document, also noted that the Federal Reserve System, a *private* banking institution, has the wherewithal and is indeed exercising its ability to manipulate international gold and silver standards to create recessions and depressions.

"Who are those Federal Reserve people responsible to?" asks Cadillac John. "Not to the U.S. Government or the American people. We didn't vote them in and sure as hell can't vote them out. The Federal Reserve controls not only U.S. currency, but the economy of the entire world. Who carries out its orders? Jewish bankers. Who do they report to? Rothschild and Rockefeller and their other One-Worlder cronies.''

All of this, as far as the extreme right is concerned, is a part of the Jewish plot for world domination as outlined in *The Protocols of the Learned Elders of Zion.* This document is considered by most scholars to be a forgery which includes material dating back to the Middle Ages and has undergone many fictive transformations through the centuries. It was reborn in Czarist Russia and used to justify the vicious pogroms against the Jews throughout the late nineteenth and early twentieth centuries, particularly following the failed proletarian revolution of 1905. James Ridgeway, in *Blood in the Face,* refers to the *Protocols* as "the greatest continuing fabrication in history to withstand the scrutiny of an age of supposedly rational thought," and in *The Web of Hate: Extremists Exploit the Internet,* the ADL calls it "a classic in paranoid, racist literature and the most notorious political forgery of modern times." Seedline Christians hold it to be the truth, and it is generally regarded as the truth by non-Identity Christians involved in the racialist movements.

In any case, *Protocols* has been reborn yet again in the United States, and several versions are offered through Identity mail-order ministries. Henry Ford's *Dearborn Independent* newspaper published a series of articles in the 1920's that indicate his belief in the *Protocols.* The articles, though largely written by W. J. Cameron, were compiled into Ford's book *The International Jew—The World's Foremost Problem.* Many others in the movement have shaped their actions around both their faith and this adjudged "fictional" notion of conspiracy.

In short, the *Protocols* states that Jews will pass as Christians, set the Gentiles against one another, disseminate lies through the media, gain control of the government, centralize it, create a welfare state, institute progressive income taxing, and eventually create one worldwide Zionist government. That is the political aspect but it is also the religious aspect. It answers the *why* of conspiracy theory as applied to white supremacy: The one-worlders—the descendants of Satan through Cain—hate the Aryan sons of Adam. Their jealousy is boundless and they make every attempt to promote the idea that, by participating in a Zionist version of Christianity, all men of every race will become equal. And, from the Identity perspective, both the Jews and the chosen know this to be a false concept.

But false concepts are part and parcel of conspiracy and certainly a component of ZOG. *The International Jew* speaks to Jewish influence on and control over a wide range of American institutions and holds them accountable for everything from prostitution, racketeering and other forms of organized crime, to mind control through the media, cinema, music and even organized professional sports.

To follow Wickstrom's line of reasoning in the *Posse Noose Report,* after the economic crisis has come to pass, the helpless and confused mass of citizens will be at the mercy of the Zionists who have in place contingency operations which include incarceration and forced relocation, perhaps even a "reservation" system—in essence, a well-constructed Aryan Holocaust planned and ready, complete with mass grave sites. Wickstrom asked the readers of his tract to consider the implications:

Add it up:

1. Planned crisis by: monetary crisis through the banks, internal Jewish communist revolution, or limited Soviet nuclear attack upon major military installations and industrial cities.

2. Mass evacuation into preselected rural host areas. In the Civil Defense Preparedness Manual, Point #1 stresses no firearms permitted by [he probably meant "to"] evacuees.

3. Civil Defense Shelters have been emptied of food, medicines and other survival equipment.

4. Rural host areas have established mass burial sites. Massive amounts of disposable body bags have been distributed.

Please, bear in mind that the Jews controlling our government on the local, state and federal level, are selling the American people down the river. (Ridgeway, *Blood in the Face)*

Charles Lee makes the observation that the economic element is certainly an effective and integral component of the eventual subjugation of the world. "Average people just don't understand," he says. "World economy is too large, too complicated. Oh, they'll know something is wrong. They'll know they're being screwed over but even if there is revolution, even if you have a gun, who do you shoot? How do you fight the world market?"

For most of the racial right, you fight the Jews. It is clear that anti-

Jewish sentiments were and are high among some rural Western farmers who constitute a portion of Americans represented by the radical right. Arthur Kirk, like Gordon Kahl, was a Western farmer and Identity Christian. Kirk, facing foreclosure on his Nebraska farm in 1984, again like Kahl, took up arms against the agents of the Synagogue of Satan. A partial transcript of Kirk's phone conversation with a police negotiator, prior to his death at the hands of a police SWAT team, is included in Ridgeway's *Blood in the Face*. The transcript reads in part:

> God damn fuckin' Jews, they destroyed everything I ever worked for, I've worked my ass off for 49 God damn years and I've got nothing to show for it. By God, I ain't putting up with their bullshit now. I'm tired and I've had it and I'm not the only God damn one, I'll tell you that . . . Farmers fought the revolutionary war and we'll fight this son-of-a-bitch . . .

Arthur Kirk died convinced he was struggling against one-world government oppressors. Arthur Kirk died convinced that he was being destroyed by a Jewish conspiracy.

The conspiracy theorists of the racial right are unequivocal in echoing Kirk's belief regarding the Jewish conspiracy and equally certain that this conspiracy is evil, destructive, and anti-Christian, manifested through the federal government and their oft-noted Gonzo-Gestapo tactics. The loss of individual rights and liberties in the United States is but a component of Satan's plan for world dominion, and the Jews' plan for accomplishing it is, of course, outlined in *The Protocols of the Learned Elders of Zion*.

There are many elusive and intricate elements involved in the conspiracy theory as it applies to One-World Government, ZOG, or the New World Order. And these complexities are made even more difficult when consideration is given to the fact that none of them are absolutely universal throughout the radical right.

However, the Identity Christians of the racial right, who may offer evidence of a similar nature to make their point, are ultimately convinced by Scripture that Jews, doing the work of Satan for destructive purposes, are behind it all. In *The Real Hate Group* Pastor Peters refers to a February 1994 ADL Special Edition " 'Theologian' of Hate: 'Pastor' Pete Peters." Quoting from this article, he then goes on to invite the reader to participate in the flattering status of also being marked as a "hater" by the ADL.

The question of who exactly constitutes the ADL and why they are allowed to gather intelligence on private citizens is a galling one for those on the extreme right. Charles Lee asks an important question. "Who are these people and by what authority do they keep tabs on me, or anyone else for that matter? Who do they answer to? Who appointed them to keep track of 'hate' groups?"

Jim Stinson also has problems with the watchdog organizations. "Listen," he says, "something happened to these people in Germany fifty years ago—to hear them tell it. I wasn't even alive then. Now Yids all over the world are rallying around this 'Holocaust' thing, shouting 'never again.' And they've built a holocaust museum right here in Houston for a bunch of Kikes who supposedly died in Europe."

"That's a little strange if you think about it," Charles Lee adds. "I was asked a while back what I thought about that museum. I said I didn't think anything about it. I don't know if six million Jews were slaughtered or not and, frankly, I don't care if they were. Come to think of it, even if they were, I don't have a problem with it. It probably made the world a better place. But the point is, what does the holocaust have to do with me? Am I supposed to feel guilty about it? Do I owe them something if it did? As far as I'm concerned the Jews should be building monuments to all those dead Aryan Americans who fought the war for them. Or have they forgotten that part?"

"The Jews have never been concerned with anyone but the Jews," Jim Stinson says. "But anyone else who doesn't follow the ADL party line is a bigot and a racist. The Christian Defense League is a hate group but the Anti-Defamation League is a protective organization? For who? Are they concerned with protecting me? My life? My rights? Hell no, they're not. They'll spy on me, violate my rights, slander me, or do anything else they can to harm or discredit me because I speak my mind and my mind is not politically correct."

"Yeah," Lee adds. "You can't get much more politically incorrect than Jim—unless you're talking to Cadillac. But being politically incorrect doesn't make you wrong necessarily. The FBI and God knows who else in the federal government are nosing around in our business all the time, but at least they have to answer to someone, at least there are a few laws left to protect my rights. One or two, maybe. But the Jews don't answer to anyone. No one. You try to hold them accountable for something and the next thing you know you're anti-Semitic. You're a radical, a hater. Let me tell you something, you've got to go a long way to out-hate the Jews."

And, from this perspective, the one group which ultimately bears the brunt of Jewish hatred is the White Christian, Aryan Israel. "If you don't believe the Jews still hate Christ and the followers of Christ," Lee says, "just call a synagogue. Take your pick. Call them up and ask them if they believe Jesus Christ is the Messiah, the Savior, the Son of God. They'll tell you no. Jesus Himself has explained who the Jews are and how they feel about Him. They hated Him when He was on earth, plotted against Him, crucified Him. They still hate Him and anyone who believes in Him. Don't take my word for it, talk to a Jew.

"You never hear them changing their religion to include Christ, do you? Then why in God's name do the Judeo-Christian churches change mainstream religion to accommodate the Jews? Politically correct or not, the Jews haven't changed through the ages. They're still the Seed of Satan; they're still the killers of Christ. Nothing anyone says or does, no matter how hard they try to pretend otherwise, will ever change that."

It can be considered a given, as far as the racial right is concerned, that the Anti-Defamation League of the B'nai B'rith is merely an American arm of the Israeli State Security Police, or Mossad, which is generally held to be similar in nature and in function to our Central Intelligence Agency. But for the conspiracy theorists, the role of the Mossad is expanded far beyond that which is generally understood by others. In fact, if one accepts and follows this line of reasoning and the idea that the U.S. government is indeed under the control of ZOG, then eventually "independent" groups such as the ADL, as well as the FBI, CIA, and all other government agencies, will eventually, if indeed not presently, answer to the same entity—the Rabbinical Council of the Synagogue of Satan, represented by the Mossad.

The whole purpose of the ADL, according to the radical right, is to discredit anything the white supremacists might try to present to the American public to warn them of this situation. The function of the ADL can then be seen as an effort to twist and otherwise distort the public's view of the Klan, Aryan Nations, National Alliance, skinheads, and every other white nationalist organization on earth. By labeling such organizations "hate groups," the ADL attempts to avoid the general acceptance of the truth of the myth of racial equality; they attempt to control the dissemination of the truth of the Scriptures, they attempt to keep concealed the real identity of White Israel. Like the "Ministry of Truth" in Orwell's *1984,* the function of the ADL is to fabricate lies.

This is the reason that those in the movements are labeled "haters" by the majority of the American public, who get their information from organizations such as the ADL and from the most questionable of sources on earth—the Jewish-controlled media and the Jewish-controlled government. It is the contention of the Identity Christians that if this same public opened their eyes and their minds to the truth—the *real truth* contained in the Scriptures, as well as the real truth of Jewish barbarity throughout history—then this perception would dissipate among Aryan Americans like the proverbial snowball in Hell.

Chapter 34, "The Great Masquerade," in the AIT Bible study guide shows some of the ways in which Jews have promoted the misconception that they, rather than Anglo-Saxons, are entitled to the name Israel, and it foretells the fate of dissemblers. "God Himself put enmity between HIS children and SATAN'S CHILDREN," it says, "and wars which the wicked started against us ended quickly with tremendous victories in our favor." It continues:

Since God has given us the victory whenever we remember that we are HIS CHILDREN and have nothing to do with the children and the ways of Satan, the only way to conquer and enslave or destroy us is to make us forget this division between the CHILDREN OF GOD and the CHILDREN OF SATAN, get us all mixed together so our ways will be corrupted with theirs, our children will learn their evil, our government will be controlled by their power, and they will make enemies of God like themselves.

How are Satan's children able to do this? By a great masquerade, in which they pretend to be God's children, and have corrupted most of our clergymen until these no longer tell us who *we* are.

All masquerades must reach an end; and this one is almost finished. It has nearly succeeded in bringing us to destruction. But God will save us, because we are HIS CHILDREN. . . . Masks will be removed and our true identity revealed.

That is, look to your ancestry, recognize that you are Israel, God's children; stop masquerading as "Gentiles"; and tear the mask off Satan's children who masquerade as you.

The real truth, as delineated in James K. Warner's undated "Land of the ZOG" (Aryan Truth Network), is also an identification of the Jews:

The Antichrist's number is 666. The six-pointed star [the Star of David] has 6 points, 6 lines, and 6 triangles. As America goes the way of Rome, as our

White Race enters the twilight of its very existence, we shall finally realize what that odd mark signified all along.

Modern Seedline defenders of the faith hold that the militancy of the Jewish country Israel, the Middle-Eastern nation of impostors, should serve to convince anyone of the true nature of the Jews. Their subterfuge, their viciousness toward the Palestinians and the hatred they hold for Palestinians and the rest of the Arab world would speak for itself if Americans could get the uncensored, un-politically-correct truth.

And that truth, always in the forefront of the Seedline Identity movement, is that not only are Jews *not* a persecuted people, they *are* in fact the most notorious persecutors of other peoples in history.

# CHAPTER TEN

# Of Spiders and Flies: Conspiracy Theory

**W**ithin hours of the Oklahoma City bombing in 1995, media reports speculated that Moslem fundamentalists were behind the event, perhaps even the same group associated with the bombing of the World Trade Center two years earlier. At the same time, there was a negative reaction by both the media and the public at large when Radio Baghdad referred to the bombing as "an act of domestic terrorism." The idea that the blast was caused by an American bomb—built, planted and detonated by "average" American citizens—seemed too much for fellow citizens to swallow. No Islamic movement claimed responsibility, nor was there any evidence that the Arabs were behind the crime. However, speculation continued even after the arrest of Timothy McVeigh and Terry Nichols.

Oklahoma City dominated conversation for weeks following the explosion. In Clear Lake City, Texas—conservative, button-down, NASA country—a gentleman in a restaurant remarks, "It wouldn't surprise me if the Feds did it themselves. Hitler needed his Reichstag fire, maybe the BATF needs the bombing of the federal building." Others also suggest that the federal government is not innocent. As David Van Biema observes in his June 1995 *Time* article, "Militia":

> Mark Koernke runs through his standard talk: the universal-conspiracy theory featuring the U.N.; the Rockefellers; the Bureau of Alcohol, Tobacco and Firearms; Bill and Hillary Clinton and others . . . apocalyptic visions: the

hundreds of thousands of foreign troops on American soil; Americans enslaved and implanted with microchips . . .

Perhaps the conspiracy goes like this: Under the control of an evil cabal of international plotters, the criminal Congress of the United States passes laws under the direction of the puppet leader President, laws which are designed, in the long run, to render the good citizens of the United States helpless. Disarmed, dependent on government and unrepresented in any significant manner, these citizens are then ripe for the picking by those who plot the one-world government. However, the citizenry is not yet to the point where they can be led like lambs to slaughter. Following the public outcry over the Ruby Ridge and Waco incidents, the government agencies associated with those fiascos (the BATF, FBI and Federal Marshals) need something to rally the public behind them. Something like Oklahoma City.

The explosion that ripped apart the Alfred P. Murrah Federal Building, damaged other buildings up and down the block and left 168 people dead and some 500 injured, occurred the week of the anniversary of the final Waco assault. Neither the investigators nor the members of the far right are prepared to believe that the date of the explosion was chosen at random. Not only is April 19 the anniversary of the Waco Branch Davidian conflagration, but it is also the eve of Hitler's birthday (April 20, 1889)— a fact not lost on the racial right—and is four days beyond the April 15 income tax filing deadline, which many members of the far right organizations consider a more appropriate date for an assault against the government. In any case, in terms of symbology, the week of April 15 through 20 is fraught with meaning. The far right knows this. So does the government. And both know that April 19, 1995, was not the first time the Alfred P. Murrah Federal Building had been targeted for a bomb.

Ten years prior, early on the morning of April 19, 1985, Special Agent Danny Coulson and the FBI's SWAT-type Hostage Rescue Team were positioned outside an Identity-survivalist-paramilitary compound in the Ozarks whose members were known to have assault weapons, hand grenades, machine guns, land mines, rocket launchers, and a burning hatred for the government.

The group called itself The Covenant, the Sword, and the Arm of the Lord; its leader Jim Ellison called himself "King James of the Ozarks," and its spokesman was scholar and Seedline Identity teacher Kerry Noble, an ex-Baptist preacher. Eighteen months earlier, in November 1983, the

CSA had begun preparations to bomb the Murrah Federal Building in Oklahoma City, "to let the government know that the right-wing has spoken."

As related by then-CSA member and second-in-command Kerry Noble in his 1998 book *Tabernacle of Hate: Why They Bombed Oklahoma City,* in mid-November 1983, Richard Wayne Snell and another member made several trips from the secluded and heavily fortified CSA compound near Mountain Home, Arkansas, to gauge what it would take to damage or destroy the nine-story Murrah building that housed several federal agencies. They found that the building had minimal security and was easily accessible by both bomb and rocket. Leader Jim Ellison had ordered CSA's munitions expert, Kent Yates, to devise a system of rockets that could be launched toward the federal building and would totally destroy it. As Noble recounts the conversation, someone asked if there weren't also children in the building. "The sins of the fathers are visited upon the children," Ellison replied, and they needed something with a large body count to make the government sit up and take notice.

It was estimated, Noble says, that about five hundred people would die in the Murrah building when the CSA launched their rockets from a trailer parked down the street. But in late November or early December 1983, Yates was injured when a rocket exploded in his hand. The attack was called off. "It was interpreted as a sign from God," Noble says, "that another plan was to be implemented. Had God not intervened, I believe CSA would have begun its war against the government with an attack on the federal building at that time."

What had begun in 1971 as a quiet, rural Christian community called Zarephath-Horeb, Noble says, by 1981 had evolved into a violent, paramilitary, right-wing supremacist group that built bunkers and practiced military-style maneuvers. Noble's book includes a panoply of right-wing leaders who visited or otherwise had contact with the CSA—among them Louis Beam who gave Ellison the nickname "Warlord," Robert Millar of Elohim City, the late Robert Miles of the KKK and Mountain Church of Michigan, Richard Butler of Aryan Nations, and various members of The Order who, under the leadership of Robert Mathews, would soon gain nationwide attention.

During the five-day period April 15–20, 1985, a series of events would link the CSA, The Order, and Aryan Nations in a flurry of terrorist acts that stretched from the Missouri-Arkansas border to Seattle, Washington. Five days prior to the FBI's 1985 stakeout of the CSA compound, two Missouri state patrolmen were shot with a MAC-10 fully-automatic machine-pistol by David Tate of the Aryan Nations who then fled on foot into the nearby woods, leaving behind a vehicle loaded with machine guns, ammunition, and hand grenades. Law enforcement officials believed that he might be headed for the CSA group's headquarters across the Arkansas border. By April 19, as many as 200 law enforcement officers, including Special Agent Danny Coulson and the FBI's Hostage Rescue Team, had set up roadblocks and surrounded the CSA compound. As Noble tells it:

> Later that same afternoon the news worsened. Fourteen members of another right-wing organization known as "The Order" became wanted fugitives when federal indictments were handed down that morning by the Grand Jury in Seattle, Washington. The indictments included charges of holding-up armored cars in Washington State and California, counterfeiting, and murdering a Jewish radio talk show host, Alan Berg, in Denver, Colorado.
>
> Two of the fourteen were ex-CSA members. Two others were currently hiding on our property, now surrounded as we were, along with two more Order members not mentioned in the news reports.
>
> In addition, then-Governor Bill Clinton had just signed into law a new anti-paramilitary statute designed by the Jewish Anti-Defamation League (ADL), which we believed would be used to make our group illegal.
>
> That same day, Order member Frank Silva was arrested near Rogers, Arkansas . . . [and] joined Order member Ardie McBrearty—arrested April fourth—in the county jail.
>
> In Fort Smith, Arkansas, on Friday, April 19, 1985, the Order's "Declaration of War" was revealed at Silva's bond hearing.

In addition to the fact that the FBI's roadblocks had kept five of the CSA's prime warriors from returning to the compound, living inside the grounds were the wives and children of the CSA members.

After a four-day standoff, Kerry Noble and Danny Coulson met on a dirt road outside the CSA compound and negotiated the peaceful surrender of both CSA leader Jim Ellison and Noble himself. The Covenant, Sword, and Arm of the Lord—the organization that the FBI had labeled the nation's second most dangerous domestic terrorist group, second only to The Order—was disbanded quietly and without loss of life.

Fifteen years since that day, Noble comments that his book *Tabernacle of Hate* is the first book written from first-hand experience by a leader within the hate movement, by someone who understands and once taught

its theology and propaganda. And, he adds, the subtitle to his book—
*Why They Bombed Oklahoma City*—is evidence that he knows what he
is talking about. "The OKC was added to my book title," he says,
"because our group originally planned that same bombing, giving me an
insight into WHY it was bombed, and why it had to involve more than
one primary individual."

The investigation which followed the Oklahoma City bombing turned
up clear evidence that the perpetrators were involved in a plot against
the federal government. A localized plot perhaps, but a plot nevertheless.
Investigators were thorough in their attempts to tie McVeigh, Nichols
and company to many right-wing organizations, and it seems there are
some loose ties there. After all, at the time of McVeigh's arrest, he
allegedly had in his possession a copy of *The Turner Diaries,* a fictional
account of the future race war which is almost a bible among many of
the separatists. And allegedly he had visited Elohim City, a militant
Identity enclave in eastern Oklahoma, and he was present during the
Branch Davidian stand-off in Waco, and he allegedly had visited Aryan
Nations in Hayden Lake, Idaho.

The point of all this?

Deceit. If McVeigh can be tied, or made to appear to be tied, to
organizations such as Aryan Nations or Elohim City, those ties may then
be used to justify further repression of white patriot groups on the part
of the federal government. By scapegoating McVeigh and other true
patriots (like those in the movements), the federal agencies devoted not
to protecting, but to stripping us of our God-given rights as citizens, can
then justify Ruby Ridge, Waco, and all other such oppressive efforts, part
and parcel of the international plot. And if such actions as these can be
made to appear proper and—though regrettable—for our own good, then
basically the government is in position to say "See, we told you so; we
told you *they* were dangerous." And as for the dead? Conspiracy theorists
certainly understand the old adage that one cannot make an omelet without
breaking a few eggs.

"Why are they trying to tie McVeigh and Nichols to Identity organizations?" asks a Missouri Seedline adherent. "McVeigh, as I understand
it, is a devout and practicing Catholic. He may be a racist but, as far as
I know, he's not Identity. As for Nichols, the man is a race-mixer, for
Christ's sake. He was married to a Filipino. Does that sound like someone
who believes as we do?

"Whether they did the bombing or not, they've already been tried and convicted. The government needs them to be guilty so they're going to be, no matter what the real truth may be. And no matter what beliefs they hold, the government is going to do everything in its power to marry them to us and, more than likely, they will be successful as far as the average American is concerned.''

It is generally accepted by historians that Adolf Hitler and his S.S. minions were responsible for the torching of the German Reichstag building in 1933. But why would a government attack itself? The answer is simple: to consolidate power. After blaming the burning of the Reichstag on the Communists, Hitler was then able to succeed in banning the German Communist Party by law. Legislation (a body of edicts, actually) was enacted which suspended the law and government of the Weimar Republic and set up a state of martial law in which one man, the Fuehrer, had all the power. This consolidation of power is perhaps the most important outcome of the event. Autonomous German police forces were then centralized against the "red threat" and the German populace was left to the often not-so-tender mercies of the S.A., S.S., and Geheime Staatspolizei (Secret State Police) or Gestapo.

But that was Nazi Germany, not the United States. After all, such manipulation on the part of government could never happen here. Still, it is argued by those in the anti-government movements that expansion of presidential powers was occurring in the United States at the same time that Hitler was consolidating his power in Germany. Conspiracy theorists point to what they call the War and Emergency Powers Acts (which actually encompass legislation regarding banking, commerce, production, transportation and other aspects of governmental regulation) under which Franklin D. Roosevelt utilized executive orders to expand the function and role of government and governmental programs.

Roosevelt declared that he would not necessarily circumvent the approval of Congress in the face of an emergency but would in fact address national crisis of any kind with a broad use of executive power to meet any emergency—an executive power equivalent to that expected and necessary as if the United States were invaded by a foreign power. The Great Depression constituted one such emergency and the policies of the New Deal certainly caused government to be seen in a new and often unflattering light. Conservative ideology holds that the programs instituted during this time were not only a misuse of federal power but a Constitutionally illegal usurpation of power.

Conspiracy theory takes this idea even further.

Dr. Eugene Schroder, DVM, of Colorado—who is held in very high esteem in far right wing circles—lectures, writes books and distributes films on the War and Emergency Powers Acts (1933) which he claims has stripped U.S. citizens of the rights guaranteed them by the Constitution. A long-time activist in strict Constitutionalist causes, Schroder maintains that the events of the 1930s have actually established a dictatorship in this country and that many Americans alive today have *never* lived in a free country. In reference to the Emergency Banking Relief Act, combined with the Trading With the Enemy Act of 1917 to further expand executive power, he quotes from Senate Report 93-549 (1973): "Since March the 9$^{th}$, 1933, the United States has been in a state of declared national emergency." The report goes on to say, "A majority of people of the United States have lived all their lives under emergency rule. For 40 years, freedoms and governmental procedures guaranteed by the Constitution have, in varying degrees, been abridged by laws brought into force by states of national emergency." In short, Schroder maintains that, since before Pearl Harbor, the United States has been governed under martial law. Essentially, an emergency was declared but never undeclared.

This sentiment is echoed across the spectrum of the ultra-right but it does not stop with the questionable legality of powers assumed by the government. Many conspiracy theorists believe such events as the bombing of Pearl Harbor ~ and the questionable "attack" of U.S. Naval vessels in the Gulf of To     which pulled the country into the quagmire of the      war, w     minently avoidable incidents. At the same time, it    postulated that     events were also necessary to advance the cause    the global conspirators—the faceless "One-Worlders"—whose agenda is at odds with national sovereignty wherever it may be found.

Conspiracy theory sees a method to the madness of history which goes beyond a mere explication of the development of nations and the conflicts both within and between those nations. A. Ralph Epperson, selfproclaimed expert and author of the 1985 book *The Unseen Hand: An Introduction to the Conspiratorial View of History,* boldly asserts, "The Conspiracy's one unchanging purpose has been to destroy all religion, all existing governments, and all traditional human institutions, and to build a new world order." Nothing, particularly as far as politics are concerned, ever happens without a purpose.

But wait a minute. Is it not the *Communists'* purpose to destroy all religion, all existing governments, all traditional institutions and to build a new world order?

Simply stated, yes. Suppose, however, that through the efforts of a number of organizations which are part of the conspiracy, the sovereignty of nations throughout the world—including the United States and, for that matter, the Communist nations—is being undermined and slowly, yet relentlessly, given over to this New World Order. And suppose that Communism, that most dreaded of threats to the free world, is actually a front for *this* order.

Pastor Ray Barker of the Christian Israel Covenant Church of Colville, Washington, in his taped sermon "The Plot Against Christianity," asks the listener to consider the truth of Communism by exposing the Jewish influence behind it: Karl Marx is actually Karl *Mordechai,* to begin with, and Leon Trotsky is actually Leon *Bronstein.* Barker cites a list of Jews throughout history whose true identity is not apparent, part of the great Jewish ploy of changing their names to non-Jewish-sounding names. The Bolsheviks behind the Russian Communist Revolution, he says, were New York Jews.

Then Communism itself is not the thing we should fear. It is the more secret, more powerful organization driving the proletarian movements which should concern us. Barker and Epperson are by no means the first, nor surely the last to articulate such fears. It is, of course, necessary to understand some of the groups in question and the manner in which conspiracy theorists make connections between these groups and world events to fully appreciate how such theory is applied. Then there is the matter of historical revisionism, which must also be examined as a factor of conspiracy theory.

Historical revisionism, in this sense, does not simply entail alternative explanations of historical events. Revisionism, as applied to conspiracy theory, may also include the "rewriting" of history from present day standards and judgments, or essentially slanting history for specific purposes (as Big Brother's government does in Orwell's *1984).* These "rewrites" are particularly conspiratorial when made or utilized to justify current policy, to change perspectives of defining events (such as the Civil War) and advancing the agenda of the "unseen hands." The new history, from a racialist perspective, is evil in nature, conceived by evil beings (Jews) and directed toward the white race in an evil manner for evil purposes. It is designed to foment rejection of and violence toward the white Christians and their way of life.

For the Identity Christian, history itself is another element in the ongoing struggle between good and evil begun in the Garden. It is important

to note that Identity Christians, and some other fundamentalist faiths, view prophetic history as the only history which really matters. All that has ever happened, or is ever going to happen, has already been addressed scripturally. This does not mean that historical interpretations are not given some credence, or that Identity Christians are not interested in history. Indeed they are. And certainly, they see conspiracy in current interpretations.

Revisionist historical views, for the conspiracy theorist, are absolute necessities as far as the establishment of one-world government is concerned. The utility of changing facts to fit situations or, worse yet, to create political agendas and popular opinions, is manifestly apparent and equally appalling. But above all, from this perspective, it is absolutely effective.

If the United States is in danger from such conspirators, who are they? Who misrepresents history in order to manipulate nations? Who is delivering the republic into the hands of the one-worlders?

The Masons are one such suspect organization. A secret fraternal society which has its origins in the stone-cutters' guilds of Europe, over time the Masons were seen as a status symbol organization for the middle class and were the recipients of patronage from the nobility. Major opposition to the society has traditionally been from the Catholic Church, which viewed the teachings of Freemasonry to be contrary to the teachings of the Church, and Hitler, of course, granted Masons the same status as Jews, blaming them for everything which had gone wrong in Germany. The Masons, oddly enough considering the position of the church, have a long tradition of supporting religious tolerance and the ideas of the equality of man. There are those in the movements, however, who see the Masons as insidious, influencing politics throughout their history with the intention of shaping governments and subverting national sovereignty to the designs of international Freemasonry.

For many conspiracy theorists, the Freemasons are an integral element of one-world government. Says John B., a Houston area militiaman, "We are *already* living in a dictatorship—have been since FDR sold us out . . . we don't have to worry about Communism overseas, we got it right here . . . anyone who's a Thirty-sixth Degree Mason or above is part of it. The rest are little fish, but Thirty-sixth degree or above, they know all about it."

Along with the Freemasons, the Council on Foreign Relations (CFR) and the Trilateral Commission (TC) are also elements of the one-worlders.

These organizations are not seen by conspiracy theorists as truly separate entitites. Such groups, in fact, share the same goals and ideology regardless of the false front they display for the public.

The CFR, for instance, presents itself as a non-profit and nonpartisan "think-tank" dedicated to the exchange of ideas which promote better understanding of U.S. foreign policy and international affairs. It is composed of leaders in academia, public service, the media, *et al.*, who are citizens of the United States or permanent residents who intend to become citizens. The CFR is not part of the government and is not financed by the federal government. Education through various studies and programs is the expressed goal of the Council on Foreign Relations. Education which they believe will be pertinent to the global community, aware of increasing international responsibilities and obligations, particularly on the part of the United States. For the enlightened conspiracy theorist, the CFR's real goal is to help create a one-world government.

The Trilateral Commission, like the CFR, presents a non-threatening agenda to the public. The TC claims to be an organization of "influential" representatives of American/Canadian, Japanese and western European states dedicated to issues of world peace, trade, alleviation of poverty, economic development and enhancement of global relationships between nations. Again like the CFR, the Trilateral Commission is not a branch of government, nor is it funded by government. The members of the TC meet annually in one of the three regions to discuss matters such as arms control, peacekeeping, finance, third world development and other topics on which they issue publications as well as serve as "advisors" to government officials from time to time.

Conspiracy theorists, however, note that the power wielded by the "elitist" individuals associated with the CFR and TC is considerable—people like David Rockefeller who, according to A. Ralph Epperson, was the power behind the election of Jimmy Carter in 1976 and, oddly enough, may well have been the power behind the "firing" of Nikita Khrushchev in 1964.

In a speech to a group of Christian activists in Orlando, Florida, in 1993, James Wardner, DDS, former teacher and now far right activist, conspiracy theorist and author, speaks to the intricate web of conspiracy woven over the United States. Using charts labeled to indicate the connections between the Council on Foreign Relations and Trilateral Commission to the New World Order, Wardner illustrates the proliferation of membership of the CFR and TC throughout the government under several administrations including Reagan, Carter, Bush and Clinton. His contention is that, regardless of who one votes for, one gets proponents of the CFR and TC—the elements of the New World Order.

Wardner states facetiously, "I want you to know there's no conspiracy . . . there is no conspiracy . . . there's no need to worry." His irony is met with laughter as he continues. "But it's interesting that the Bible is full of conspiracy . . ." He goes on to quote Psalms 31:10, 56:6, 64:2, and 71:10; Jeremiah 11:9; as well as Acts 4:25–28 and Acts 9:23 (which speaks to the Jewish conspiracy to murder Christ).

Although Wardner does not overtly refer to ZOG or the Jews or to Christian Identity, he does drop a few names such as Eustace Mullins and Linda Thompson. Mullins is the virulently anti-Jewish holocaust revisionist and author of *The Secret Holocaust: A Primer for the Aryan Nations Movement* in which Jews are blamed for the European slaughter during World War II and virtually every other atrocity that has ever happened in the world. Thompson is an attorney, a militia activist and producer of the video documentaries *Waco, the Big Lie,* and *Waco II, the Big Lie Continues*. These works offer questionable proof of a federal plot to first murder, then cover up the murder of the Branch Davidians.

Wardner exhorts the audience to circulate, network, to "get to know one another and ask questions of those who understand, who know the truth." He states that almost anyone in government is willing to write off his concerns by noting that membership in CFR or TC is nothing to be concerned about. But, he also claims, "if we replaced the TC/CFR labels on the names with ADA [American Dental Association] everyone in America would be concerned because the price of services would go up."

Wardner's lecture has a much broader appeal than the inflammatory rhetoric of Tom Metzger, Louis Beam, Neumann Britton or other more strident members of white supremacist and Christian Identity factions. The conspiracy theories advanced in Orlando might be embraced by more mainstream Christian activists, or those who adhere to apocalyptic visions of the coming Armageddon. And, it must be noted, a good many new members of the radical right have slipped over the line from the often marginalized ultra-conservative factions of more mainstream conservative ideology.

In any case, as far as the right wing conspiracy theorists are concerned, the point remains that these members of CFR, TC, United Nations and other multinational groups are a danger to the sovereignty of the United

States, to what's left of the republic and the Constitutional rights of the citizens and to the Christian faith. Wardner contends that the policies of the CFR and TC are already implemented and are the driving forces behind economic realities and policies affecting the nations of the world. He also contends that there are, already in place, social controls—mind control—exerted through CFR as an element of the New World Order. The policies and influence of CFR control print and video media, educational institutions and the quality and content of public education, textbooks and nearly every other aspect of American life.

It is particularly damning, in the eyes of the far right, that the CFR and TC advance ideas that are included in the party platforms of the Republican Party, the Democratic Party, and the Communist Party. The leaders of these parties are powerful players in the arena of world politics.

"The vote doesn't matter," observes Mark of the Texas Aryan Nationalist Skinheads. "It doesn't make any difference whether or not you vote for a Democan or a Republicrat . . . it's still the Jews. The only difference I can see is the liberals screw you fast and the conservatives screw you slow."

The United Nations? One-world government.

Organization of American States? One-world government.

The Council of Churches? One-world government.

The Bilderbergers? One-world government.

The Federal Reserve? One-world government.

One-world government? The Jews.

Such conspiracy theories can extend far beyond the arena of conventional politics—to illness, for example. From a conspiracy viewpoint, it is not profitable to cure Acquired Immunodeficiency Syndrome (AIDS), which, of course, is curable and much easier to acquire than we are led to believe. The internationalists who control the government, the faceless dictators, are more interested in money and power than in lives. And, since the encompassing goal is one-world Zionist government, it is quite logical that a sick and dying population is easier to control.

Then there is the matter of ZOG's control of the Food and Drug Administration (FDA). Diet, for instance, is a topic important to many Identity Christians, Seedline Christians in particular. Since they do identify themselves as the Israel of the Scriptures, it should not be surprising that they feel themselves bound by the dietary laws. Virtually every Identity ministry's mail order list includes tracts with dietary information—some from Old Testament law, some from ordinances, some a matter of common sense, with natural foods and herbs high on the list—and women's sections of newsletters sharing hints about health and food preparation as well as other household hints.

Logic and the modern availability of refrigeration notwithstanding, a preponderance of the faithful eschew pork products and most attribute their good health to the wisdom in Old Testament dietary laws that still work. The subject of healthy eating seems to be an Identity-wide issue that takes on more ominous overtones when intermarried with governmental control over food products.

Identity Pastor Earl Jones of Christian Crusade for Truth of Deming, New Mexico, is a retired military rocket engineer and intelligence officer and publisher of *Intelligence Newsletter*. Speaking at the 1997 Branson Super Conference of Christian Israel Congregations, Jones points to the inclusion of FDA-approved toxins in a wide range of foods consumed by the American public. He claims that American consumers are ingesting a plethora of additives, flavorings, preservatives, synthetics, ad infinitum, which cannot be and are not healthy.

The 18 June 1997 *Washington Post* article "Spit, Don't Swallow: New Toothpaste Warning Labels Give Brushers Pause" turns this belief into certainty. Author Don Oldenburg cites the recent case of an eight-year-old New Hampshire girl who read the warning label on her tube of toothpaste. In small print it said: "If you accidentally swallow more than used for brushing, seek professional help or contact a poison control center immediately." Her father was surprised. "When did they start putting a poison warning on toothpaste tubes?" he asked.

But that is the message of the new warning labels required by the U.S Food and Drug Administration on all fluoride toothpaste tubes "shipped as of April 7 [1997]." Says an employee at the Princeton, New Jersey, laboratories where the toothpaste is made, "When I receive the fluoride here, it has a skull-and-crossbones on it." One wonders why, if an oral product contains poison, the FDA would approve it at all. "It is always a kind of a trade-off," says a vice president of another company which markets "natural" toothpaste. This second company fruit-flavors the toothpaste to encourage children to brush, but still includes fluoride as an ingredient.

The name of the game, from this perspective, is profits. And issues of bottom-line profits far outweigh issues of the health of "Goyim cattle." The damage done to consumers through the ingestion of these toxins is not a problem for the Jews. After all, as impostors to the title Israel, the

Jews eat "Kosher," and follow the dietary laws written for the people they are bent on destroying. But the damage done by ZOG's Food and Drug Administration does not end with the adulteration of food products.

The presence of FDA-approved toxins in not only prepared foods but in household products such as cleansers and sprays, makeup as well as toothpaste, is no accident. According to Earl Jones, women who work at home are 55% more likely to die of cancer from these products found in virtually every home. An important goal of household hint newsletters is providing information on alternative cleansers and personal products.

The presence of dangerous products such as these, purposely containing toxins and licensed as safe by the Jewish-run government, is no accident as far as the Identity faithful are concerned. But through the sharing of information, Jones says, the forces of Satan that want to destroy God's chosen will be foiled. "You—Kingdom, Covenant, Christian Identity, whatever you're called," he said, "you are the people who are the great teachers. They up there recognize the infrastructure, but they can't destroy us."

Such thinking extends to all other aspects of American life, purposely corrupted by those who would enslave the world's population. Sports, for instance, is something that seems entirely innocent, and most Americans would undoubtedly have a difficult time considering something as innocuous as baseball part of worldwide conspiracy. However, it is reasoned, upon closer examination, professional sports may not be the innocent diversion it appears.

"The whole idea of sports is to turn people's minds away from politics," according to militiaman John B. "That's the whole thing. Everybody gets caught up in rooting for their teams and nobody pays any attention to politics or what's going on. Do you know, there are folks out there who can tell you the batting average of their favorite player and what he did last night, but they can't even tell you the name of their congressman? That's the kind of thing Communists can count on."

"I think a lot of these conspiracy theories are really out there sometimes," Charles Lee states. "I mean, I liked sports when I was growing up. I liked watching them and I liked playing them. I don't have time for them today but I don't see anything particularly wrong with sports in general. But you can't deny there's a certain thread of truth in the idea. The average American *is* happy as long as his stomach is full and he has his television so he can watch his favorite nigger dribble a ball up and down the court."

Conspiracy theorists note that, along with sporting events, such things as soap operas, game shows, circus events such as the trial of O. J. Simpson and the endless, mindless situation comedies constantly bombarding the viewing public are the real "opiates of the people." With nothing more to command his interest, the average American is never aware of *what* he is actually losing to the one-worlders, much less *when* he is actually losing it.

As far as Charles Lee and the White Camelia are concerned, we are being programmed by "the one-eyed Jew-Tube" to consider unnatural and un-Christian situations—such as interracial marriage, unwed motherhood, fictive ideas of racial equality, tolerance for homosexuals and the perverted lifestyle they lead—as natural, acceptable and innocent. Thus, the white supremacists perceive the television and film industries as Jewish-dominated control devices, molding us into a nation without focus, without morals, without purpose, without Yahweh.

The deleterious effect of television is not just an issue for white supremacists, however. America is filled with "Christian Soldiers." And some of these self-identified Christian activists are not the soldiers of the Klan, Aryan Nations, and other Identity Christians. Those associated with the Christian Coalition, for instance, who generally operate through acceptable political means to advance their causes, are equally upset with the "spiritual toxicity" of products delivered by the entertainment industry. These individuals are often as steeped in conspiracy ideology as the more right-wing and racialist organizations. In fact, certain fundamentalist factions hold that Christianity, the Bible, and any overt trappings of religiosity—or more specifically, Christianity—will one day be forbidden by law in the United States.

Cadillac John believes this as well: "I fully expect to go to jail for my beliefs. It says right there in the Bible, 'you will be brought before the Sanhedrin,' which means high court, but not to worry because God said 'I will put the words in your mouth.' So, I'm not worried and I am *not* backing down from my beliefs."

The federal government's interpretations of the separation of church and state, through court decisions forbidding the practice of government-sanctioned worship or religious instruction in the schools, are just one example of how the process has already begun. Thus, a good number of Christians point to the prophecy in the book of Revelation, insisting that such conspiracy exists as part of a foreordained struggle between good and evil:

And he causeth all, both small and great, rich and poor, free and bond, to receive a mark in their right hand, or in their foreheads; And that no man might buy or sell, save he that had the mark, or the name of the beast, or the number of his name. Here is wisdom. Let him that hath understanding count the number of the beast: for it is the number of a man; and his number is Six hundred threescore and six.    (REVELATION 13:16–18)

The "beast," of course, is a Satanic entity which cannot be separated from the Prince of Darkness. If one accepts the prophecy of Revelation, is it not understandable that one might possibly view such vaguely disquieting organizations as the Council on Foreign Affairs, the Trilateral Commission and the United Nations in a somewhat suspicious light? Does it not follow that one might ask, "which earthly entity has the power to mark people in this manner and how might this mark be made manifest?" Social Security numbers? Driver's licenses? Census data? Bar-codes on products at the supermarket? A national identification card? Fingerprint identification? DNA identification? Implantation of a microchip?

One woman, a fundamentalist Christian of the non-Identity variety, makes the observation, "They already have a central computer somewhere in Europe that has access to every bit of this information. And do you know what they call this super computer? It's called the 'Beast.' You can't believe in prophecy and at the same time believe that this is some kind of coincidence."

It is important to note that there is a strange area, a doctrinal no-man's-land, in which it is almost impossible to ascertain where the views of the traditional religious right leave off and the more virulent racial views of Christian Identity begin. Jack Van Impe Ministries on Trinity Broadcasting Network, as well as other ministries, produces (and offers for sale) books, television programs and videotapes addressing such Satanic conspiracies. One such video is the *666 Conspiracy: The United States of Europe and the New World Order* which includes arguments that, indeed, national identification, driver's license info strips, etc., are part and parcel of one-world Satanism. Hal Lindsay promotes his "end times" ministry with sales of his books in the millions of dollars. Pastor Adrian Rogers's sermons warn of an encroaching One-World government and a New World Order.

The anti-Christ conspiracy, from Seedline Identity teaching perspectives, is real, ongoing and underpinned by the Jewish usurpation of the title "Israel." From that basic starting point, a complex web of deception begins to emerge in the eyes of the true believer. The Zionist plot is indeed designed to create a one-world government and that government is "the beast" and its ruler Satan.

Since the Identity Christian believes the Jews are already in control of the United States government, it is understandable that there exists a separation of church and state and that all manner of false religion is elevated to an equal plane with, or even placed above, true Christianity. In the eyes of the Identity Christians, this is a deplorable attack on the morals of the country and another attempt to mask the identity of Aryan Israel. The efforts of the conspirators also explain the destruction of the white race through forced integration, encouraged intermarriage and the manipulation of cultural mores through media-controlled, politically correct programs.

However, these are some massive undertakings and, given the true nature and goals of such efforts, they cannot be advanced without a good deal of subterfuge. Hence we have programs such as welfare, ostensibly to aid people but actually designed to enslave them and render them dependent on the government. Governmental programs, from this perspective, have an almost Orwellian double-speak quality about them. We have freedom of religion, which is actually put into practice as freedom *from* religion. We have social security, which actually creates social insecurity. We have free trade agreements which undermine our national sovereignty, place us at the mercy of foreign governments and curtail our ability to trade freely. We have sex education in schools which undermines the morality of our children and promotes illicit sexual activity. We have Planned Parenthood, which is actually planned murder and the destruction of the unborn, not to mention the destruction of families. Jewish bankers control the economy and make it impossible for the white middle class to stay afloat as the Zionists create recessions and depressions to suit their purposes.

It is the worldwide financial institutions—ultimately benefiting the wealthy cabal of financiers who pull the strings to bring about one-world government—who constitute the Zionist Occupational Government, ZOG.

The late Pastor Sheldon Emry in his undated *Billions for the Bankers, Debts for the People* speaks to the socioeconomic conspiracy evident in the Jewish-instituted and controlled Federal Reserve System, global economics and their effects on American culture. The "would-be despots" in control, he says, use profits from the massive debts to create a web of economic enslavement. Under the guise of "doing good," they create dependence; under the guise of "discovering cures" for disease, they deliberately prevent real cures; under the guise of "improving education," they degrade our educational systems. Ill, poorly educated, and subservient people are easier to control and are less likely to understand what is being done to them.

Equally weak are the victims of social unrest and the morally bankrupt. The manipulators in control encourage the use of drugs and alcohol, the practices of racial intermarriage, sexual promiscuity, abortion, pornography—everything which debilitates the individual morally and devaluates the family—and they make a mockery of family and morals, patriotism, the Christian religion, all that is honorable. The new "rulers," Emry says, want to change every social order among the populace, except for the economic system by which they rob and rule. Our people have become slaves to bankers, "conquest through the most gigantic fraud and swindle in the history of mankind." The key to their power over us, Emry reminds us, is "their ability to create 'money' out of nothing and lend it to us at interest. If they had not been allowed to do that, they would never have gained secret control of our nation."

Other proponents of conspiracy theory also note the importance of controlling a country's monetary system. Conspiracy theory, as explained by Epperson, holds that the Rothschilds and other Jewish bankers have been in control of Europe for centuries. Because they controlled the money, they also controlled the governments of European nations. This provided them the wherewithal to create wars, loan money to fight those wars, and reap huge profits from the seemingly endless conflicts between the European nations. Just prior to the Civil War, the conspirators decided that the United States should also become a part of the monied class' assets.

As Epperson explains, the Jewish bankers fomented the Southern insurrection in order to create a National Bank in America. In addition, the Southern states were joined into a Confederacy, each retaining sovereign rights and rights of secession. Should the South have won the war, then it would be conceivable to arrange the continuing secession of the states from their own Confederacy and the financiers could count on the National Bank of Virginia, the National Bank of Tennessee, the National Bank of Louisiana, and, in fact, a national bank in each of the singular states. This done, each state with its own currencies, each state with its own resources, it would not be a much larger task to create conflict between any of these several sovereign states and re-create the small warring factions so easily manipulated in Europe. All the while the people of the United States believed the awful slaughter of Civil War was grounded in issues of states rights and slavery.

But the Army of the Republic emerged victorious and such plans were stymied—for a while. Still, a National Bank *was* established in the United States. And now the Federal Reserve, a private agency, controls the currency of the United States. According to conspiracy theory, every recession and every recovery occurs at the discretion of this entity which has both the power to cause inflation and the power to end it. And Jews control the worldwide purse strings.

And, of course, it does not end there. "This Satanic government has injected itself into every aspect of our public and private lives," Charles Lee states emphatically. "It tries to control what we think and how we think. If we disagree or voice opposition to any of its pet projects, promotion of homosexuality, integration of the races and so on, the next thing we know we find ourselves under investigation, in court, in prison, or with federal thugs kicking down our doors."

Given such a bleak outlook, what can any citizen do when, like David confronting some faceless, monolithic Goliath, he finds himself contending with such an overwhelming foe? He fights. Not just with ballots, or rhetoric, or party affiliation, but with any means at his disposal.

There is, of course, one glaring inconsistency with conspiracy theory and the idea that a small group of wealthy internationals have controlled the nations. If this is the case, all the nostalgia and longing for the purity and freedom of the government of the founding fathers is an illusion. So is the often-admired Fascist movement of Adolf Hitler.

If, for the sake of argument, one assumes all the elements of conspiracy theory as fact, then the government of the United States has been ruled by this group *since its very inception.* If one assumes these individuals, through financial chicanery and control of currency, inflation, and recessions, create and destroy leaders, then one must by necessity assume that the depression in Germany, through which Hitler came to power, was controlled as well. If one follows this line of reasoning to its logical conclusion, then Hitler was *allowed* to come to power—in fact, was even manipulated into power—by these same individuals and eventually destroyed at their discretion. If this is true, there has *never* been any true freedom nor any true rebellion. Identity Pastor Ray Barker, in his taped sermon "The Plot Against Christianity," claims not only that Hitler *was* a Jew, but that Nazi Germany and even the British Israelite movement supposedly arrayed against the Jewish people were also created by Jews in order to garner world sympathy and support.

There are many in the movements who undoubtedly would dispute the above conclusions, as indeed does Charles Lee, but it is nevertheless the logical end-point of this line of reasoning. Still, the relative nature of freedom, both historically and in the world today, can be explained by the theory of the Angelic Conflict, the War of Eden. And conspiracy theory, certainly not inconsistent with Identity doctrine, is understood as an expression of the struggle between the children of light and the children of darkness.

Conspiracy theory notwithstanding, Tom Metzger, leader of White Aryan Resistance (WAR) is often quoted on his beliefs that the white supremacist movement is about racial survival and that *any* means of ensuring that survival is acceptable. The Klan, too, holds this belief, as do the Church of Jesus Christ Christian, Aryan Nations, the Aryan Brotherhood and each threatened special interest group in the nation. For the ''leaderless resistance'' this is not merely an ideologically driven struggle but a call to arms over life and death issues over which control can be, and must be, exerted against ZOG.

# CHAPTER ELEVEN

# Race Relations and Integration: Racial Suicide on the Installment Plan

As far as the members of the movements are concerned, the Zionist conspirators' plans to corrupt America have met with wide success. They argue that toxic and un-Christian ideology, expressed in terms of official policy and social norms, is manifested daily for those who care to pay attention. And certainly, the members of the movements pay attention. The natural order of the world, as they see it, is collapsing into chaos, often supported by well-meaning, though misled, white Christians who have been "programmed" through the active efforts of ZOG to view this chaos as normal. A key element of the plot to bring down the white race is the Jewish "myth" of racial equality advanced as fact. The idea of equality, in turn, drives the policies of integration which racialists maintain has proven to be a dismal failure. Given this reality—coupled with the racial strife as experienced in a nation where people of various cultures and races are thrown together to clash and struggle for dominance—separatism is the only program that makes sense and ensures tranquility between the various races.

Racialists believe that factional rivalries exist everywhere. Racial prejudice exists everywhere. Ethnic conflict exists everywhere. Many on the racial right contend that racism is innate, that every individual is born with it and that ethnocentrism is as natural and God-given as any other instinct. And, following this line of reasoning, racism is impossible to eradicate. Since one cannot get rid of it, then one must find a way to live with it, and the conclusion of the separatists—both black and white—is separate nationhood.

But, they also note, race is not the only divisive element. Nations may also subdivide along religious and political lines. And it is true that sometimes other, often quite surprising distinctions emerge between peoples. In the Dominican Republic where there is a large population of black people, prejudice is based on the "shade" of blackness and hair texture. In Mexico where a huge proportion of the population bears the brown reminder of the original inhabitants of the land, a good deal of prejudice is directed toward "los indios" whose identity lies in tribal units.

Admonitions in virtually every culture's holy book notwithstanding, loving one's other-race, other-religion neighbor is often more in evidence on paper than it is in practice. In the case of the extreme racial right, ethnocentrism that celebrates the similarities in one's own group actively embraces the other side of the coin, xenophobic reaction against the differences of other groups.

That racial and ethnic differences exist is not in question. Why they create blanket pre-judgments and a tendency toward segregation—whether this preference is innate in the human psyche, or we learn racism through some sort of sociocultural osmosis that we are unaware of, or racism is taught in a conscious and calculated effort—is an issue for debate on any side of the various racial lines. Difference *is* noted. Only the type and degree of xenophobic reaction varies.

If one assumes that such prejudice is indeed innate, then the present climate of racial tension in the United States should not be surprising. In fact, it would be much more surprising if it did not exist. The members of the movements maintain that prejudice and ideas of separatism are not the sole domains of the white race. They reference the Nation of Islam, a black separatist group surprisingly similar to Christian Identity in terms of belief, to make their point and to illustrate the racial double standard of America.

The Nation of Islam would like an area covering five to seven states as a black homeland. A separate black nation, pulled out of the melting pot and splashed onto the map of the former United States, sounds ludicrous to some. However, such nationhood is a stated goal of Nation of Islam whose idea of Islam is racially based and also encompasses the concept of the chosen. And there have been precedents set—Israel, the Jewish homeland, Pakistan, the Moslem state carved out of India, Bangladesh, the nation of Bengalis. The separatist agenda of Nation of Islam, though certainly not their claim to be the chosen people, is met with whole-hearted support by the white separatists. And such demands are racist. Nation of Islam, as far as the racialists are concerned, is most definitely a racist organization; and its leader, Louis Farrakhan, is most definitely a racist.

"You might say it takes one to know one," Jim Stinson states.

Pastor Richard Butler of Aryan Nations has called Farrakhan "a black patriot who hates jews and Whites." Butler believes similarly about the necessity for separate states as an intrinsic natural given. "Blood will tell," he says. "This old saw has a meaning that crosses all cultures. The essence of life is in the blood. We witness strife between the various cultures that have been forced to occupy the same territory."

Minister Farrakhan organized the "Million Man March" on Washington, D.C. (October 16, 1995) to promote the responsibility of black men as fathers, husbands, workers, and human beings. Of course, such a campaign is a laudable cause. Minister Farrakhan called for an end to drug use, violence, and dependency on government in the black communities—as well as advancing the cause of good old family values and respect for one another in these same communities—all laudable causes. There are few in America who can take exception to such an agenda. However, there are those who have problems, not necessarily with the issues or the followers in this particular event, but with the leader. Some critics referred to the event as nothing more than a black KKK rally.

A caller to Michael Reagan's (son of former president Ronald Reagan) talk show that same week, posed the question, "What if a march like that had been organized and led by David Duke?" A valid question. What if David Duke, former Imperial Wizard of the Louisiana Klan, with a positive history of racism and separatism, were to organize a "Million White Man March" focusing on the same issues? The supremacists know what would happen. The same supporters of Farrakhan's efforts would condemn the efforts of Duke. Duke's years of racist rhetoric and activism would overshadow his positive message of responsibility. And the marchers themselves would be viewed in at least a slightly suspicious manner.

Cadillac John Thellin does not believe anyone among the white separatists holds the slightest idea that any white separatist leader would be tolerated—or given any credit at all—for an attempt to organize such a rally. In fact, Cadillac John also maintains that "no white man whatsoever would be able to get away with organizing anything *just* for white men." The fact that Farrakhan has been given any credence, for those in the movements, is a further example of the double standard and proof that whites today are routinely discriminated against.

Charles Lee also notes such double standards. "The Klan has been teaching the same message of racial and individual responsibility for over a century and all we ever get is put down for it. Whites are told it is wrong to have an organization, association, or group that promotes our race or that its membership is predominately white or all white. At the same time, non-whites are given approval to organize one group after another. In many schools around the country, blacks can wear black-power T-shirts with a black fist on front, but white students are expelled if they brandish a white power symbol or Confederate flag. If you join a pro-white group that promotes the history, heritage, or culture of the white race, you are given thumbs down and called a hater and a racist.

"Christian civilization, culture and history will cease to exist and all because of lies from those that want their culture to be the dominant one in America. White Christians are under attack, and the double standard rules imposed on our people strengthen our opposition while weakening our race."

Mark, leader of the Texas Aryan Nationalist Skinheads, states that Farrakhan "realizes that the two races cannot live together. And he knows the Jews are Satan Seed." Mark is an ardent supporter of separate racial nationhood. Like many others in the movements, he views it as the only way to ensure the integrity of the various races and the only hope of peace between them. An inescapable component of the racialist agenda is the idea of racial purity, racial survival.

"We must secure the existence of our people and a future for white children."

The above "14 words" of David Lane (incarcerated member of The Order) pretty well sum up the underpinning philosophy of the supremacist movements as far as race relations are concerned. It is extremely clear that even beyond government oppression, one-world government, the "reverse discrimination" of affirmative action and other government programs, the soldiers of God fear the dissolution of the white race into the "mulatto zombies" described in *The Turner Diaries*. The implications of identifying the true heirs to the covenants, Aryan Israel, add an additional degree of urgency to the efforts of the separatists to secure an Aryan homeland in the United States, based on biblical principles and the omniscient Word of Yahweh.

These principles demand a clear separation of the races and acknowledge the Christian Identity belief that inherent differences between the races exist, which precludes successful integration. For the separatists, integration has proven to be a dismal failure and that failure is directly attributable to the fact that integration is contrary to the laws of God and nature. Those on the racial right speak to differences between the races that far exceed the color of one's skin. Not the least of these is the belief among many Identity Christians that non-white races, Pre-Adamites or "muds," have no immortal souls, or at least lack the divine spirit infused into white Adamic man.

Of course, Charles Lee and the members of White Camelia, Imperial Wizard Darrell Flinn and all other Klans have always carried the message of segregation. Lee maintains that his racial beliefs are *not* rooted solely in hatred. In soft, even tones, he draws an allegory by way of explanation. "If you have family pets," he says, "no one expects the cat to sit up and beg, roll over, play dead—that's the dog's job. It is totally unrealistic to expect the dog to keep the home free of mice, climb trees, or do anything the cats usually do. A man would have to be a total idiot to hate a cat for being unable to be a dog or vice-versa. It is the same between the races.

"Look at the great cultures of the world. Where are the black architects? The black explorers? The black military leaders? Black philosophers, mathematicians, theologians? Where?

"Oh, the revisionists of history point to the pyramids and so forth, but does that really equate? Left to themselves, niggers would be running around Africa, living in mud huts and eating each other. That they are civilized at all is through the efforts of white Christians. If you take the white man, the white mind out of the equation, civilization falls, it's as simple as that. One need only look at history and present world affairs— if he's honest with himself—to know the truth. How effectively are blacks running Rwanda? South Africa? Zimbabwe?

"I've had black people come up and ask me, 'Why do you people in the Klan hate us? Why don't you respect us as fellow human beings?'

"I always tell them, 'I don't hate you, per se. I hate integration and the myth of equality. There is no racial equality. There never has been. There never will be. It is a simple fact that He created racial inequality with His own divine purpose in mind. Where we, as a society, get into trouble is that we try to ignore God's natural law."

Darrell Flinn and his wife, Anna Lynn, echo the same sentiments in regard to inherent racial differences. Sitting over a seafood dinner in a

Cajun restaurant in Lafayette, Louisiana, the Flinns draw a good deal of attention from other diners. Which is not surprising since both are wearing T-shirts proclaiming their affiliation with the White Kamellia Knights. They also have a rather high profile due to their public images as co-hosts of *The Klan in Acadiana,* a public access cable program airing weekly in Lafayette.

Anna is young and pretty with a trace of Michigan in her accent. A relatively recent convert to the supremacist cause, she is nevertheless passionate about her beliefs. "I never really gave the issue of race any thought at all when I was growing up," she says. "In the small town where I grew up there was only white people. The only black person I ever knew was a little girl who had been adopted by a white family. We were friends—she has even spent the night at my house—but it's like . . . well, she was more like a little black white girl, I guess. When I left Michigan to come down here, that's when I discovered the differences— the real differences—between the races. And it's a much greater difference than simple skin color."

Darrell Flinn, like Charles Lee, points to natural difference.

"I may be a lot of things, but I'm not a liar. And I'm not a hypocrite but in one way. Yahweh created black people. And because He created them, He must have a purpose for them and they must have a place in His scheme of things. I think it's hypocritical of me to be judgmental in this regard because they can't help what they are and all they are doing is being what they are. I know that. But I can't stand them. I absolutely hate a nigger just for being a nigger."

The idea of "nature" of the races transcends all political and philosophical differences among the constituents of the racial right. Charles Lee says, "Aryans should be true to their natures, blacks should be true to theirs. In fact, we have to be. As for respect? I tell them, 'How can I respect you? You don't respect yourselves. You don't take responsibility for yourselves. You complain and yell the white man is holding you down. Yet, in your own communities, you murder each other, rob, steal, rape, buy, sell, and use drugs. I don't see any white slave masters down there cracking a whip and making you do these things.' How am I responsible for that?

"I'm not saying every black is a criminal or that every criminal is black. That's ridiculous. But what I am saying is that black people are a more violent people. They are disproportionately represented in crimes and in prison. Shouldn't this tell us something about them?

"When I talk about racial differences, this is what I mean. When I was a kid growing up in Port Arthur, white people used to leave their homes unlocked. Since integration, they can't do that. What happened? Did we assume skin color was the only difference between the races? Couldn't we see what was going on in their neighborhoods? Did we expect them to be grateful? To fit in? To leave us alone? Now our neighborhoods look like prisons—burglar bars on the windows, three or four locks on every door, our old people and women afraid to walk the streets at night, or the daytime either for that matter. All of this can be laid at the door of liberals, at the door of the idiotic 'equality' laws.''

Among such groups as the Ku Klux Klan, there has traditionally been a somewhat patronizing attitude held toward the black race. The Klan, as an organization, seems to shoulder the ''white man's burden'' as caretaker for the more ''impetuous'' races—whether the races in question agree to this arrangement or not. Whereas this is an infuriating affront to black Americans in general and has been historically dangerous for more than a few, it is, in the eyes of the Identity Christian, part of the Divine Will.

This sentiment is voiced by J. B. Stoner, former Klan leader who served time for the bombing of a black church in 1958. Speaking before a convention of separatists in 1993, he notes that blacks are unable to govern themselves and, in a larger sense, unable to control themselves.

In the ''Old South'' whites, charged with keeping the blacks in line, were quite effective in maintaining societal order. ''No one liked to see a white officer beating a nigger with a billy-club. I never took pleasure in seeing that sort of thing . . . blood flowing and all . . . but I did take pleasure in being able to walk the streets at night without fear . . . in places like Birmingham, Mobile, Dallas, or Atlanta, Georgia. Do you want to try that today?''

And, as one might expect, the overwhelming response to that question was an emphatic no.

The Klan, Aryan Nations, and other supremacist organizations all adhere to the basic concept that there is *no* such thing as racial equality. And, since there is no racial equality, the idea of an integrated, balanced society of multiracial equals—each as intelligent, industrious, creative and capable as the other—is a liberal pipe dream.

Mike Hallimore of Kingdom Identity Ministries devotes a good deal of his time to patiently explaining the scriptural attitudes his ministry holds toward the non-white races. He, too, speaks to inherent inequalities.

"I think inequality is pretty obvious," he says. "I think it's obvious to most blacks as well. It all boils down to how you define equality and, even then, inequality in terms of superiority is still obvious. If you take sports, for instance, and set putting a basketball into a goal as the standard measurement, then blacks are clearly superior to whites. But, if you set other standards such as academics or scientific achievements, isn't the reverse true?"

Hallimore insists he does not base his perceptions on blind hatred or hatred of any kind. "I don't hate the black race at all," he says. "Not at all. I am a Christian and I believe that Christians should express the love of God. God loves all his creations in their proper order." As a member of the chosen people, the Servant Nation charged with the steward-ship of the world, Hallimore holds that the erroneous promotion of the idea of equality, generally perpetrated by Jews, is detrimental to the black race as well as the white. He is certainly not alone in his thinking.

The general consensus among white supremacists is that it is cruel to teach black children that they are on equal footing with white children only to have them discover for themselves that this is not true. When blacks, competing on an equal basis with whites, fall short in terms of performance and abilities, becoming aware of innate inequalities in the process, it is bound to be hurtful. The disappointment they feel, it is argued, must undoubtedly be increased by the awareness that they have been lied to. From this perspective, the whole idea of equality between races has made the realities of inequalities that much more difficult to bear, led to increased tension between the races and contributed greatly to decline of American society as a whole.

"This whole 'Great Society' thing has failed," Cadillac John says, shaking his head. "Our society was great, and could be great again, but not until we get these silly notions of racial equality out of our heads.

"Now, I have no problem with a man trying to get ahead. Hell, I'll help him anyway I can, and I don't care what race he is, but I'm not about to sell myself out in the process. People say that white racists build themselves up at the expense of other people. That we put other people down to feel good about ourselves. That's bullshit. White Christian Ameri-cans are the ones being put down. I don't go out of my way to antagonize black people. But any time I stand up and tell the truth, there's always somebody somewhere wanting to holler 'racism.' Okay, racism it is then. But it is still the truth. We are *not* equal."

Thomas Jackson, in his article "What is Racism," *(American Renais-*

*sance,* Vol. 2, Number 8) argues the point of view held by those in the movements: Explanations for any black failure always become an indictment of white people, lest logic venture into the forbidden territory of racial equality. ''If blacks are equal to whites in every way,'' he says, ''what accounts for their poverty, criminality and dissipation? Since any theory of racial differences has been outlawed, the only possible explanation for black failure is white racism.''

Such articles, repugnant as they may be to many Americans, articulate the feelings of a significant number of others and raise important questions for mainstream America. But however troubling such questions might be, they are questions which are already answered for the racialists. The issue of racial inferiority/superiority, from a Christian Identity reading, is clearly addressed in the Bible and leaves no room for doubt. Yet, the non-Christian Identity white supremacists are equally clear on issues of race.

Those on the racial right argue the idea that the natural laws of hierarchy hold true within races themselves, but that the difference between the races is more than physical appearance, hair texture, or pigmentation. The contention then is that this situation is right and proper, and demands acknowledgment.

Arguments advanced to prove black physical and genetic inferiority include questionable arguments—from a medical perspective—of profound differences in the structure of blood, susceptibility to specific diseases, and other issues which are generally rejected by anthropologists, physiologists and other twentieth-century professionals who study such phenomena.

The AIT's Chapter 95, ''Anthropology Confirms the Bible,'' addresses these very issues, beginning with the qualifications of those whose criteria provide a measurement:

> Through grants and funding by large tax-free foundations, many members of the profession of Anthropology have sold their integrity for the price of a ride on the highly profitable ''liberal band-wagon'. All this has worked well, on the unsuspecting public, to help evolve the ''one race'' or ''Brotherhood of Man'' idea . . . Dubbing a scientist a ''racist'' is a cowards way of avoiding the responsibility of an intelligent refutation . . .

On the subject of intelligence:

> Various studies have been made of the comparative average weights of white and negro brains with the results that all fall within the range of about an 8

to 12% lower weight for the negro brain . . . As a racial average, the negro brain is lighter than the white and this in turn indicates a lower average level of intelligence.

And blood:

A tremendous fact developed is that the human races are not the same—*but particular kinds of living things.* The blood of the white Caucasian differs in molecular construction and hereditary factors from that of the Negro. . . . the 'social engineers' and misguided 'do-gooders' devoting their energies to race mixing as a basis for social adjustment now are proven wrong from every scientific point of view. Race mixing is bound to result in race suicide. The Red Cross and other blood banks who have mixed blood of the races for transfusions—under pressure from minority groups—are guilty of a crime against humanity.

Identity, as argued by the racialists, is lost through race mixing whether it is black/white, white/oriental, oriental/black, black/Latino or any combination.

"This is probably the most important aspect of the separatist movement," Lee explains. "Racial survival. This is the message Pastor Butler preaches. This is the cause I've been working for the last twenty years. Not hatred of other races but love of one's own. I don't see anything wrong with that. I believe that any white man anywhere on earth should know there's a homeland for him, where he can come and be with others of his kind. I believe the United States of America should be that homeland."

It is not the individual race's place, or lack of place in society which is entirely at issue for the Identity Christian. Instead, the underlying issue is the subjugation and eventual destruction of God's chosen people, White Israel. Identity again becomes the issue, or the perceived loss of identity. And this is not just an issue of physical, racial identity, but of spiritual identity. As Mike Hallimore has pointed out, consistent with Seedline doctrine, Adamites are "spirit men."

"It's not really about intelligence or performance or culture," Hallimore says. "Although those differences are apparent. The key difference is found in the Scriptures. White people are the children of God, invested with the spirit of God. Other races know God as their Creator. Only white Israel people can know God as their Father. *That's* the real difference."

Identity Christians lament the fact that the majority of white people in

America are unaware of their purpose and their place in Yahweh's grand plan. For the most part, they admit, so are the other races. There are those, however, who are completely knowledgeable of the genocidal conspiracy—racial destruction through intermarriage *is* genocide for the white supremacist—even if it is self-inflicted. But many Identity Christians would argue that technically it is *not* self-inflicted, since it results from the propaganda of ZOG and the deliberate superimposition of foreign anti-Christian values on white society.

From the Identity point of view, miscegenation—the mingling of the races—is a genetic battle the darker race will win through contamination. Thus, they maintain, the clever Sons of Satan, the Jews, have orchestrated the diabolical philosophy of integration, ensuring race mixing and the breeding of the "goyim cattle" that their Talmud teaches exist to serve them.

Cadillac John explains, "The product of such a union is what the Scriptures call a *mamser*. In most Bibles this is translated as 'bastard.' But if you read it in context, 'bastard' doesn't make any sense. God says you will not allow a *mamser* to enter the congregation of the Lord, even unto his tenth generation. Does that mean if your parents aren't married that your blood line is cut off from God for ten generations? Does that make sense? Is God going to hold against you something your parents did?

"The word *mamser* is more accurately translated as 'mongrel' because it means the parents were of two different races. The blood-line is polluted, unclean. This is an abomination in the sight of God. Non-White blood even ten generations later is too much. It's all about the blood.

"If a white woman marries a black man and gives birth to his child, then that child is a *mamser*, a mongrel. Now, suppose that woman divorces the black man and marries a white man. She gives birth to another child, by a white father. Is that child white? No it is *not*, because the woman is polluted. *She's* black and the child's still a *mamser*. It's all in the blood.

"Now, people can argue that any damned way they want to, but I can read and it's in the Bible. A *mamser* can't help what he is, but that doesn't change the fact he is what he is. And nothing, *nothing* changes the word of God.

"For the races to mix is against God's law. You will not accept a daughter from 'their' house for your son. You will not allow a son or daughter from your house to go to theirs. You won't hear any mud-loving preacher in these Judeo-Christian so-called 'churches' telling you the truth about that. But that does not change the fact that it is the truth.''

But if there is a pervasive mixing of the races—if intermarriages occur on a grand scale and progeny remarry into both pure race and impure races, ad infinitum—then all races would eventually be destroyed through assimilation. And what Dr. Pierce, in *The Turner Diaries,* refers to as ''the racial basis for our existence'' will also be destroyed.

Even more disturbing for the adherents of Christian Identity is the belief that a ''black gene'' is dominant. The new race would undoubtedly be a darker race and Aryan Israel would be lost in the gene pool of the pre-Adamites and the Seed of Satan. God's grand plan would fall beneath the schemes of the Prince of Darkness.

Other Identity Christians insist that Yahweh Himself warns the children of Israel against such miscegenation, as is noted in Numbers 25. The act of Phinehas, who runs the sinners through with a javelin—thereby pleasing Yahweh, who establishes the Phinehas Priesthood—sets a precedent which many Americans find immensely disturbing:

Race mixers, breakers of Yahweh's law, are to be put to death.

# CHAPTER TWELVE

# The Welfare State: Immigration, Drag Queens and the Judgment of Yahweh

**W**ith their morning coffee, Americans are jolted by the headlines: babies found in dumpsters, politicians involved in graft, corruption and sex scandals; abortion doctors, clinic employees, and sometimes patients attacked—even murdered—by anti-abortion activists; racial crimes on the increase; gay bashing on the increase; crime in general on the increase; bombs planted in federal buildings and at the Olympics; news stories which are, at the very least, extremely troubling. In the eyes of many, including the racialists, such situations are not the problems in themselves but symptomatic of a much larger problem.

We are reaping the whirlwind sown by the Unseen Hand. Our nation is in crisis because it is supposed to be in crisis, consistent with the goals and agenda of those who seek global domination. The problems which face us are immense and pervasive. Crime, drug use, overcrowded prisons, familial violence, child abuse, pornography, AIDS, abortion, and the murder rate in cities such as Detroit, Houston, New York or Los Angeles, which routinely exceed in terms of annual raw numbers all the murder rates Western Europe has to offer—these are relentless issues which daily confront the American citizen. And millions are perplexed by our sad state of affairs.

If one tunes the radio or television to a Christian broadcast network, of which there are usually several to choose from in any given area, biblical answers are abundant and the one most prominent answer is that the end is near at hand. In fact, there are many who are absolutely convinced that we are already living in the end times. Apocalyptic visionaries point to twentieth-century America, then to the book of Revelation where, they maintain, the truth is clear. God's promises are being fulfilled. The prophecies are being realized.

From this perspective, our human frailties and the supernatural involvement of the Prince of Darkness explain the moral, social, political, and international crises of America. We have strayed from God, from the Christian principles which made our country great. That is how we've gone wrong, allowed the ''good old days'' to slip away, lost our direction, had our values up-ended, our priorities inverted and come to such a state of affairs.

But where do we go from here?

Not a hard question for true believers: to Hell or back to God.

''The only possible path for any people who want happy, fulfilling productive lives is to follow the Laws of God, as they are written in the Holy Bible,'' Charles Lee says. ''I want to follow those laws. I don't think they're that harsh. Maybe because I'm not so arrogant as to think I know better than God.

''I don't think a person has to have a degree in theology or political science to see the practicality of the Laws of God, either. And these practical laws have not changed. God said Israel should remain a separate people. We haven't and look where we are . . . the crime . . . people on welfare who never contribute . . . only take and take and take. God said homosexuality is an abomination. Look at America. Where did AIDS come from? People can say what they want but I believe it is a judgment from God. That isn't politically correct, but I believe it. People say it's spread heterosexually, but it's not. Unless one of the people involved has been engaging in the filthy, perverted faggot lifestyle. Accepting abominations . . . queers, race mixers, followers of foreign gods . . . false gods, is a sure way of dooming a people and a culture.''

Identity Christians, consistent with a number of more orthodox denominations, basically view our problems as a fundamental continuance of the struggle between God and Satan. For them, the perceived decline of the republic is not a surprising occurrence because they understand the agenda of the Beast. In fact, they understand this decline as an event which is taking place right on schedule. However, supernatural influence notwithstanding, there are plenty of human elements involved. The decline of the nation, certainly indicative of the supernatural struggle, may also be understood as the calculated, systematic and carefully implemented plan to destroy the country, dissolve its sovereignty and bring it under the cloak of one-world government.

This plan will not necessarily come to fruition through force of arms. Rather, it will occur when a helpless population, undergoing a number of carefully formulated crises, yield to their savior—not Christ, but the government. The populace will have to do this in order to survive. If, indeed, the final element is force of arms, this will occur after the population has been weakened and hobbled through gun control, welfare, abortion policies, increased taxation, increased regulations, socialized medicine, social programs, integration, affirmative action, and other destructive policies implemented by ZOG.

Concerns about such issues are not the sole domain of the movements but are shared by any number of Americans. These individuals may have a wide range of various social, religious and political philosophies and equally varied interpretations of the meaning and origin of programs such as welfare. Still the consensus may be unanimous that such programs, however well-intentioned, are destructive to both society and to those who ostensibly benefit from them. Clearly this is a shared ideology among those of the far right and of the more mainstream right.

With one glaring exception.

Racialists hold that there is nothing ''well-intentioned'' about the efforts of ZOG to enslave Americans. Welfare, for instance, is falsely presented in a positive light—as a humane and necessary method to alleviate the suffering of fellow citizens—to make the concept more palatable to Americans who blindly follow the siren call of Jewish propaganda. But, as far as the racialists are concerned, it is merely another Jewish trick to build the power base of the Seed of Satan and further entrench ZOG as a powerful global entity.

''If you don't think welfare is part of all this,'' Charles Lee says, ''you're ignoring reality. There are people out there, mostly blacks, who have never known anything but government handouts. They don't know how to pull their own weight, even if they wanted to, which a lot of them don't. It's keeping them alive—barely—but it's killing this country. [St.] Paul says that the lazy don't deserve to eat. I believe that. But I also believe there are a lot of people, of all races, who are crippled this way by the government. They can't do any better because they don't know any better.

''Of course, if you challenge a congressman on welfare—whether they're Democrat, Republican, or Independent—they'll almost always tell you that these people can't make it without our help. There are a lot of good Americans who want to help, and there's nothing wrong with wanting to help. I think most Americans are good-hearted and generous. But they are misled. We're not helping anyone with welfare. We're hurting them and hurting ourselves. The only real beneficiary of welfare is the federal government.''

''And you can bet your ass if something's good for the federal government, it's bad for the American people,'' Jim Stinson interjects.

Among the Identity supremacists, the responsibility for the welfare state rests with the Jews, abetted, of course, by the Judeo-Christian churches and their toxic ''churchianity'' and these same well-intentioned but misled white Americans.

As Epperson notes in *The Unseen Hand,* the methodical aspect of the situation is apparent to those who care to make an honest examination. The standard of living for the worldwide masses must move to common ground, a median, if the one-world government is to be established. For example, in America it must be lowered, in Ethiopia raised. But in all cases, it must be near subsistence. When that has been accomplished, the individuals and organizations behind the conspiracy—the unseen hands which control governments—will have a firm power base. Individuals scraping to get by are much more involved in day-to-day existence and direct all their energies toward a one-day-at-a-time approach to life. They are easier to manipulate, less able to organize, and grateful to any hand, seen or not, that might toss a few scraps from the table.

Zionist plots notwithstanding, race is elemental to the welfare argument as, in the long run, is nationalism. Just as black Americans are held to be more prone to criminal activity by both the racial right and any number of other Americans, they are also seen to be over-represented on the welfare rolls. However, it begs stating that the reality of the situation is that the majority of welfare recipients are white.

Cadillac John also acknowledges this reality. ''I'm not surprised by that. And the number of white people on welfare is going to get even bigger with all this affirmative action keeping qualified white people out of work, keeping them poor and hopeless. What I'd like to know is how many of these white people on welfare are the third or fourth generations to get it? How many of them are professionals at living off the government?

''And it's not just black people doing this,'' Cadillac John maintains. ''You've got illegal immigrants from all over hell and gone coming to this country and heading for the welfare office before they've got their suitcases unpacked. Damn people have a welfare check coming before they've got a mail box to put it in. It's killing our country and the productive people here. Every time a Mexican swims the Rio Grande, he either goes on welfare or takes a job away from a white American, born here, who needs that job just as bad as he does.

"Then you hear politicians bleating and moaning about human dignity and how we've got to take care of these people. Why? They're criminals. They're trespassers. They're here illegally.

"I'll tell you what. If we really wanted to help these people, this is one problem we could solve within thirty days. All we've got to do is line a couple of armored divisions up along the border and head into Mexico killing every one of those crooked, bribe-taking sons-of-bitches in power we can catch over there until the Mexican people have their country back. That will solve illegal immigration. While we're at it, it wouldn't hurt to turn around and do the same thing here."

E. Raymond Capt takes a more moderate stance. "Not all of us [Covenant Identity Christians] are so worked up over the idea of immigration. Illegal immigration is another thing, it is a problem. But as a Christian and an American, I have no problem with legal immigrants. But we do have to be realistic about the number of people we allow in and realistic about our resources."

Tom Metzger, of WAR, notes in his essays that every foreigner in this country is here because white Americans allow them to be and that their place here relies on the graciousness and permission of white America. At the same time, it also seems that anyone who is not white American fits Metzger's definition of foreigner. Still, it is Metzger's contention that it is even more important that these recipients of white American good will realize such graciousness and permission may be withdrawn at America's discretion and should be withdrawn if immigrants become a burden. Of course, Metzger also notes that due to the displacement of white workers, free medical care, Social Security benefits and welfare, foreigners—non-whites—have already become a burden and should leave now—while they can.

"It is not hate to repatriate non-whites," Mike Hallimore states, "or to have them remain in their own country and prosper among their own people. The issue is not one of legal or illegal immigration, but of race. If White Christian immigrants from Canada, England, Germany, Scandinavia, etc., want to come to this country, that doesn't concern me; they would be welcome. We have plenty of room to assimilate quality members of our own race and Christian culture.''

It remains a given that America is still the land of milk and honey as far as a significant portion of the world is concerned. Pastor Richard Butler maintains that immigration will soon be exceeding the white birth rate (due, in part, to the policies of abortion) and that Aryans are already a minority in the world and rapidly becoming so in America. Still, most of our subjects eschew blaming the immigrants who come here for seeking a better life. Cadillac John notes with a laugh, ''Blame them? No, I don't blame them. If the shoe was on the other foot, I'd be swimming that river in a heartbeat.'' He becomes serious. ''But even if I don't blame them for wanting to better themselves, we just can't have it.''

Nor, some believe, should we have to contend with the attendant diseases and unhealthy practices brought into the country by foreigners whose medical care is yet another drain on the welfare system. As noted in Richard Hoskins's *The Vigilantes of Christendom,* from the earliest days in Christian society, disease-bearing strangers have usually been quarantined, separated, and avoided, not even to be touched. Not only does today's government *not* practice these defenses, government increases taxes in order to finance this willful breaking of God's commandments—not to mention ignoring the rule of common sense.

''We don't have the resources to take in any more 'huddled masses,' '' Jim Stinson says. ''We can't even take care of our own people.'' Stinson, like many others on the racial right, notes that the attraction of America is not so much what we have to offer—which is considerable—but what is present in their countries of origin. Poverty, war, disease, oppression, famine, ignorance, ad infinitum, are the driving forces behind the immigration waves. If, as Cadillac John has pointed out, these problems are resolved in Mexico, as well as Haiti, China, South America, Africa and other departure points, then immigration will dwindle. Likely, so would welfare payments.

But no one on the racial right believes such problems will be resolved. They will not be resolved because they have been too carefully implemented. And they have been carefully tailored to create just such profound social and economic upheavals. These situations, at present, may be understood as an explanation for the tendency of an individual to flee the depression and despair of his homeland for the greener pastures of the United States or other countries which present better opportunities. However, the overall purpose of widespread poverty and strife is to soon remove even that option. It is argued that if the one-worlders are not stopped, there will be no greener pastures for anyone. The entire world population will be in the same boat—and that the boat will be a leaky one indeed.

Identity Christians and conspiracy theorists of the racial right see the Zionist bankers as the source of financial manipulation, capable of creating economic crises both nationally and globally which, of course, have far-reaching effects on the middle class and those dependent on government largesse. These crises may also be seen as the source of wars and political unrest through which bankers establish themselves as the "shadow government." And the shadow government ensures its power through the welfare state and oppressive income tax, along with the global trade agreements which have a negative impact on nations such as the United States. The lowering of educational standards, promotion and tolerance of homosexuality as "an alternative life-style," substandard medical care, unregulated abortion, establishing secular humanism where the guiding hand of religion once held sway and splitting the family are all elements of this one-world conspiracy. The resulting increase in crime, drug use, and other examples of moral and social decay, particularly among juveniles, are simply symptoms of spreading contagion. Yet, rather than posing a problem to those in power, the resulting chaos is conducive to the further entrenchment of those who, posing as saviors, rape and pillage the masses.

For any number of conspiracy theorists, the "enemy" one-worlders are atheistic, multinational, perhaps Masonic, somehow connected to the United Nations, and generally communists. On the racial right, this power base is considered to be entirely Zionist, though African, Asian and Aryan "stooges" are utilized whenever possible. The overriding belief which is woven through the often disparate groups which constitute the white supremacist movements is that liberalism is communism and communism is Judaism. Thus, there is a clear demarcation between non-racial and racial conspiracy theorists. But, regardless of who may be holding the reins, the conspiracy hinges on racial fragmentation and welfare, in combination with affirmative action as an essential tool to bring about antagonistic divisions between the races.

But race is certainly not the only issue in regard to government programs. Equally disturbing to the radical right is the shelling out of public money, drawn from the taxpayer, to care for drug addicts—considered disabled under the Americans with Disabilities Act—and homosexuals afflicted with AIDS. In the eyes of Identity Christians, drug use and abuse are self-inflicted problems and the whole idea of ''subsidizing'' drug addiction is galling to the point of being unbearable. It is the general consensus, not only of the racialists, but of millions of others, that welfare and SSI payments to drug addicts only go to acquiring more drugs and, if there is any good derived at all from this practice, it is only the fact that for short periods of time, the recipients of these funds may be too stoned to steal.

Mark, Chad, and several other Texas Aryan Nationalist Skinheads, all claiming the faith of Identity, discuss an anti-drug rally they have been considering holding in Pasadena, Texas, in 1997 and the feasibility of gaining permission of city government to do so. Since our first interview the skinheads have relocated to a blue-collar neighborhood in the part of town known as ''Old Pasadena'' nestled at the foot of refinery row.

''I doubt they will let us do it,'' Mark says candidly. ''We don't really care for druggies and that's no secret. But we do believe that sometimes good people get caught up in bad things. If this is the case, then people should be given a chance to do better. A chance. Most people would back us on that.

''But if that doesn't work out . . . well . . .'' he lets the sentence trail away. Mark, like Cadillac John, notes the widespread emergence of ''pharmaceutical entrepreneurs'' in neighborhoods and the damage that follows. ''If someone refuses to clean up their act,'' he adds, ''then maybe folks in the neighborhood should clean it up for them. Drug prevention works if you do it right.''

And ''tough love'' with a vengeance constitutes doing it right. In a nutshell, if someone is using or selling drugs in your neighborhood and you are serious about stopping them, then hurt them—and hurt them badly. There should be no unclear messages in one's actions. If they insist on persisting in this behavior, kill them. This, it is held, will greatly reduce the attraction of drugs and the temptation to use them.

Rob, an unaffiliated skinhead from Oceanside, California, holds no religious beliefs. His racialism is based on the fact that ''I just don't like niggers,'' but his position on drug users and homosexuals is rooted more in his social consciousness and pragmatism. ''I don't particularly like queers, either, and I think they're bad news as far as society is concerned. But I don't go out of my way to mess with them, as long as they don't fuck with me. If we're lucky, they'll all die of AIDS anyway. But drug addicts are another matter. They're dangerous to innocent people. They'll rip you off, kill you if they have to, just to get high again. Killing a drug addict isn't murder. It's more like euthanasia. They walk around like 'Night of the Living Dead' anyway. Killing them is doing them a favor.''

Whereas a number of members of the movements agree with Rob in a general sense, they also speak to the pervasive use of drugs as part of the one-world conspiracy. In addition to all other factors discussed, drug addiction is another way of crippling the population. Not just in terms of illegal drugs, but in terms of prescription drugs, dangerous substances provided to the public through ZOG's Food and Drug Administration. Likewise tobacco and alcohol, distributed with the blessings of government, which are debilitating to users of every race. And it is not only the bodies of the populace that are being poisoned but minds as well.

"God created *Adam and Eve* not *Adam and Steve.*" Mark jokes, "The way I read it, [the Bible] God says, 'be fruitful and multiply' not 'go out there and screw other men and die out as a species.' I don't see how people miss that part.''

Such immorality, the Identity Christians maintain—which is thoroughly condemned by Yahweh—is being presented by the Jewish-media as an acceptable, sometimes even a desirable alternative lifestyle. "Coming out of the closet" characters and "Flamers" are common to network programming, and their presence on cable is apparent to the most casual of observers. The contention then is that the mind-numbed Aryan sheep, under the mesmerizing control of the Jew-tube, accept at face value the false and damaging notion that homosexuality is okay.

Identity pastor Van S. Herrell, in notes accompanying his Bible translation, *The New Testament: Anointed Standard Version,* points out problems that may explain how even Christians are misled by relying on the King James translation of the Bible. According to Pastor Herrell, the guidelines compiled by the appointees of King James, a notorious homosexual, reflect their need to be sensitive to the king's true nature. As a result, there are two specific instances in which the word "homosexual" was translated indirectly, using other words and obscuring the intent of the passage.

An accurate reading of the scriptures, therefore, reveals to the Identity Christian a true picture of how God feels about homosexuality, a response anything but tolerant. One need only read Pastor Herrell's translation of the famous passage in Romans 1: 18-32 for this to be made perfectly clear.

AIDS, for the Identity Christian, is a visitation of God's judgment on the homosexual and, for that matter, on the black race since it seems they are disproportionately represented in reported cases. "Thank God for

AIDS!'' exhorts J. B. Stoner at the 1993 Aryan conference in Spokane. ''Thank God! Because it is of God and by God that AIDS is visited upon the wicked.''

Others share this opinion, but some have an ambivalent attitude toward it. In the August 1990 *Liberty Bell,* Robert Frens writes, ''The American nits have an insatiable appetite for sheer nonsense whether it is about 6 million ghosts or 6 million sunspots, both capable of damaging your psyche with cosmic juices.'' None of this, however, seems to match what he calls ''the on-again-off-again AIDS threat.'' He admits being perplexed about it, even though some thousands of ''our more talented perverts will be the benefactors of the only weight loss method that really works.'' Frens also notes that there are strong indications that one risk factor might be racial in nature, but conflicting information and disagreement about this virus leave unanswered questions.

The party line of the movements is simple: AIDS is not the problem, it is the cure. First, the government is less than forthcoming about AIDS— what it is, where it comes from, how it's spread. And secondly, it poses no threat to those who live a Christian lifestyle. Pete Peters notes that the Jewish media would have one believe that AIDS is something all Americans should be concerned with but, in reality, the only real risk groups in America are homosexuals and drug addicts. And, despite media propaganda to the contrary, like-minded Identity Christians see both groups as a blight upon the land.

Cadillac John fairly vibrates with rage when he speaks of homosexuality in American society. ''Homosexuality is *not* okay! How in the hell can anyone—I don't give a damn how stupid they are and I've flat met some stupid ones—how can anyone read the Bible and make an ignorant statement like that? Did silly old God, overreacting as usual, rain destruction down on Sodom and Gomorrah because of a harmless 'alternative lifestyle'? Was He kidding when He said for a man to lie with a man is an abomination? Now, because of the lies of the Jews and Judeo-Christianity, we even have homosexual churches—so-called Christian churches. There is *no* such thing as a homosexual Christian! There can't be. Look up the verses for yourself . . . that's what people ought to do anyway. God hates, loathes, and despises homosexuals. Woe unto you, sodomites, there is no place for you in the Kingdom of God.''

Strict biblical interpretation holds with the Scriptures, the literal word of God. Identity Christians overwhelmingly reject the idea that individuals are born homosexual. They reject the idea that homosexuals have the right to be left alone to practice vile perversions among a Christian population. They reject the idea that homosexuality is not a teachable, acquired behavior, advancing instead the notion of homosexual "recruitment" from among a heterosexual population—particularly young boys. They point to the current, much-publicized glut of child pornography on the Internet and the attendant "recruitment" cases as examples of this truth.

Charles Lee refers to the Scriptures when presented with hypothetical situations: Suppose a man keeps his predilections to himself and elects to practice his "vices" with another consenting male—behind closed doors, sans public demonstrativeness, or the seduction of young boys— in other words, to remain deeply closeted. Isn't that his business? Since the matter is between him and God, would Lee really like to see the man flogged, imprisoned or otherwise punished?

"What I really had in mind was more along the lines of public execution," he says. "I don't believe the Scriptures were created for our convenience. I don't believe they were ever designed to change as society changed or the world progressed or whatever. For me, they are etched in stone. I know that makes me a dinosaur and an outcast among modern Christians. I'm not ignorant of that, I was raised Lutheran. But there it is, the word of God. What can I say?"

Mike Hallimore agrees. "The Bible doesn't say that we should get together and vote on what should be legal or illegal, right or wrong. Our God tells us these things. As a Christian, I must believe in the perfection of the Laws of God—and I do. I don't have any qualms at all in stating that a Biblical theocracy, based on Scriptural laws and principles, is the perfect and most appropriate form of government."

In January of 1996, two half-brothers, Daniel Christopher Bean, 19, and Ronald Henry Gauthier, 21, admitted attacking a pair of gay men in a Houston bar. Forty-six-year-old Frank Mangione was stabbed to death and his companion of sixteen years, Kenneth Stern, was beaten, allegedly because the gay men had made sexual advances toward Bean and Gauthier. The young men claimed to be members of the German Peace Corps, a neo-Nazi group, and both maintained that the attack, in which Mangione was stabbed 35 times, was justified because of the sexual advances. As they said, "Where we come from, a man just doesn't do that."

Bean, who had the initials of the German Peace Corps tattooed on his arm, was sentenced to a life term in prison. In June 1997, Gauthier was given ten years' probation. In a 28 June 1997 *Houston Chronicle* report by Stefanie Asin, Lane Lewis, president of the Houston Gay and Lesbian Political Caucus, says that Gauthier's probated sentence was unjust, that both men were equally guilty of Mangione's murder. "It makes it even more heinous," Lane says, "when the murder is based simply on bigotry and ignorance."

Identity Christians disagree. Killings such as this, they believe, are based on Scripture. But strict Identity adherents carry the rule further, applicable even if a homosexual exhibits no overtly homosexual behavior. As noted in Herrell's translations of Romans I, the simple fact that a man *is* homosexual makes him "worthy of death." In fact, as the passage points out, anyone who condones or accepts such perversion is worthy of death. Lesbianism is a lesser crime, according to Hallimore, an "uncleanness" rather than an abomination. This is because it involves women, who are held to a different standard of behavior. Among the core Seedline beliefs of Kingdom Identity Ministries is the statement that, according to biblical principles, homosexuality is a capital offense.

From a Seedline Identity perspective, men such as Bean and Gauthier are not murderers. Neither are those who kill race traitors. Assuming the mantle of the Phineas Priesthood, consistent with the commandments of Yahweh, they are doing the work of the Lord.

# CHAPTER THIRTEEN

# Circus Maximus: Talk Shows, Media and Other Blood Sports

It was a movie *The Klansman,* oddly enough featuring the young O. J. Simpson, that opened Charles Lee's eyes to Jewish-controlled Hollywood. "I remember going to the drive-in theater," he said, "and seeing O. J. Simpson running around in the woods, jumping over logs and shooting Klansmen. They showed several Klansmen attacking an individual's home and they were wearing their white robes—with a full moon out. I remember thinking to myself how stupid it would be to carry out an assault wearing that particular garment, visible to everyone because of how bright it was. Then it dawned on me. I realized that this movie had been produced for propaganda purposes. I don't think I've ever seen a movie involving the Klan, with the exception of *Birth of a Nation,* that wasn't anti-Klan propaganda, that didn't present false Klans."

Lee notes that since most Americans believe the reports they hear on television and radio and what they read in the paper, these same Americans are misinformed about the nature and motives of the movement. Hollywood compounds this problem by its representation of Klansmen and other racialists in contemporary film. Thus, from his perspective, the Klan that the public thinks it knows is a mythological blend of history and propaganda, a false Klan. The general public cannot understand the activities of white supremacist organizations like the Klan, because all the information they are presented is slanted toward discrediting such groups.

For instance, if one believes the reports one hears on television or reads in the mainstream press, then the image of a cross burning brightly against a stark night sky is meant to convey terror, to intimidate blacks or Jews or other targets of racial hatred. The blazing cross is also considered by many to be blasphemous, the desecration of one of the most sacred icons in Christendom.

Lee maintains that nothing could be further from the truth. ''We tell people and we tell people,'' he says. ''No matter how many times we say it, it's always twisted around by the press.'' He runs his fingers through his red hair, leans back in his chair and gestures for emphasis. ''It's not a cross-burning. It's a cross-*lighting*.''

His usually stoic demeanor breaks for a moment, frustration evident in his voice. ''The cross does burn, of course, but that's not the point. It's not some kind of Satanic thing or a desecration, but a Christian ritual that originated in the Scottish highlands. It represents the light of Jesus Christ in the world, the advancement of the Christian faith. Do the news reports ever tell you that?''

''Cross-lighting is also a call to arms,'' Jim Stinson adds. ''The old clans of Scotland would signal with burning crosses on the hillsides to call their people. We're doing the same thing—calling our people.''

Cross-lighting, to be sure, is a powerful image. Which is precisely why it is featured in nearly every video essay and written work that has ever addressed the issue of white supremacy or the Klan—including this one. And just as certainly, the ritual lighting of the cross is customary and expected at major Klan events. Still, it might be supposed, the lighting of the cross could prove a rather shocking experience to the uninformed observer. Robed, hooded men and women standing in the dancing circle of orange lights—with their right arms raised in the stiff salute most closely associated with Fascist Germany—and shouting ''white power'' can certainly be a powerful, even intimidating experience.

''Sure, cross-lighting has been used in the past to intimidate people,'' Charles Lee explains. ''And it *was* used by Klansmen. But nowadays you hear things like . . . I don't know . . . some black family has a cross burned on their lawn and 'Ohhhhh, it's the Ku Klux Klan.' More than likely it's neighborhood kids just fooling around. But the media never reports it that way. No, you'll hear about the burning cross but you'll never hear about who *really* put it there.''

Both Lee and Stinson contend that misinformation about the movement is regularly presented to an unsuspecting public by media sources who have their own agendas. ''It's no accident,'' Stinson says. ''They know better but the truth doesn't fit into their scheme of things. It seems to me that some reporters have their own preconceived ideas and beliefs and they're not willing to consider the fact that they might be wrong. But for the most part, particularly when it concerns white people who support their own race, the press sees it as their mission to discredit us and they're not going to let truth get in the way of that mission."

Pastor Pete Peters, in his essays and sermons, regularly takes the news media to task for the way they falsify stories about who he is and the purpose of his mission. He contends that the truth is in awfully short supply in mainstream media. Referring to writers as "slithering scribes" and "lying whores" in one of his sermons at the Branson Conference, Peters is not shy about expressing his feelings about dishonest reporters. He relates a story of one writer who made a brief appearance at LaPorte Church of Christ while Peters was away, spoke briefly with Peters's secretary, then went back to his office and wrote a slanderous feature article that made it appear he had interviewed Peters. From the pulpit, he maintains that he will not speak with writers because "Jesus my Lord tells me, 'Do not cast your pearls before swine lest they turn upon you and render you asunder!'" He is met with applause and a chorus of "amens."

The research staff of National Vanguard Books (William Pierce's organization), in a 1993 article "Who Rules America?" in *National Vanguard,* addresses "the alien grip on the news and entertainment media" held by the Jews. The article names "media bosses" such as Leonard Goldenson of ABC, Laurence Tisch of CBS, and Sumner Redstone of Viacom, as well as Samuel Newhouse of the print media and any number of other Jews and minions of Jews who are actively engaged in anti-American propaganda. In essence, these individuals are held accountable for promoting interracial unions, unwed motherhood, drug use, homosexuality, promiscuity and all manners of filth and evil as normal and natural ways of life. At the same time, they "make" the politicians most sympathetic to their cause and "break" those who run counter to ZOG's agenda. They filter the information the American public gets through national and local news reports and otherwise present lies in the guise of truth by either overt commission or covert omission of vital facts.

Racialists contend that through this control, Christian patriots such as Gordon Kahl and Arthur Kirk, pushed to the breaking point by a heartless and soulless government, are held up as aberrations, "wackos," objects of scorn. Timothy McVeigh and Terry Nichols are convicted before their case ever comes to trial. Any racially conscious white man who loves his race and his people, who objects to miscegenation or affirmative action, who questions the truth of the Holocaust, is branded a bigot. Any organization which upholds Second Amendment rights, preaches preparedness and racial pride, questions the motivations of government or kicks any of the sacred cows of ZOG is labeled a "hate group." Anyone who speaks out against the oppressive policies of government or who supports the "traditional" American values of our forefathers is either ignored and never mentioned at all, or held up to ridicule. The contention of the National Vanguard researchers is that this is not a random or accidentally occurring situation but a methodically thought out and systematically initiated plan.

A unanimous belief among the movements is that, where they are concerned, such propagandistic smear tactics are certainly the rule rather than the exception and that such tactics are entirely intentional and purposeful. Bob Sherman, for instance, an Israelite Christian from Arkansas, tells an entirely different story about certain incidents from the version presented to the public.

"I couldn't believe the things the press and television stories had to say about Joan and Gordon Kahl," Sherman says earnestly, speaking a little louder than normal, to be heard over the lunch hour noise in the Branson, Missouri, restaurant. He pulls at his gray mustache as he speaks, his blue eyes intent as he turns in his seat. "We were neighbors for a time and Gordon was a fine man and good friend. He would go out of his way to help anyone—and did. The media portrayed him as some kind of psychotic killer, and he wasn't like that at all. What would you do if you were confronted by federal agents and one of them shot your son? That's what happened to Gordon. I know what I'd do.

"I know all the press reported that the agents were fired on first. I knew Gordon and I don't believe it. The press doesn't tell you that they had already tried to kill him twice before. Once by sabotaging the engine of his plane and once by poisoning his food while he was in jail. And when they raided his home the first time—Gordon and his family weren't home, thank God—they shot the place to pieces and killed his dog. For no reason other than it was there and it was alive, I guess. But what does that matter, really?

"It doesn't even matter who shot first, though they'll never get me to believe it was Gordon Kahl. The point is that Joan [Kahl's wife] was in the car, ducking and flattening herself against the seat and bullets were flying all around. Yorie [Kahl's son] was lying bleeding on the ground, and the agents were continuing to fire their weapons. What's a man—a man who loves his family—supposed to do? In my mind, it was self-defense. There were four U.S. Marshals—Kenneth Muir and Robert Cheshire who both died, Carl Wigglesworth who took off after Scott Faul then hid until it was over, and Hopson. U.S. Marshal Hopson had been hit and was lying in a ditch. He said to Gordon, 'Don't shoot me again. I'm all done.' Gordon took his gun and walked away. Does that sound like some kind of cold-blooded monster? But that's not the way the media presented it.

"Then there was that made for TV movie ["Bitter Harvest," based on the book *Bitter Harvest* by James Corcoran and starring Rod Steiger as Kahl]. I couldn't believe that film. They portrayed Gordon as a violent racist who attacked a black man while incarcerated, then beat another in a restroom before stealing his car, always spouting off racial slurs. That wasn't the Gordon I knew. Gordon didn't even use the word 'nigger' and never talked bad to people. He wasn't like that. At no time did he ever go after anyone. They always came for him. There's your twisted, psychotic maniac for you."

Sherman is clearly angry as he leans forward, though his tone is even and controlled. "You know they cut off his hands and his feet don't you? They did that because they thought they'd killed the wrong man. It was destroying evidence. The same reason they burned the body. There are some who still believe they got the wrong man, that Gordon somehow got away. He didn't. Gordon Kahl is dead, all right, murdered by the same trigger-happy federals who killed their own man, Sheriff Gene Matthews [of Lawrence County, Arkansas]. They pinned that on Gordon, too. After all, what was he going to say about it?

"Yorie Kahl is in prison. He's been there for fifteen years for the crime of preparing to defend himself, and stopping a federal bullet in the process. But I guess that's not too newsworthy and, after fifteen years, I don't see any movie of the week telling Yorie's story, or talking about the years of hell Joan's been going through trying to get him released and trying to get people to pay attention to what really happened."

But then, no one in the movements expects fair treatment from the establishment media. The print and television media are powerful tools, they claim, powerful weapons which are used against the racial right to advance the cause of the Zionist one-world conspirators. It is a simple enough process to understand. If one considers the role of the media in national politics, for instance, it is clear that there have been issues raised in terms of fairness or bias in reporting national events. Usually the challenge is that the reporting is slanted to the left in both television and the print media. In the 1992 Presidential election, conservatives complained that the media were much harder on Bush than on Clinton—which, of course, the Democrats strongly denied. This objection was raised again in the 1996 election in which Clinton defeated Dole.

Militiaman Carl Haggard observes that following the Oklahoma City bombing, the militia were targeted by an opportunistic press and equally opportunistic video journalists who painted militias in the worst possible light, lumping everyone under the general umbrella of racist, anti-government revolutionaries which, he maintains, is *absolutely* not true.

The contention is that reporters take quotes out of context, create stories where there are no stories, accept questionable information and present it as truth without secondary verification, slant everything toward sensationalism and, even when they know they have erred, never retract or correct those errors. Our subjects believe that the whole idea of fairness, of reporting factually, is abandoned by those who cover the racial right.

"I did an interview a few years ago at a West Texas television station," Charles Lee recounts. "I was prepared to talk about my beliefs, the Klan, what we hope to accomplish and why. But that really wasn't what they wanted. They wanted to talk about night-riders and lynchings and all the standard things we're used to. I told them that as far as my involvement was concerned, I didn't know anything at all those subjects other than history. They must not have liked that very much. I've never been invited back. Another time I was being interviewed by a magazine reporter, a friendly enough guy, when the photographer asked about the dragon embroidered on my sleeve. I held it up for him to see, he took a picture, and the next thing I knew I was on the cover of the magazine looking like Dracula, as if I had been trying to hide my face." Lee grimaces. "And people ask why we don't give interviews."

The white supremacists also note that political correctness, expressed in equal respect for all minority groups whether they be racial, homosexual, non-Christian religion or minority Christian religion, is expected and tolerated by modern Americans. They maintain that Black Panthers, Nation of Islam, League of Latin American Citizens, La Raza Unida, Asian American Coalitions, and numerous others have been and are treated seriously and deferentially by the media. But not the white supremacists.

The members of the movements make some serious arguments when it comes to discussing the validity of talk show presentations. First, they contend, none of the various talk shows are interested in serious dialogue but only in sensationalism. In any given hour, where roughly one-third of the time allotted is devoted to commercials, there is little time for serious discussion of anything. Secondly, the sensationalistic aspect outweighs any other element of the presentation. The contention is that talk shows appeal to our most base and voyeuristic impulses. In addition, the audience participation element is a vital component of most talk shows even though at times it seems that its only purpose is to allow worked-up members of the audience to vent their emotions and hurl insults (and sometimes other things) at the ostensible ''guests'' who constitute the panel. Most members of the movements discount the format as a legitimate forum for discussion or for the dispensation of information. In fact, the talk show has little credibility among the racialists as a legitimate anything.

''It's a circus,'' Charles Lee states.

And if the talk show is a circus, everyone involved is reduced to the status of clown—including the host. Geraldo Rivera, for instance, is a constant source of both amusement and aggravation for most of the racial right. As one observer notes, ''Geraldo Rivera does for legitimate journalism what HIV has done for casual sex.'' On one episode of his talk show, Rivera, filming on location, had a brawl with a member of a racialist organization after the member remarked, ''You're half Spick and half Jew, you're not welcome here.'' The racist punctuated his remark by pouring a beverage at Rivera's feet and on his shoes. Rising to the occasion, Rivera grappled with the offending accuser and a few ineffective punches were thrown. Mark, of the TAN Skinheads, notes ''Rivera can't decide whether he wants to be a professional wrestler or a newsman. Actually, he's not very good as either one.''

Probably the most widely remembered of Geraldo Rivera's encounters with the white supremacists was the episode of his program which featured Roy Innes of the Congress on Racial Equality, and John Metzger (son of Tom Metzger) of White Aryan Resistance. Following a confrontational format, the already heated dialogue escalated to name-calling before degenerating into an outright brawl. Innes attacked Metzger and began choking him, other WAR members rushed to Metzger's defense and punches were thrown—as well as furniture. One errant chair connected with Mr. Rivera, resulting in a broken nose. The on-camera fireworks, however, were well received by the viewing public. The Geraldo Show's ratings shot through the roof and clips of the brawl were aired across the nation on both national and local news reports.

A salient point, made not only by the racialist right but by more conventional observers as well, is that both incidents did not have to be aired. "The Geraldo Rivera Show," like other talk shows, is taped. The "mano a mano" scuffle and the racial mini-riot were aired, anyway. And the members of the movement maintain they know why.

"Ratings," Darrell Flinn states. "That's no secret. The only reason they do anything is ratings. Anyone who thinks talk shows are about issues or helping people is sadly mistaken."

As far as the movements are concerned, this is a reality they've been dealing with for years. Darrell Flinn, for instance, has appeared, along with his wife Anna Lynn, on "Hard Copy," a number of episodes of "The Jerry Springer Show," and other productions of this type. He understands the trade-off well.

"I know what they're about and I know they're using me. I'm using them, as well. Once I told a host that appearing on his show gave me a chance to reach more people in one afternoon than I could reach in a lifetime of rallies and speaking engagements. I don't care how I get my message out as long as I get it out."

Messages, racialist or otherwise, are not the point of talk shows nor the concern of the various hosts. Flinn maintains that his organization understands this and basically supports his efforts. However, there are many among the movements who deplore talk show appearances and generally shun the limelight altogether. Some, such as a Seedline theologian from Arkansas, hold that it is necessary to maintain a low profile so that issues of prestige, ego, or personality do not eclipse the more important message of the Scriptures. Others, such as Louis Beam and Pete Peters, who have been consistently hoodwinked by supposedly "objective" reporters, moderators, commentators and such, simply have no trust left to give and avoid the media altogether. Still others do not see that the benefits obtained from such appearances outweigh the risks. And all, or nearly all, expect to be tricked and misrepresented. This, of course, all comes back to the Jews.

"You never see someone lead a story with 'We're here tonight to talk to some white men who love their race and are proud of their race,' do you?" Jim Stinson asks over his coffee. "Uh-uh. No. 'We're here to interview the vicious, hate-mongering, kill-'em-all-let-God-sort-'em-out, hooded, night-riding, cross-burning Ku Klux Klansmen.' That's the party line. And why not? Hell, if I owned a TV station or two, I'd be pretty hard on the Jews.'' He grins. ''It's not like we're each other's favorite people.''

But even though they joke about the treatment they get in the press, there is another side of the Jewish control of television the white supremacists find little humor in. And that is the constant barrage of genocidal propaganda that daily clogs the airwaves. And this control extends to the film industry as well.

''Hollywood is totally controlled by Kikes,'' Cadillac John notes angrily. ''It is totally decadent, totally corrupt. You tell me something they've put out in the last twenty years that's worth two bits. Everything, every damned thing that white Christians have considered a sin for generations is now 'politically correct' because it's been presented that way in television and in the movies. People don't even read the Bible anymore. They get what little teaching they get from some crooked son-of-a-bitch like that Jim Bakker.

''If you go to the movies what do you get? Race mixing, sex, sex, sex—premarital, extramarital, homosexual—faggots being presented like sexual perversion is just as harmless a choice as what ice cream you want from the store. Women having babies out of wedlock. You get the same thing on TV and all that Murphy Brown stuff. You see things on prime time television, situation comedies, that polite company never even mentioned when I was a kid. Hours at a time of some of the most perverse, sickening, un-Christian, and morally degrading bullshit imaginable. Then you look at the credits and who produces it? A goddamned Yid. Man, Americans are out there laughing at shit that ought to make them cry. It ought to make them mad.''

And, indeed, anger is the response of many Americans and certainly a universal response among the soldiers of God.

Charles Lee maintains that white Christian Americans are vilified in film and television programs and that white viewers seem totally unaware of the shame they are being subjected to, the subliminal guilt which is introjected into them. ''Militia people or just average Americans who might want to exercise their Second Amendment rights to keep and bear arms are always portrayed as lunatics, gun nuts, psychos. You tell me that's *not* propaganda. If and when you see a white racist portrayed on television or in the movies, how is he portrayed? Is any consideration given to his point of view? His beliefs? No. He's totally evil. Totally filled with hate for hate's sake. Out to kill for the hell of it. No purpose, no beliefs, no mind half the time. A mad dog.''

For example, the film *A Time to Kill,* based on the John Grisham novel, portrayed the Klan as vicious indeed. The film opens with two white racists who kidnap, rape, beat, urinate upon and then hang a small black girl. After they are apprehended, the two racists are gunned down by the young girl's father. The Klan becomes involved in terroristic activities directed toward the attorney defending the father. A riot involving the Klan and the ''good'' citizens of the town breaks out and a young black man hurls a fire-bomb from a roof top to incinerate the Grand Dragon. The black father is exonerated, the white Klan defeated, and justice prevails.

Realism?

''That's Hollywood for you,'' Mark notes. ''They don't know the first thing about what we believe. Or if they do, they don't care about it when it comes to making movies. In the first place, if someone in the movement rapes a child—even a black child, *especially* a black child—there's a pretty good chance we'd take care of him ourselves. Everyone I know is serious about observing God's law about race-mixing. We don't do it. Everyone I know is serious about obeying the laws of God. Faggots, child molesters, drug addicts, we have no use for them. As far as we're concerned, they should be killed and the sooner the better. We're certainly not about to come to their defense, no matter what color they are.''

Charles Lee concurs. ''I wouldn't have had a problem with that incident. Two race-mixers were punished. It doesn't matter to me who punishes them. It's like the O. J. Simpson thing. A nigger kills a race-mixer and a Jew.'' He nods. ''It's a case of natural consequences.''

Perhaps a more ominous overtone of the film, as far as the racialists are concerned, is a more subliminal message than the obvious ''racialists are evil'' message. The plot of the film is wrapped up neatly as the two brutal white men are killed by the outraged father, the equally brutal Klansmen are run to earth and held accountable for their actions and everyone lives happily ever after—including the black youth who murdered the Grand Dragon and is never arrested or charged with anything.

''Oh, but that was justice,'' Mark says facetiously. ''Righteous retribution. It's not murder if you kill a racist, is it?''

It is a common belief among the separatists that the presentation of such films and related materials are indeed part of a systematic program to discredit white Christians and promote violence toward them, to promote racial intermarriage and homosexual lifestyles among the white race. And to do this in such a manner that the vast majority of unsuspecting viewers are never even aware that they are being poisoned in small dosages or aware that they are lining up to pay for their own demise.

Pastor Richard Butler, in a 1992 sermon at Aryan Nations, notes that the long range goal of ZOG, which controls the media, is the elimination of the white race. Race-mixing, considered unnatural and forbidden by God, is portrayed on film as not only acceptable but desirable. And racial equality, as a prelude to race-mixing, constitutes racial genocide and can be considered another means by which the white race will be destroyed.

Television programs such as "Different Strokes," "Webster," "The Jeffersons," etc., were only the beginning. "Russell Simmons Def Comedy Jam," "The Fresh Prince of Bellaire," and any number of more modern bearers of the racially damaging tradition are seen as more than merely offensive, as far as white separatists are concerned. They are deadly. The toxic propaganda of racial equality, of race mixing, is lethal.

These programs not only promote the sin of miscegenation, the racialists are quick to point out, but they also illustrate the reverse racism that is widely practiced throughout American society. To illustrate this, the white supremacists pose some difficult questions: Why is it, for instance, that comics on "Russell Simmons Def Comedy Jam" (HBO) can liberally sprinkle their routines, not only with objectionable racial slurs but with ethnic humor that makes whites the butt of jokes? How is it that comics such as Paul Rodriguez, Martin Lawrence, Eddie Murphy and others can make fun of whites in their speech, movements, dancing, etc., yet white comics are crucified if they attempt the same thing with other minorities as the butt of the joke? When Ted Dansen showed up in blackface for a Hollywood affair, as a joke—with his black girlfriend, Whoopi Goldberg—he found himself harshly censured by his Hollywood peers and much of the rest of the nation, for his "racist" behavior.

Some in the movement note that—although popular old programs such as "Amos and Andy" are currently labeled racist—beginning in the 1970s and continuing today, network programming is more racist than ever before. Television allows blacks to use words like "nigger" to one another, but whites cannot use the word. Furthermore, blacks are allowed to use racial slurs toward or about whites, such as "honky," "cracker," and "white boy," but whites are not allowed the same privilege. And, of course, there are movies such as *White Men Can't Jump,* the title of which is offensive to many. Which, as far as the racial right is concerned, raises even more questions.

"What if a film were made titled *Black Men Can't Coach?*" Mark asks. "Everyone in America would be upset about that. And why would they be upset? Because it's racist, of course." But then, he notes facetiously, "Only whites can be racist. Just ask any nigger."

"When do you think the networks are going to lend their support to a 'Miss White America' beauty pageant?" Lee asks. "Is that racism? How often do they support the National Association for the Advancement of White People? As much as they do the NAACP? Is that racism? If black people have been treated badly by television in the past, is treating white people badly now going to make up for it? No. What's going on in television and in the movies today is bad for the white race and it's equally bad for the black race. That's because the people who control the television and film industries don't give a damn for either race."

The same can be said for any of the media—newspapers, magazines, radio, film, television—but movies and television undoubtedly reach the largest number of people. Since movies eventually end up on television, this makes television the most efficient avenue for the dissemination of misinformation and propaganda. And a most valuable tool for those who disseminate lies as a part of their One-world plan.

The consensus of the racialist right is that the "Jew-tube" is just one more manifestation of the reign of the Beast.

# CHAPTER FOURTEEN

# White Camelia: The Modern Klan

## WHAT IT'S LIKE TO BE A KLANSMAN IN TODAY'S SOCIETY

To be a Klansman in today's society makes me constantly wonder if anyone knows what it's like to give your heart and mind to the truth of Christ and Yahweh, and to be hated and ridiculed for those beliefs, especially by people that don't even know me.

I'm always trying to make sense of everything I read and everything I see going on around me and holding back my disgust for those that I feel are responsible for the lies that my people so easily accept as truth.

I see drug dealers, gang members and other criminals killing and being killed all the time with no sign of fear from these individuals. But we Christians that are promised life everlasting seem to stand back and let things get out of control because of our fear and because of the Judeo-Christian preachers and the government constantly telling us that these problems will be taken care of. But they never are.

My hateful thoughts toward my enemies sometimes consume my logic. But I am always mindful of the mistake and great wrong it would be to take any kind of action out of hate or ignorance.

As a messenger of Yahweh I am always praying that what I have expressed to my people will make them thirst for more knowledge. And that what I have told them will never escape their minds.

As a Christian I don't need to see what will take place in the future

because Yahweh has told me what will happen, therefore I know it will
be. But knowing what the future holds doesn't make it any easier living
in the present.

So, when I'm asked, don't you get depressed or do you ever feel like
giving up, my answer is "yes." But it is my faith that sustains me and I
start out every morning with the thought that every new day means one
more day of Satan's rule behind me and one day closer to the second
coming of Christ.

My wife also reads Psalm 91 every morning, which I suggest that
everyone should read for spiritual fortification.

—Charles Lee, Grand Dragon, White Camelia Knights
of the Ku Klux Klan, Texas. June 1, 1997.

**"I** guess I got involved with the Klan as soon as I came back from
Vietnam," Cadillac John Thellin says, "and really saw just what in
the hell I'd been fighting for. About the time I found out that, I couldn't
get into college. Because of all the affirmative action crap, I got turned
down by nineteen of them in one year's time." To say that he has some
bitterness is to put it mildly. As he himself declares, "I am full of hate."

If John Thellin was initally motivated to join the Klan by white American
blue-collar economic dissatisfaction—currently held by sociologists as
the primary reason driving new members—that focus changed as he was
introduced to the concepts of Christian Identity and white Israel. The
doctrines of Identity and supremacy, as advanced by the White Camelia,
provided Cadillac John new eyes with which to view the world—a new
basis for understanding it.

The traditional philosophy of the Ku Klux Klan fits the tenets of the
Identity faith like a custom suit, although not all Klansmen are Identity
Christians nor are most Identity Christians Klansmen. Despite doctrinal
variables which, after all, create differences that appear to be quite subtle,
Christian Identity is congruent in major areas of belief. In a like manner,
the Klan is consistent in major areas of belief with most white Christian
patriot organizations.

The Klan has always promoted itself as a Christian organization, family-
oriented and dedicated to sound American values. Charles Lee, in his
official capacity as Grand Dragon of the White Camelia Knights of Texas,
refers to his ten-acre tract north of Cleveland, Texas, as "the Church of
the Piney Woods." Like those in many other Christian denominations,
he believes a church exists wherever two or more believers come together

to worship and Yahweh is, of course, invoked at every Identity Klan gathering.

Non-Christians are welcome at such gatherings, providing certain criteria are met. First, one must be white—*all* white, a pure-blooded Aryan. And even if one does not believe, one must at least be willing to entertain certain ideas—that Christ the Son of God came as ransom sacrifice for the sins of mankind (white Israel), was delivered into the hands of the Jews, was crucified, rose from the dead to ascend into heaven and will return to establish His kingdom on earth. If these criteria are met, then the rest—the false teachings of Judeo-Christianity or the willful insanity of atheism or agnosticism—can be ironed out later.

Many Identity Christians, including Charles Lee, hold the belief that all white people are born Christian, born under the Covenants, born under the law of Yahweh. Yet these individuals remain ignorant of their birthright, their Christian identity, because they are immersed in the false religions of mainstream "churchianity." It is not then surprising to those in the movements who claim the title *Israel* that a large number of white people reject the unsatisfying doctrines of Judeo-Christianity and turn their backs on religion altogether.

In the eyes of Seedline adherents, atheism is a capital offense as specified in scriptural law. However, atheism forged through exposure to Judeo-Christian teachings may not constitute "true" atheism. Jim Stinson notes that rejection of a false God does not necessarily entail rejection of the true God and that, in this case, ignorance of the law is indeed an excuse. He maintains that one cannot reject the word of God without first hearing the word of God. "Many white Christians who call themselves atheists are not rejecting God," he says. "They're rejecting Judeo-Christianity. Most of us [Identity Christians] agree that if you haven't heard the law and don't understand it, then you can't be held accountable for what you don't know."

Charles Lee agrees and he, as well as other members of White Camelia, sees carrying the word and the law to uninformed white Christians—the lost sheep of Israel—as an integral component of their organizational mission. "I believe what Christ says," Lee explains, addressing the outreach efforts. "Christ says, 'My people hear my voice. They know it and they follow me.' That's good enough for me. But we can't get through to everyone. Some people are in too deep into false religion. They've been misled too long to turn it around. It's unfortunate but true."

Such ministry is the active expression of faith, the works without which faith is dead. And among the true believers, faith drives their actions and shapes their hopes, their world views and their visions for the future.

Like Charles Lee, Cadillac John's passionate beliefs are embodied in the Klan. Thellin sees himself as a true patriot, a true American, a true Christian. And the Klan epitomizes everything Cadillac John stands for, what he believes America is all about. "God *commands* apartheid!" he says. "It's in the Bible. The founding fathers—white Christian racists—knew that. White slave-owners founded this country for other white slave-owners. Like it or not, you can't get around that. For over two hundred years, we got along just fine with white conservative policies. Then we got into the great society and integration . . . equality for all. We are *not* all equal! The Klan understands, even if no one else will. It's all common sense."

The Ku Klux Klan came into existence in 1866 (although Lee claims some Klan references to 1865) in Pulaski, Tennessee. Founded as a "social club" for Confederate veterans, the Klan soon became politicized to combat the harsh policies of Reconstruction. According to contemporary Klansmen, battling Carpetbaggers and other unsavory elements—protecting white Christians from oppression, preserving the Southern way of life, as well as restoring recently freed blacks to their proper status—became the true mission of the Invisible Empire. It is a history of which those of the White Camelia are quite proud.

Outlawed during Reconstruction, though certainly not neutralized, the Klan resurfaced in 1915 and reached its apex in the 1920s when it was indeed a source to be reckoned with on the political scene. The Klan of the Roaring Twenties was strong enough to have members elected to public office, to sway elections and to influence political policies. Public support of the Invisible Empire at the time was so great that many members in the community were quite open about their affiliations. Merchants, for instance, proud of their Klan involvement, would display signs in the windows of their shops reading, "Support America: Trade with a Klansman." The acronym TWAK (Trade with a Klansman) became a seal of approval prominently displayed in many businesses and a visual statement of white patriotism.

The Klan also became more national during the twenties. Though long considered a phenomenon of the Southern culture, Klans existed in such Northern cities as Detroit and Chicago. Indiana, in fact, boasted the largest Klan membership during the twenties. However, after this brief period of glory, the Klan once again faded into the background of American society. Though strength of the organization and membership has waxed and waned throughout the years, the Klan has never gone away. At a gathering near Vidor, Texas, in 1993, a Klan speaker tells the audience of interested citizens, "This is Klan country. It always has been and it always will be. My grandfather and your grandfather knew the Klan. So will our grandchildren."

History paints a violent image of the Ku Klux Klan. Night-riders, white sheets trailing behind them, blazing crosses, whippings, lynchings and terrorism come immediately to the minds of many at the very mention of the name. Cadillac John, Charles Lee and Jim Stinson do not deny Klan involvement in these historic activities any more than they will deny the intimidation value of cross-lighting in the past. However, they are quick to point out that the Klan most Americans are familiar with—that portrayed by the media—is *not* the White Camelia they know. It is not *any* Klan they know.

Charles Lee grew up in Port Arthur, Texas, and, like many other youngsters in the integrated public schools, he was taught the theory of racial equality. He was taught that the only difference between the races is skin color. However, he developed his own ideas and maintains that living among non-whites convinced him that the whole idea of racial equality was simply not true.

"I mean, it's a nice concept and everything," he says. "And I have no bones to pick with people who believe that equality is desirable. World peace is desirable, too. I'm just saying that whether it is desirable or not, it is simply not possible."

In the early 1970s, the already race-conscious, socially and politically conflicted Lee went into a Klan bookstore in Louisiana where he met then Imperial Wizard, David Duke. By 1975, Lee had made his commitment and has been a Klansman ever since. In 1978, along with Louis Beam, he was working for the Klan at a bookstore on Red Bluff Road in Pasadena, Texas. Beam, following a number of run-ins with the federal government, eventually moved on to become Ambassador at Large for Aryan Nations for a time, and free-lance writer for *Jubilee* as well as publisher of his own periodical *The Seditionist*. Charles Lee, on the other hand, remained in Texas and has risen through the ranks to become leader of White Camelia. Throughout the years, Beam and Lee have remained good friends and associates.

Lee notes that when the Klan is mentioned today, whether in the media or simple conversation among non-racialists, the most common description ascribed to it is "hate group." This descriptive rankles Lee.

"Do you think a guy can run that long on hate alone?" he asks. "I don't think so. He'd either end up dead or in prison. Sure, I hate a lot of things going on in the world, and, of course, I hate the enemies of God, but I've been a Klansman for twenty-one years because of my beliefs. My faith keeps me going. I have times, even today, when I get up in the morning and wonder what's the point of all this. I get discouraged just like anyone else, especially when I meet with so much resistance from white people who don't understand. But it all comes back to faith. Without that, well, without faith nothing means anything."

Jim Stinson echoes those sentiments. "I was a Catholic for years . . . raised just down the road from here [South Houston]. I was even an altar-boy. In all those years I spent in the Catholic Church I don't think I ever picked up a Bible, much less opened it. I read it every day now and I help my daughter—I'm a single parent—to understand it. We're learning together. I don't pretend to understand everything, but then that's why you study."

Lee and Stinson, Cadillac John, and thousands of others stand united in the disclaimer—despite the allegations of their enemies—that the Klan is not a hate group. There is hatred, they admit, but it's righteous hatred, consistent with the will of God. Pete Peters, though not a Klansman, sums up this subtle difference at the Branson conference where he states, "It's not hard to understand. If you're against God, then I'm against you." In short, to love God is to hate his enemies—those who pervert His teachings, who violate His commandments, who array themselves against His people. The members of White Camelia, Identity Christians of the Church Militant, understand this concept well.

Charles Lee sees White Camelia as a Christian political organization with a cause to advance. Because their cause is a generally unpopular one, one which is not "politically correct," he contends that the federal government, the media, Hollywood, and everyone with an ax to grind attempt to discredit it. The public, programmed by the media, buys these distorted reports and becomes even more convinced that the beer-swilling lynch-mob of murderous bubbas portrayed in popular culture is the true Klan.

"The White Camelia Knights of the Ku Klux Klan is a Christian Identity Klan," Lee says. "The most important thing we do is convey the truth of Yahweh, of Christian Identity. If someone chooses to take direct action based upon these beliefs, then that's their choice. We are not engaged in criminal activities nor are we inciting others to commit criminal activities. Some Judeo-Christians become extremely hostile at the Klan whenever this subject [Identity] is mentioned. But we are followers of Christ and, even if our beliefs are unpopular, they are still correct.''

These beliefs certainly put Klansmen at odds with mainstream society. The Ku Klux Klan, in general, is against race mixing, homosexuals, integration, affirmative action, immigration, the "quota" system, oppressive income tax, welfare, GATT, NAFTA, CFR, Trilateral Commission, Israel, Jews, hate crime laws, gun control, the ZOG federal government, the United Nations and any number of other practices, organizations, and individuals, many of which are elements of more socially acceptable political views. Like other organizations, they consider education a large part of their agenda and spend a good deal of time not only trying to get their message out, but attempting to counter-balance and correct the propaganda that they maintain constitutes contemporary American education. Why, then, are Klansmen met with such scorn when they try to advance their political agenda?

"Because we're the Klan, man," Stinson says, smiling. "And you know the Klan is nothing but a hate group." Then he becomes serious. "I got a letter a while back, from [a former Houston police officer who killed two black men in separate incidents, ostensibly in the line of duty. The authors never saw this letter]. We were the only ones who stuck up for this officer when everyone in the world was down on him—including his buddies in the department. Everyone tried to distance themselves from him but we supported him. The bad old Klan.

"Anyway, he said he was sorry it took him so long to thank us. He appreciated what we did. We do this sort of thing all the time but we don't get any recognition for standing up and saying, 'Hey, the guy's doing his job; what he's been trained to do; what we pay him to do.' But we do it anyway. It's right.''

Because they are the Klan, it is reasoned, there will never be anything positive about them presented to the American public. In fact, many Klansmen argue, there will never be anything simply honest presented to the American public in regard to who Klansmen are and what they do. But bad press is not the only concern of the white racialists of the Ku Klux Klan. Because they are the Klan, they maintain, they themselves are subjected to all sorts of discrimination, often the same discriminations they are accused of perpetrating against others. Because they are the Klan, they are excluded from participating in social, political, educational and civic activities—no matter what the cause or how worthy it might be— participation which other organizations take for granted.

Darrell Flinn, Imperial Wizard of the Knights of the White Kamellia of Vidor, Texas (formerly in Lafayette, Louisiana), is particularly outraged by this discrimination.

"What I want to know is, if there is room for everyone in this country, why are white Christians being squeezed out?" he asks. "I'm just finishing up my degree in education, and I'm being prevented from doing my student teaching because of my political and religious beliefs and affiliations. I am a veteran in good standing of the United States Army, a former officer, and the V.A. wants to cut my educational benefits because they say that, as a Klansman, I'm unemployable as a teacher. Is that right? Marxists are allowed to teach. Faggots are allowed to teach. People who belong to the B'nai B'rith, the NAACP, the Black Panthers, the ADL, the Nation of Islam are allowed to teach. The educational system loves them. You know, my organization was even denied the opportunity to participate in the 'Adopt a Highway' litter control program. Can you believe that? They won't even allow us to pick up trash on the side of the goddamned road."

The reverse discrimination, though galling, is something all Klansmen and Klanswomen have come to expect. A good deal of the public acceptance for such practices—which the racialists maintain would be met with public outrage and outcry if perpetrated against an organization such as the NAACP—is based on the public's lack of understanding of the movements.

"Most people who contact us have a misconception about who we are and what we do," Lee explains. "Media people, of course, are looking for sensationalist information which they twist around to make us look bad. We've grown to expect that, and that goes a long way toward explaining these public misconceptions. But I got a call from a white couple whose daughter was living with a black man. I listened to what they had to say, even though I knew where it was going. It seems their daughter had taken up with this guy and he got her hooked on crack and they thought maybe he was using her as a prostitute and they were really concerned and wanted to do something about it. What they really wanted was for me to do something about it. In fact, after they told me all this, the mother asked, 'well, what are we going to do?'

"Well, *we* weren't going to do anything," Lee says. "But it wasn't easy telling them that. I understand their concern for their daughter, and

I believe it was sincere, but they didn't know anything about the Klan or they wouldn't have been calling. I guess they thought I'd call up a few of the boys and we'd put on our robes and hoods and go out and lynch the guy. Well, that's not what we do. Not that I don't believe in righteous violence—I do—but like I've said before, the black man was just being who he is. If this couple had understood the commandments concerning race mixing they would have known what they were asking. They would have known it wasn't the black man who was violating the law. He's not Israel and he's not bound by it. *Their* daughter, a white woman, is the one bound by the law of God. Their daughter is the one worthy of death.''

Several days before our interview at Kelley's restaurant, both Lee and Stinson had been at a rally in Conroe, Texas, supporting the efforts of Michael New. The young Army medic faced a pending court-martial for refusing to wear the shoulder patch and blue beret of the United Nations as part of a multinational peace-keeping force. Lee met the soldier's parents, spoke with them and offered his support. He did not, however, identify himself as a Klansman. "It wasn't a political or recruitment thing," Lee says. "I'm sure everyone in White Camelia supports the News. But I wasn't speaking for White Camelia, I was speaking for Charles Lee." (New has since been discharged under less than honorable conditions for refusal to obey a direct legitimate order.) Up front, vocal, and within established legal limitations, Lee maintains that the White Camelia advances the cause of traditional values such as "old time" religion, and he defends the rights of white Americans against the forces joined to destroy them.

These efforts certainly include political activism. White Camelia holds rallies, organizes marches, prints and distributes information tracts, conducts prison ministries and education and, according to Lee, engages in other legal means of advancing the political agenda of racialism and the religious agenda of Identity, and Lee himself once ran for Governor of Texas.

"I actually got more votes than I expected," Lee states.

In the early 1980s, white shrimpers found themselves at odds with immigrant Vietnamese shrimpers on the Texas Gulf Coast. Texas shrimpers felt they were losing their ability to compete in the industry, that they were, in effect, being driven out of business by the Vietnamese. Cadillac John, claiming that the Vietnamese had an unfair advantage over the white shrimpers, vehemently contends that not only were the Vietnamese fishermen the beneficiaries of special exemptions from established legal limits, but they were receiving federal funds.

"Everybody pays Social Security," he says. "Social Security is for old people who've worked all their lives . . . cripples, widows, orphans and people who are just too damned tired to go on. What gives the government the right to give away your tax dollars to the goddamned gookers? Over five-hundred dollars a month, just for stepping off the fucking boat? But that's not all. They gave them grants, twenty-five thousand dollars . . . not loans, mind you, that you have to pay back—grants! Why? How many white men got a federal grant to buy a boat?

"And if that wasn't enough, all the white shrimpers got to drag two hours in the morning and two hours in the afternoon. The gookers could shrimp twenty-four hours a day, seven days a week, including raiding your traps and stealing your shit! What's right about that? How are you going to stay in business like that? A lot of people didn't."

Though these claims are not substantiated, members of White Camelia hold them as truth, noting that, of course, no government official would ever admit such practices ever existed. Still, Cadillac John, Charles Lee, and other members of Louis Beam's Texas Knights—this group was part of the national organization, Knights of the Ku Klux Klan, prior to the formation of the present White Camelia—formed an armed boat patrol. They "rode shotgun" for the white shrimpers to demonstrate support and solidarity and, according to charges by the federal government, to terrorize and intimidate the Vietnamese. Lee disagrees. "When the Klan got involved with the white shrimpers, it was the shrimpers who came to us and not the other way around. Some of these guys [the Vietnamese] were fresh from Vietnam and they weren't at all reluctant to use violence and intimidation. Some boats were burned and at least one white man murdered. Of course, we immediately came under federal investigation and eventually ended up in federal court. And, as always, the feds couldn't make a case because there never was a case to begin with."

In another incident, in 1992 the Klan rallied to support some rather vocal citizens in the city of Vidor, Texas, in their attempt to block what Charles Lee describes as "forced integration" of a federal housing project. In all fairness to Vidor, many citizens were outraged and outspoken against both the efforts to block the integration and the presence of the White Camelia. But Lee is careful to point out that it was *not* the Klan trying to block the integration, but the citizens of Vidor. Dressed in his robes, the Grand Dragon stalked across a stage draped with Klan banners and

Charles Lee, Grand Dragon of the White Camelia, Ku Klux Klan of Texas, puts on his robe and hood. (*Photo by Myra Barnes*)

Charles Lee, Grand Dragon of the White Camelia, Ku Klux Klan of Texas, speaks at the "Church of the Piney Woods." (*Photo by Myra Barnes*)

Grand Dragon Charles Lee
displaying the dragon
embroidered on his sleeve.
(*Photo by Myra Barnes*)

White Camelia Klan meeting place
(*Photo by Myra Barnes*)

Klan's practice range in the woods.    *(Photo by Myra Barnes)*

Klansmen of Texas White Camelia. Front row far right is Charles Lee.
*(Photo from Charles Lee's personal collection)*

White Camelia Klansmen prepar[...]
for a cross lighting ceremony[...]
(*Photo from Charles Lee* [...]
*personal collectior* [...]

Cross lighting ceremony.
(*Photo from Charles Lee's*
*personal collection*)

"Cadillac" John Thellin.
(*Photo by Ed Collins*)

Jim Stinson and Charles Lee in
front of the Klan bus.
(*Photo by Ed Collins*)

Darrell Flinn, Imperial Wizard of the Louisiana Knights of the White Kamellia, Ku Klux Klan, speaks at a Klan rally.   (*Photo by Ed Collins*)

Display table and Klanswomen at a Vidor rally.   (*Photo by Ed Collins*)

Items on display at a Klan rally.
(*Photo by Ed Collins*)

Charles Lee, Richard G. Butler, and Kent Davis at the July 1997 Aryan Nations Congress in Hayden Lake, Idaho. (*Photo from Charles Lee's personal collection*)

Louis Beam, former Klan leader and Ambassador at Large for Aryan Nations, outside courthouse during the "Boat Patrol" confrontation with Vietnamese shrimpers in 1981.   (*Photo:* Houston Chronicle)

Mark of the Texas Aryan
Nationalist Skinheads.
(*Photo by Bob Daly*)

Chad of the Texas Aryan
Nationalist Skinheads.
(*Photo by Bob Daly*)

Texas Aryan Nationalist Skinheads Mark (left) and Chad (right) in Jenkins
Park, Baytown, Texas.   (*Photo by Bob Daly*)

Author H. L. Bushart with Mark and Chad (White Power T-shirt), Jenkins
Park, Baytown, Texas.   (*Photo by Bob Daly*)

Skinhead transportation, complete with Nazi and Confederate flags.
(*Photo by Bob Daly*)

Typical skinhead footwear, combat boots.    (*Photo by Bob Daly*)

Police checking skinheads' identification, Jenkins Park, Baytown, Texas.
(*Photo by Bob Daly*)

Anti-Jewish graffiti with "gang-tag" marking found at Fort Travis,
Galveston, Texas.　(*Photo by H. L. Bushart*)

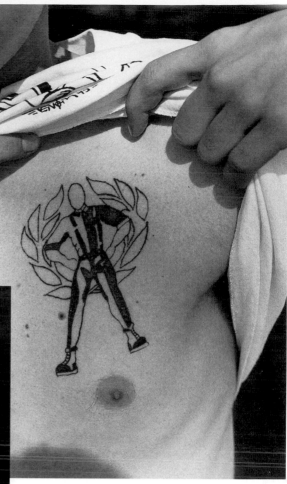

"Faceless Aryan Warrior" tattoo, displayed
by Chad of the Texas Aryan Nationalist
Skinheads.   (*Photo by Bob Daly*)

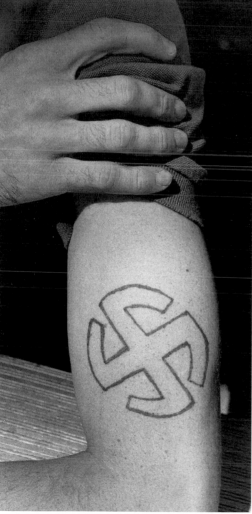

Circular swastika, crest of the 5th S. S.
Panzer Division Wiking, displayed by Mark
of the  Texas Aryan Nationalist Skinheads.
(*Photo by Bob Daly*)

Brigadier General Carl D. Haggard, militiaman and advocate of the
Second Amendment.  (*Photo supplied by Carl Haggard*)

"Black helicopters do exist. Location: classified."
(*Photo from Carl Haggard's personal collection*)

Billboard in Branson, Missouri, April 1997, "The Legend Lives,"
featuring old-style Klan night riders.  (*Photo by Myra Barnes*)

Confederate flags to ask the rhetorical question, "How can you people in Vidor be discriminating against the niggers when there are no niggers in Vidor?" The question was met with resounding approval. Lee spoke the evils of integration, of race mixing, of the federal government's interference into private lives and dictating how white citizens must live. As a result, the government again took exception.

Currently, Charles Lee, as the representative of White Camelia, is being sued by the government for the involvement of the Klan in Vidor. He has also been pressured by government representatives to provide a membership list of Klansmen involved with White Camelia—a list which Lee maintains not only does not exist but has never existed. He takes it all with a grain of salt. "On and off throughout my years in the Klan, I have been under state and federal investigations for illegal activity," he says, "and each time these allegations of criminal activity have been dismissed. Not because we are smarter or more clever than the agencies that have investigated us, but simply because we are a Christian and political organization that has not committed any criminal acts or violated anyone's rights."

It is Lee's contention that, just as with any other political organization, Klansmen have the right to gather, speak and distribute information, to support any cause they find worthwhile, to march and engage in other acts of non-violent protest, without interference from federal, state, or local government. However, he also contends that he knows—as every other Klansman in America knows—that even though this is his right, it is not actually the case. As the leader of a suspect organization, he believes he is never free of scrutiny.

"My lawyer Rife Kimler and I recently met with some federal agents," he says. "FBI. The threats are a little nicer now, a little more veiled, but they're still there. I know my movements are monitored and I believe my phones are tapped."

Darrell Flinn holds this belief as well. Flinn, for instance, has no private phone at his residence. He carries a pager and is subject to returning pages from public phones all over Lafayette. "It's my civic duty," Flinn says, grinning. "As a good American citizen it is my responsibility to avoid the waste of public funds whenever I can. There's not much I can do about the federal agents who follow me around and take pictures, but think how much money I'm saving the taxpayer in phone tap expenses."

And, even if the government is not monitoring their phones or their movements, Flinn, Lee, Stinson and others claim that every racialist leader in America knows—or should know—that he is being monitored by others.

"Not too long ago," Lee says, "my organization was set up to distribute literature along Highway 59 [Texas]. A car pulled over and a couple of women began taking our pictures. They pulled slowly alongside our bus and were just snapping away at everything. One of our members walked over and asked who they were with. Well, one woman stuck her jaw out and said she was with the ADL. I don't know, maybe she expected him to faint or something. He just smiled again and said 'Okay, I thought maybe you were feds,' then went back to what he was doing. They finished taking pictures for their files and drove away. It's supposed to be intimidation, but when it happens so often you come to expect it. I think it violates our rights, but I don't expect it to stop."

"That kind of thing happens all the time," Jim Stinson says. "Both the feds and the public are willing to ignore due process wherever we're concerned. They say we're a 'terrorist' organization and I guess that gives them the excuse they need to harass us, to monitor us, to threaten us and to trample our rights as citizens—rights which anyone else in this country, even foreigners and illegals, can take as a given. Well, after all, we are the Klan."

Charles Lee also addresses the relationship between the Klan and the agents of the federal government. The adversarial stance assumed by the two entities dates back to Reconstruction and certainly has continued throughout the twentieth century. Lee maintains that federal agents have a long and established history of infiltrating the Klan and other supremacist organizations—and not just to gather intelligence. "Anytime you go to a Klan gathering and you hear someone talking about planning an assassination, blowing up a federal building, or perpetrating other acts of violence, you can bet the feds are involved somewhere. Beginning in the sixties, I guess, with that whole Civil Rights thing down in Mississippi, the FBI came up with the new tactic that 'if you can't beat them, lead them.' It's pretty likely that some of the people who represent themselves as Klan leaders and who try to convince people to engage in acts of terrorism are on the federal payroll.

"The way I understand entrapment, if I come to an undercover agent and say 'hey, I want to bomb someone, will you help me, or provide me explosives or something,' then I am guilty of conspiracy and they have the right to arrest me and charge me with that crime and prove it fairly in court. But if a federal agent comes to me—and here I am minding my own business, exercising my rights as a citizen, doing nothing illegal—and he says to me, 'hey, I need you to help me bomb a building' or 'hey, I need you to kill someone for me,' well, that's another matter.

"I'm probably going to tell them to go to hell, if you want to know the truth. But suppose I'm a little more naive than that. Suppose I say, 'Well, I don't know. I'm not sure that's right. I'm not sure I want to go that far.' But the agent doesn't accept that. He says something like, I don't know, maybe 'I thought you were serious about your commitment. I thought you wanted to be active in the movements. I thought you believed in all this.' And he persuades me, or shames me into following along, *that's* entrapment. That's going to someone who has no inclination at all toward doing something illegal and tricking him into criminal activity. It's a pretty good tactic if you can get away with it—and the feds usually can. Look at Randy Weaver."

Lee also claims firsthand knowledge of the scenario he describes. It is his contention that there are any number of Klan groups, infiltrated at their highest levels—"law enforcement-approved Klans"—whose only purpose is to allow close surveillance of the membership. And, in addition to providing opportunities for surveillance, such law enforcement-approved Klans provide the wolves in Klan clothing the opportunities to lead astray those who wish to take a stand based on their heartfelt convictions then charge and convict them in a court of law, eventually delivering them to federal prison.

"Of course, the feds do this to other individuals and organizations as well," Lee states. "We know that federal agents have infiltrated Aryan Nations, militias and many other white Christian organizations in the past. It's a fact of life that every white Christian patriot has to deal with. And these agents were not just there to spy, which is a big part of it, but they were there to promote criminal activity, to try to destroy our legal organizations from the inside. Even though they failed, as always, they still keep trying.

"Like that deal up in the Davis Mountains with the Republic of Texas. Have you ever—anywhere, anytime— ever heard of any law enforcement agency releasing a prisoner in some kind of 'hostage exchange'? It just doesn't happen. But that's exactly what happened with McLaren's 'soldier.' I don't know what the rest of America thinks about this, and I certainly can't prove anything, but I believe as sure as I'm sitting here that the man is a federal informant. That's why they let him go."

Lee is referring to the hostage situation in May 1997 in the Davis

Mountains near Fort Davis, Texas, when a non-racialist separatist group known as the Republic of Texas—which is actually one of three distinct factions claiming that title—took two of their neighbors hostage in response to the arrest of two of their members on weapons charges. The hostages were released after Robert J. Scheidt, a Republic of Texas member, was released from jail and rejoined the group at their "Embassy" compound, which was actually a few dilapidated house trailers, sheds and crude bunkers. After a tense week-long stand-off, the ROT officials eventually surrendered, with the exception of two men who slipped away—one of whom was later killed in a shootout with law enforcement officers. The other escaped into the desert toward Mexico and in September 1997 was captured in Walker County, in East Texas.

"Think about it," Lee continues. "They have an armed stand-off up there. Didn't the news reporters tell everyone how dangerous it was? Why in the world would law enforcement put that citizen's life at risk by taking him from Austin to Fort Davis and letting him go inside? Why would they let him go inside if he believed in McLaren's cause? And—when it came time to surrender—wasn't this guy the first one out? No matter how you add it up, it only makes sense if you consider the man an informant."

Also in May 1997, three men and one woman affiliated with the True Knights of the Ku Klux Klan of central Texas, headed by Grand Dragon Bob Spence, were arrested and charged with a plot to blow up a North Texas oil processing plant.

Charles Lee shakes his head. "The government-approved Klan in action. Everyone around here knows Spence has been an informant for years. Don't get me wrong. I have nothing but respect for the members of that Klan who joined the Klan for a true and honest purpose, and I'm certainly not putting them down. But the True Knights is a false Klan because of its leader, not because of its members.

"Those four people who got involved with Spence's group and found themselves charged with conspiracy have been misled, misdirected and more than likely entrapped. They have been misled intentionally in order to create good press for federal agents and to oppress white Christian organizations. I don't doubt that Spence, with the full blessing of law enforcement, either initiated the plan or did everything he could do to encourage it. And I have no doubt these people are going to prison while Spence walks around a free man looking for other targets."

According to Director of Commission of Human Rights William Hale's sworn testimony, Spence came forward with allegations of the involvement of Charles Lee and Jim Stinson and other Klansmen in a plot involving an assassination list which included Texas Attorney General Dan Morales and Mr. Hale. Under questioning by Rife Kimler, Lee's attorney, the deposition reads in part as follows:

**Q. Regarding Robert Spence, you have identified him as being an informant for the Commission on Human Rights. It that correct?**
A. Yes, sir.
**Q. When did he begin his role as an informant for the Commission on Human Rights?**
A. To the best of my recollection, he came in—made his first contact with me sometime in February of '94.
**Q. February of '94. And you say that he made his first contact with you. Am I to understand by that that he initiated the contact?**
A. Yes, sir.

As the deposition continued, Mr. Hale testified that Spence's motivation was based on the fact that he was angry with Michael Lowe, Grand Dragon of the Knights of the Ku Klux Klan, a national organization based in Harrison, Arkansas. Spence, according to Hale, felt that he was being taken advantage of by Lowe who had persuaded Spence to sign tax documents which made him responsible for sales taxes incurred by the Knights. Spence was concerned that Lowe was basically dishonest, would not pay the taxes and would leave Spence holding the bag. Charles Lee and the White Camelia were included primarily because Lowe's Knights of the Ku Klux Klan were working with the White Camelia in protesting the Vidor desegregation at the time. [However, since that time there has been a parting of the ways between the two organizations.] Hale stated that Spence had testified before a secret grand jury during an FBI investigation of the Knights, the White Camelia and the Vidor housing project situation.

Although this incident involves one particular informant, Lee maintains that it is representative of problems faced by any number of racialist organizations in their relationship to law enforcement. Lee, like Louis Beam and others in the movement, believes that eventually membership in organizations like the Klan will be outlawed. But for the present moment, the war is a war of attrition in which federal agents target individual members and engage in questionable practices like entrapment to bring these individuals down.

Cadillac John Thellin, a machinist by trade, says he has been approached by federal agents on more than one occasion, and they have attempted through chicanery and persuasion to entice him over the legal line.

"If you think about it," Cadillac says with an odd mixture of anger and amusement, "who else but a federal agent would walk into a machine shop and ask a perfect stranger about manufacturing silencers and kits to convert semi-automatic weapons into fully automatic weapons? You know, I think it pisses me off more that they think I'm that stupid than it does to know they're trying to trick me into prison.

"But that's the name of the game. I've been with the Klan for a long time and I'm fully aware that the feds know all about me. I'd have to be a complete idiot to consent to something like that."

Cadillac John did not consent. Jim Stinson, in the machine shop at the time of the incident, recounts Cadillac's response to the request. "That's one agent who had to file his report standing up," he says.

As far as the contemporary membership of White Camelia and other Klan organizations are concerned, such clandestine tactics are a fact of life. In their eyes, such efforts, though directed against individuals, are attempts to discredit the Klan as a whole and incite negative reactions toward racialist organizations on the part of the public.

Secure in their beliefs, the Identity Christians of the White Camelia—although they maintain that more than anyone else they understand the scope, the might, the subterfuge and the capacity for destruction the ZOG federalists hold—feel a total disdain for the agents of the Synagogue of Satan, which extends from the top all the way down to local government. Any harassment they receive will not come as a surprise.

"Bring it on," Cadillac John states defiantly. "I expect their worst and I'm prepared for it. But I can tell you this, no one can change my heart or my mind. I don't care what laws are passed or what tactics they use. There's no way in hell the feds or anyone else can make us or our beliefs go away." Besides, in the eyes of the Identity Christian, the days of the Satanic conspiracy are numbered.

Jim Stinson grins. "For them, it's like the old joke says, the good news is that Jesus is coming. The bad news is, He's pissed."

At the 1996 Aryan Nations Conference in Hayden Lake, Idaho, Charles Lee shares the speaker's dais with such personages as Richard Butler, Neumann Britton, and Charles Weisman. Lee speaks of the dangers of trusting too easily.

"You know, I spend a lot of my time visiting and writing white Christian patriots who happen to be in prison,'' he tells the audience. ''And do you know why they happen to be in prison? They're there because they felt they had to talk to someone . . . and people ask me all the time, 'well, who can I trust?' ''

Lee's face becomes hard, his anger apparent. *''Nobody!* That's who you can trust! *Nobody!''*

# CHAPTER FIFTEEN

# Aryan Nations: Blut und Boden

"**H**ail His victory!"

The imposing patriarch of Aryan Nations stands at the pulpit holding a cross adorned with swastikas. With a somber expression he raises his right arm, palm of the hand down, fingers extended stiffly toward the congregation in a salute with which the entire world is familiar. Above him is a stained glass window bearing the crest of Aryan Nations, an elongated "N" stretched across a shield and bisected by a sword with a crown atop it. Very similar to the crest of the 5th S.S. Panzer Division, Wiking. But then, there have never been any pretensions toward distancing the Church of Jesus Christ Christian from Nazi Germany.

Hanging from the wall is a Nazi banner, black swastika on white background, inside a circular black border, centered on a field of red. The sculpted visage of Adolf Hitler, prominently displayed to one side of the pulpit, gazes impassively and inscrutably out at the congregation and behind the lectern a two-edged broadsword hangs upon the wall.

"Hail His victory!" the congregation responds.

Pastor Butler clenches his extended right hand into a fist and brings it to the left side of his chest as he completes his benediction. For the uninitiated, the setting—the blue-shirted members of Aryan Nations security, the stiff-armed salute, the Nazi regalia—all seem as foreign, as out of place in a church service as anything could possibly be. But a church service it is, and Yashua the Aryan Warrior/Christ is He whose victory is being hailed. At this particular Identity congregation, the Seedline message has a definite National Socialist slant. The service evokes other images: of grainy black and white newsreels of the goose-stepping Shutz-staffeln of Germany, of the Nuremburg rallies, of Leni Riefenstahl's *Triumph of the Will,* of Der Fuehrer.

But this is not Berlin, the city referred to as "New Jerusalem" in sermons by Pastor Neumann Britton. This is America. This is the house of Yahweh. The house that Butler built.

Aryan Nations. *Blut und Boden.* For blood and soil.

Following the Treaty of Versailles, which ended the First World War, supposedly to end all wars of the twentieth century, the New World Order of Woodrow Wilson's League of Nations fell apart almost before it had begun. Long-standing tensions and rivalries between European nations continued to escalate in spite of hopes to the contrary. In the chaos of economic depression and armed conflict between rival internal factions, the post-war German republic crumbled under the vicious battles between the red factions, Spartacists, and the right-wing Fascist groups such as the Freikorps (Free Corps) and Sturmabteilung (Stormtroopers or Brown Shirts). A former corporal in the Kaiser's defeated army with a narrow mustache and unruly hair, bitter and filled with rage over Germany's disgrace, united the fractured republic under the banner of National Social-ism and once again, the dark clouds of war began to gather on the European horizon.

Adolf Hitler spoke to something which Pastor Richard Butler refers to as "the life law" which lay deep inside a significant portion of the German *Volk.* Long before these children of the northern storm unleashed their fury against their enemies, the perceived historic oppressors of the Germanic nations, simmering ethnic and religious differences—expressed in racial terms—boiled over the German nation. Anti-Semitism, always near at hand in European societies, surfaced and was institutionalized as an inte-gral component of Nazi party policy.

By the time World War II was in full swing, William Pelley, an Ameri-can writer and open supporter of Adolph Hitler, had founded his Silver Legion or "Silver Shirts" loosely modeled after Hitler's Sturmabteilung but never approaching Hitler's organization in terms of numbers. The Silver Legion was unsuccessful in mounting a widespread National Social-ist movement in America where anti-Nazi sentiment ran extremely high during the war years. However, the anti-Jewish element of its agenda did find fertile ground in this country. In spite of anti-German and anti-Nazi sentiments, America shared an undercurrent of anti-Semitism with its European cousins.

Butler, consistent with many other Seedline believers and National Socialists, holds that the terrible slaughter of world war is something fomented entirely by the Jews to pit white nations against white nations. While it must be noted that the extermination of Jews during World War II—which most members of the racialist right hold to be a hoax—is horrifying to most Americans, it is horrifying because of its cold, systematic and machine-like implementation which is numbing in its emotional void. Butler, Lee, and almost any member of the movements will, to a man, point out that Jewish blood shed in this particular holocaust is a drop in the bucket compared to Aryan blood shed on all sides by combatants and non-combatants alike. And the common belief is that the shedding of Aryan blood, especially when it is shed by other Aryans, is of particular delight to the Zionist one-worlders. Thus, war between Aryan nations is something the Jews are eager to initiate and even more eager to prolong. This, the racialists claim, is the historic and prophetic truth of European and American wars designed to weaken and deplete the white race.

In the 1950s, Gerald L. K. Smith, a radical fundamentalist minister, anti-Jewish populist, former aide to Louisiana Governor Huey Long and well-known figure in the history of the racial right, was instrumental in incorporating the National Socialist political ideology as preached by the Silver Legion into some branches of Identity. The pre-existing anti-Semitism, of course, was not the sole domain of the followers of the Anglo-Israel doctrine. Father Tom Coughlin, an outspoken Catholic priest, had been blistering Jews in vituperative radio essays for years.

Smith became one of the central figures of the racialist right during this period, networking with different organizations and utilizing the teachings of race-conscious political theorists as well as the teachings of such individuals as Howard Rand, founder of the Anglo-Saxon Federation of America. Smith, along with several other prominent Identity leaders— William Potter Gale, who later was instrumental in the founding of Posse Comitatus; Dr. Bertrand Comparet, attorney and one of the authors of the Seedline AIT Bible study; and Pastor Wesley Swift, an ordained Methodist minister, Klansman and political activist—played key roles in the evolution of racialist ideology. Swift hated Jews and Catholics, not surprising for a Klansman of his generation, and much of what Smith and Swift taught and believed is incorporated into the movements today. These Aryan warriors of the pulpits coalesced the thinking of such figures as George Lincoln Rockwell, founder of the American Nazi Party, and Richard G. Butler of Aryan Nations who now pastors the Church of Jesus Christ Christian.

Richard Girnt Butler is a native of Colorado, where he was born in 1918. His family moved to California when Butler was in his teens. Butler studied engineering and went to work in the aircraft industry. It was in California that Butler, already anti-Jewish, anti-Communist, raceconscious, and militant, immersed himself in Christian Identity and the racial politics of white supremacy.

In 1962, Butler supported retired Colonel William Potter Gale (who, like Butler, was a veteran of World War II) in his failed bid for the governorship of California. Gale, a former member of General Douglas MacArthur's staff, was, again like Butler, a former worker in the aircraft industry and right of McCarthy in his politics. Though Butler's efforts in Gale's gubernatorial bid did not meet with success in the long run, Butler did make the acquaintance of Wesley Swift, protégé of Gerald L. K. Smith and pastor of the Anglo-Saxon Christian Congregation. Butler, raised Presbyterian, soon became a regular member.

A short time later, in response to sweeping social changes such as school integration and the Red threat hovering over America, punctuated by the Cuban Missile Crisis, Swift and Butler, along with Neumann Britton, formed California's Christian Defense League, and Butler was the first leader of that organization.

The various organizations of the movements experienced a sudden spurt of growth during the Cold War when it was widely believed that Communist troops could show up on America's doorstep at any moment. Communism, long believed by racialists to be a Jewish plot toward one-world domination, loomed on the horizon. Frightened but determined to meet any challenge to national sovereignty, many Americans swelled the ranks of Christian Patriot organizations such as the John Birch Society and the Minutemen. The Ku Klux Klan and other racialist entities also experienced this swelling of the ranks due to the galvanic effect of the Civil Rights Movements. In many cases the ideological distinctions between such entities became blurred and often disappeared altogether.

''Tom,'' a former Minuteman from Arkansas who had joined the organization in his early twenties, espouses no racialist or anti-Jewish sentiments as he summarizes his motivations for joining the group. ''The Russians,'' he says, without hesitation. ''They had missiles and troops in Cuba and I fully expected them to make a tour stop in Miami.'' Tom's response pretty well reflects the fears of the era. But he also contends that race and religion had nothing to do with the Minutemen as he understood them, that their sole purpose was to respond to the threat of global communism. However, somewhere along the way, racialist and anti-Jewish ideology certainly became a component of the Minutemen agenda.

For Richard Butler and any number of others, including Charles Lee, the blurring of distinctions between racialist, religious and political organizations can be and should be understood as a right and proper evolution. "I think it's an awakening," Lee states. "White Americans have known for a long time that something is very wrong in this country and with the world. That's why all these different organizations have sprung up. I believe such things as the militia movement, for instance, represent the awakening of white Christian America and that through this awakening the awareness of the conspiracy to destroy our nation is increasing. Once the militiamen evolve beyond this basic awareness and educate themselves to the core beliefs of both race and religion, they will understand and embrace these beliefs."

As a devout follower of Christian Identity, Pastor Butler believes in the concept of Aryan Israel and Seedline doctrine. After completing the AIT course in theology, Butler was ordained an Identity minister and took over the leadership of Swift's church following the death of Swift. In the mid-1970s Butler relocated to Hayden Lake, Idaho, where he built the Church of Jesus Christ Christian and, in 1978, established Aryan Nations as the political arm of the church.

In the Church of Jesus Christ Christian, ministerial sermons teach from the basic outlines in the AIT Bible study guide. The fundamental foundation of faith is the Bible (authorized King James Version), along with the research aids of Strong's Exhaustive Concordance and Young's Analytic Concordance for the original Hebrew, Greek and Aramaic word definitions. According to the "Standard Orders of Worship" supplied by Aryan Nations, Sunday worship services open with hymns such as "Onward Christian Soldiers" and "How Great Thou Art" sung by the congregation; prayer is observed by standing erect with head bowed and *open* right hand extended upward in an appeal to heaven (Genesis 14:22); communion is taken twelve times each year, symbolic of the twelve tribes of Israel, using unleavened bread (wafers) and communion cups of pure grape juice. Offerings are not a part of the worship service, as money is given only on a free will basis to support local requirements.

Sermon topics are undiluted Identity. Nearing eighty, even after heart bypass surgery, Butler is still an imposing figure at the pulpit. His message is one dear to the hearts of the Christian Identity congregation who listen raptly. "The war between the states, where you lost more men than you did in all the other wars combined," he says, "was fought for the nigger. The thirteenth amendment made citizens out of aborigines. Equal to you and now more equal than you by the affirmative action program . . . [we need] to establish a party . . . of people who know their identity. Who know who they are, where they came from, and why they are here."

As a proponent of the faith, Richard Butler advances the theories of chosenness. The Gospel of Pastor Butler is, in the eyes of the Seedline faithful, the true Gospel directly from God through the prophets, the gospel that race is religion, nation is race, and Aryans are the chosen people. This idea underpins the theology of Seedline Identity congregations across America. An integrated country, according to Aryan Nations' doctrine, is not a nation nor is a polluted bloodline a race.

Pastor Butler notes that the terms "race" (blood) and "nation" (blood) mean the same thing. "Nation" (bloodline) and "country" (citizenship) do not. It was America the *country* that fought the successful Persian Gulf War of the early nineties. In a sermon at Aryan Nations, he speaks to the celebration which followed the victory, from the perspective that there is a general misunderstanding of the terms *race* and *nation*. "Everybody was saying 'Oh, boy, how great our *nation,*' " he says facetiously of the media's terminology. "We had everything [racially] under the sun marching in that desert." His contention is that the United States is not one nation under God. The United States is, in fact, composed of a variety of nations, only one of which is under God. Though these nations can and do pull together at times, as evidenced in the Persian Gulf, that does not negate the fact that these various nations within a common territory have always had divisions and will continue to struggle for dominance.

The Church of Jesus Christ Christian is a Christian Identity congregation. Its political counterpart Aryan Nations has among its membership some Identity Christians, some of other faiths and others who claim no religious affiliations, as well as those who have ties to or have been involved with various Klans, skinhead groups, the John Birch Society, the Minutemen, Liberty Lobby, Posse Comitatus, National Alliance, American Front, Aryan Brotherhood, the White Patriot Party (formerly the North Carolina Knights of the Ku Klux Klan), the now defunct Covenant, Sword and the Arm of the Lord, numerous militias, and others. The ease with which these members move between organizations belies some of the ideas of the depth of disparity and infighting that is assumed to exist among them. For example, at a Klan rally one can routinely encounter skinheads—both the currently active youngsters and grown-up varieties—militia and Nations members. Rather than dissension, cooperation and interaction seem to be growing. But to a man, they are white and generally Christian. They understand the concept of race as nation.

Aryan Nations observes the admonition of Christ to carry the message to the lost sheep of Israel. They also note the admonition to "shake the dust from your feet" and move on if the message is not well received. Whereas there may and likely will be large scale rejection of this message—at least at the present—by the gullible sheep of contemporary white society, there is one area where the message of white Israel has met with a more than receptive audience, the prison system.

Pastor Butler and Aryan Nations have always been very active in their prison outreach, as is Kingdom Identity Ministries. Providing information and support to incarcerated white prisoners has resulted in a fairly successful conversion rate. Aryan Nations, through an arrangement with Kingdom Identity Ministries, provides these imprisoned white Israelites with the AIT Bible study guide and other literature of its own that open their eyes to who they really are and what purpose they are here to serve. It is reasoned that by increasing the knowledge base of such individuals, confirming their identity, instilling in them a sense of racial pride and a sense of purpose will far outstrip any contemporary non-Identity approach to so-called "rehabilitation."

As one worker in the prison notes, *"Re-*habilitation is a misnomer. You've got to be habilitated at some point before you can be *re*habilitated. Most of these guys have never been habilitated in the first place."

"Some of the convicts are a waste," admits Jim Stinson. "I mean, they'd be raping and stealing no matter what. God's Law provides for that eventuality. But there are others in there, full of anger, full of rage, and they don't even know why they're angry. These are the guys we can reach. We can help them understand."

Charles Lee, at a local gun show in 1997, waxes a bit philosophical about the inclusion of convicts in the ranks of the movements, including incarcerated members of the Aryan Brotherhood. "As a Christian, my job—and Pastor Butler's—is to carry the good news of Christ to every white person I can. Some people in the movements have a bit of a hypocritical attitude toward convicts or AB's and feel they have 'jailhouse religion.' And, of course, some of them do. But it's really not our place to judge that. I mean, is church for people who never sin? It seems to me that the people who most need to hear the message are the sinners. And I'm including myself in that. I don't know anyone who isn't a sinner, present company included.

"A few years ago, one of the Aryan Nations security officers was recommending that people should be excluded from attending their functions if they have tattoos. Well, there are Scriptural references to images and not marking your body but that's getting a little carried away. Salvation is not about what you do *before* you know the word of God. If it were, what would be the point of the whole thing?"

The Church of Jesus Christ Christian welcomes the opportunity to minister to both true believers and potential converts through their efforts inside the walls of the ZOG Gulags, both state and federal. Walls, they contend, will not stop an idea and will not stop the Word of Yahweh. Stone walls, it is reasoned, do not a prison make and the truth of God liberates one, regardless of the psychological and environmental circumstances one may be subjected to. A time is coming, they maintain, when the roles will be reversed, when Christ Himself will set free the prisoners and welcome them into his kingdom. Until then, for Pastor Butler, Aryan Nations, and all the various organizations and soldiers of the racialist right, there is much work to be done to prepare for that eventuality.

At the 1996 Aryan Nations conference, Pastors Richard Butler and Neumann Britton inducted soldiers into the army of Yahweh. Two by two, Klansmen, skinheads, Aryan Nations members, neo-Nazis—complete with Swastika armbands—marched forward to pledge their loyalty to Yahweh. Each in turn raised the two-edged sword to point it above the pulpit. "To Yahweh I pledge my honor," each declared before passing the weapon to another. After the oath of fealty, both initiates and those reaffirming their faith stepped forward to be anointed by Butler or Britton. The ministers of Yahweh made the sign of the cross upon the men's forehead with sacramental oil and welcomed them with the phrase, "I declare you a soldier in the Army of God." After the final man in the congregation had received this blessing, Butler and Britton performed the ritual upon one another.

Charles Lee states that he has been honored with conducting cross-lighting ceremonies at Aryan Nations Congress gatherings at Hayden Lake and has also been a featured speaker at such events—most recently at the 1997 Aryan Nations Conference. It is not uncommon to find blazing swastikas (cross symbol/sun symbol) also burning against the night Idaho sky. Louis Beam, former head of the Texas Knights, Tom Metzger of White Aryan Resistance, and Carl Haggard of Texas 1st Cavalry Militia, United States Special Field Forces/National Militia, 1st Texas Light Infantry Militia, and Texas Constitutional Militia, among many others, have been visitors to Aryan Nations headquarters. Many well-known activists have been frequent visitors.

Therefore, the leap of imagination it takes to infer some common unifying element among these groups is not a quantum one. This is particularly true when one considers the agenda of Richard G. Butler—unification of the white supremacist movements and the establishment of a separate Nordic nation.

Some in the government consider Aryan Nations the most dangerous organization in America. This is a reciprocal feeling because members of Aryan Nations consider the federal government the most dangerous organization in America. If the core idea which underpins all the efforts of Aryan Nations is the idea of a separate state, a racial nation—and it is—then certainly such an idea is threatening to the government of the United States. The idea of the racial homeland, however, is both unifying and divisive at the same time for the organizations of the racialist right. While it is true that most racialists believe that separate nationhood is the only solution to racial tensions in this country—and in the world, for that matter—how these homelands are to be established and, more importantly, where they will be established are bones of contention.

Though not an Identity Christian, Dr. William Pierce, former physics professor and full-time National Socialist, also believes the only solution to the problems of the nation is the formation of a white homeland. Pierce is the head of National Alliance and hosts the shortwave radio program "American Dissident Voices." Pierce is also the author, under the nom de plume Andrew Macdonald, of *The Turner Diaries* and *Hunter.* Like others in the movements, particularly in National Alliance, he is not sold on the idea of dividing the United States into territories. The official position of National Alliance is that white Americans already have their own territory. All that needs to be done is to purge all non-whites from it.

In a speech at Aryan Nations Congress in 1993, Pastor Butler called on delegates to support the idea of a racial national state solely for Aryan Israel. He contends that the government of the United States, the Synagogue of Satan, is no longer that government which the founding fathers intended. The republic, he says, died in 1865. White Americans, from Butler's perspective, are rapidly becoming a minority in their own country and the white race is a minority throughout the world. "If you took a vote [worldwide]," he says, "all white people voting together, including your babies, you'd be outnumbered eleven to one."

And, of course, it follows that in a "majority rules" society where whites are the minority, society will be structured in such a manner that Aryan culture will be subordinated to non-Aryan cultures. Laws will be established to ensure that white people will be "kept in their place" by the dominant culture. And, for those who would argue that this sums up exactly what Aryan Nations is trying to do to other races, it must be noted from an Identity perspective that the Servant Nation has been commissioned by Yahweh Himself to serve as steward of the earth and overseer of all non-Adamites.

According to Butler and the doctrine of the white homeland, the establishment of separate nations is an example of responsible stewardship. Only in a racially pure Aryan Nation will the Laws of Yahweh be acknowledged and obeyed to create the Israel that God intended.

To do otherwise, from a Seedline perspective, is insane. Integrated societies, governed by the laws of man rather than the Laws of God, are bound to be chaotic. Butler and any number of racialists share the sentiments that obedience to God entails disobedience to—and often outright conflict with—the Synagogue of Satan and laws enacted by Zionists and their toadies.

"Who was the law, Pharaoh or Moses? Egypt or God?" Mike Hallimore asks. It is his contention and his belief that every true Christian in America, every individual who puts the Laws of God first in his life becomes an outlaw in the eyes of the federal government and in the eyes of the brainwashed general public. "As part of his calling," Hallimore notes, "Moses had to kill an Egyptian." Did this not make Moses an outlaw? A radical? A terrorist under the law of Pharaoh? White Israel, the chosen few, are almost always in direct conflict with the ZOG government.

Direct conflicts are inevitable when the government—city, county, state, or national—requires a license for exercising what Identity Christians consider a God-given right. God ordains ministers to carry His word, not government-supported universities. God sanctions owning weapons for self-defense, not the BATF. God decrees how His people's money should be used, not the IRS. God owns the airways, not the FCC. God determines how white Israel children should be schooled, not the State

Board of Education. God unites a man and woman in holy marriage, not the Marriage License Bureau.

It is for reasons such as these that it is not uncommon to find Identity Christians, as well as other fundamentalist religious adherents and strict Constitutionalists, in effect "dropping out" of society. Through Aryan Nations' and other ministries' mail-order lists and at gun shows, conventions, and rallies throughout the country, one can obtain books and pamphlets detailing the steps to "disappearing" within the alien Zionist society. Already some members of the various organizations are virtually untraceable, lacking driver's licenses and Social Security cards, using forged documentation. Some have children born with no records of birth. Any number of these individuals believe that, although such "invisibility" of white Christian patriots may presently be necessary, there will come a time when every true believer can stand up and be counted, can assume a rightful place in the Aryan National state, the true Kingdom of God, governed by the Laws of God, where Yashua the Messiah will establish His throne and Yahweh of Hosts will reign as King.

Aryan Nations shares the universal Identity contention that most white people do not know these things. In fact, most cannot know these things because they have been misled by the Zionist conspiracy which keeps them in the dark about who they are, a conspiracy that feeds them disinformation in the form of falsehoods disguised as facts and history. The lies are intentional, purposeful, destructive, and designed to first enslave, then destroy Aryan Israel. Of course, one of the first and most effective steps that can be taken is to divide the white race against itself.

Yet, as Butler notes, to control past history is to control not only the present but the future. And it is the contention of Aryan Nations that ZOG controls the past and uses it to advance present agendas geared to future world dominance. In addition to disseminating information about Christian Israel and working toward the Aryan National State, much effort is expended by Aryan Nations to combat the false and misleading teachings regarding history to which so many Americans are subjected and to awaken the white race to who they are. The truth of the Second World War is but one battlefield in this war of information in which not only Aryan Nations, but other racialist organizations find themselves engaged.

Although some publications are somewhat secular and others proselytize from the perspective of Christian Identity, all vilify the Jews, identifying them as the enemies of America and the Aryan race. All advance the racial philosophy of Aryan Nations. All see the need for separatism.

All reject the idea of assimilation. All reject the idea of tolerance for other races or religions as a perversion of the intent of the founding fathers.

Pastor Butler notes that more immigrants are coming into the country than there are white children being born, and white America must waken to this fact. However, he also acknowledges that white America is lethargic, unaware, concerned with material items and creature comfort, the trappings of success which keep them distanced from their true plight. He notes that, unlike the German *Volk* of Hitler's day, today's white Americans lack the fire of nationalism, the "belly-button touching the backbone" hunger of a people striving to unite racially against a common enemy.

From the pulpit Butler notes that, unlike the Germans, "we are a new people . . . transient . . . we move from spot to spot. We haven't got within us the essence of what they [the Nazis] called Blut und Boden, or blood and soil. But we do have the inheritance, in our genes, the idea of what is right and what is wrong. We do have the ability to learn . . . we can have the same will . . . the same stick-to-itiveness . . . we can reach our racial brothers and sisters with the life law. That's exactly what Hitler did."

Historians agree that Hitler did indeed touch something common among a very significant portion of the German population. Yet the Third Reich, the reign of a thousand years, lasted only a little more than a decade. How did it fall? The veracity of the Holocaust notwithstanding, Hitler had either driven the Jews and the race traitors from the borders of Aryan Germany or neutralized them through imprisonment. His push for *Lebensraum* (living space) displaced Jews, Gypsies, Turks and others the Nazis identified as unsavory from the borders of the Aryan homeland.

"Where did they go? That's what we have to ask ourselves," Pastor Neumann Britton says from the pulpit at the 1996 Aryan Nations Congress. "All those Jews driven out of Europe, where did they go? Canada? America? And who were the real victims of a 'holocaust'? After the war several million good, German men were rounded up and marched toward Siberia. Most of them were never seen again, never heard from again. And Eisenhower—that Kike—that Jew bastard—let it happen." An overwhelming majority of racialists in Aryan Nations and like organizations believe that American troops shot the wrong people during our last European war.

They also believe this is a situation that can be remedied.

The idea of a separate nation for whites only—free of Jewish influence,

Jewish institutions, dark faces and alien tongues—has long been a part of many supremacist organizations and the spokesmen and political philosophers of the movements.

David Duke, former Imperial Wizard of the Louisiana Klan who, as a Republican candidate, once won a seat in the Louisiana House of Representatives, has gone to a great deal of trouble to shed his racist image. However, while still involved with the Klan, Duke undertook an effort to outline a map of how the United States should be reorganized to include such "countries" as West Israel (for Jews), New Africa (for blacks), Navahona (for Native Americans), New Cuba (for Cubans, Haitians, etc.), Alta California (for Mexicans), East Mongolia (for Asians), and Minoria (for other minorities). This type of plan is also embraced by other separatist organizations who hold a great deal of ill will toward non-Aryans, as well as a few non-Aryan groups who would like their own territory free of whites.

Organizations like The Order, Bob Mathews's commando group formed of Aryan Nations members, demanded a white "Bastion," a separate Aryan nation in the Pacific Northwest and Idaho, solely for the white race. Many white supremacists echo this sentiment. One of the major platforms of Pierce's National Alliance is the necessity for White Living Space, an Aryan society based on Aryan values, where young white men and women can gather to socialize and dance, but "never to undulate or jerk to negroid jazz." It is a common observation among the Texas Aryan Nationalist Skinheads, for instance, that such a separate nation would end the racial problems in America at large by providing Aryans with a homeland that would prosper while the race-mixing mongrels of the rest of America go to hell in a hand-cart.

Ministries and ministers who support racial separatism often include that fact in their statement of beliefs, but the Church of Jesus Christ Christian—Aryan Nations—includes within its body of resolutions the formal "Platform for the Aryan National State," its Preamble and ten subdivided Articles as evidence of their attention to the organizing and implementation of a separate white Christian homeland, an Aryan Republic.

Much abridged, the "Platform for the Aryan National State" contains these summarized provisions:

ARTICLE I—Only Aryans (White Race) will have citizenship and vote; only citizens will be allowed to conduct business, hold office, serve in the military or law enforcement, be free of taxation, receive loans without interest charges, have equal rights and duties, be free to work as they choose.

ARTICLE II—Non-citizens can visit the Republic, but only under the custodianship of a citizen.

ARTICLE III—All hybrids called Jews are to be repatriated from the Republic's territory, and their wealth be redistributed; it shall be a capital offense to promote Jew Talmudic anti-Christ Communism or any other crimes against nature.

ARTICLE IV—All Talmudism (Judaism), devil and heathen religions and practices will end immediately, and there will be an expansion of true Positive Christianity.

ARTICLE V—Responsibility of the educational process will be in the control of local citizens and parents; the curriculum will include a renaissance of White Aryan Heritage, Arts, Sciences and Humanities.

ARTICLE VI—News media will require that all personnel be citizens; disallow circulation of any non-Aryan media except by permission of the government, and only with appropriate comments from an Aryan cultural viewpoint; forbid circulation of material which is not conducive to the National welfare.

ARTICLE VII—The government, as servant of the nation's citizens, will protect the purity of the race and defend its territory; promote industry and livelihood; promote a program of nutritional food, eliminating the current poisonous practice damaging life and environment; support farmers and small private businesses and restore property unlawfully seized by deceit by "Usury Bankers"; care for the aged impoverished by fraud; clear out the [welfare] parasites created by the present political parties; make the killing of a White by a non-White a capital offense; confiscate all unearned wealth stolen by usury or fraud but leave inviolable the rights of lawful inheritance; nationalize all multi-national trusts; prohibit land ownership and industries by aliens; abolish the present money system with its privately Jew-owned Federal Reserve and establish a monetary system based upon a just set of weights and measures; stop feeding and arming enemy nations and force them to buy our food and technology; and immediately annul all foreign alliances and treaties with all non-White nations.

ARTICLE VIII—Wage war on those who injure and dishonor the nation.

ARTICLE IX—Abolish the current materialistic Jew-"Law Merchant" judicial system and return to a God-ordained, racially inherent Anglo-Saxon, Germanic Common Law Order.

ARTICLE X—For the foregoing to be implemented, a renewal of Racial self-respect in the knowledge of our God's Eternal Natural Law Order and the will to return to it with heart, soul and mind is imperative.

But the remedy, for justly militant Seedline Christians, involves both a leap of faith and a bold leap of ideology: Aryan Identity Christians can isolate themselves from the other races, but the Jew is the spawn of Satan. From this religious perspective, no adherent to Christian Identity, no member of the Servant Nation—despite Article III of the Platform for the Aryan National State calling for repatriation of Jews to another territory—can escape or abjure the eventual scriptural responsibility to purge Jews from the face of the earth.

The scriptural imperative is in place and unavoidable. God, Yahweh, is immutable, unchangeable and so are His laws and commandments. The Jews cannot be allowed to live among the other peoples of the world.

# CHAPTER SIXTEEN

# Jugend:
# Soldiers of the Fourth Reich

With their black jackets and Nazi regalia, thin red suspenders, White Power T-shirts, close-cropped hair, combat boots and tattoos, they are in little danger of being mistaken for members of the Vienna Boys Choir. Skinheads are in even less danger of being accepted as just another youth group. Many people view skinheads as one of any number of youth gangs in America today.

But irrespective of how they are seen by the rank and file American, they see themselves as the ''Jugend,'' the youth-wing of the Aryan movements. They take themselves quite seriously.

There are some very good reasons for the rest of the country to take them seriously as well. Some skinheads have proven to be extremely violent. The Fourth Reich Skinheads of California, for example, were stopped short in their attempt to rekindle the violence of the Los Angeles riots of 1992 by bombing the African Methodist Episcopal Church, a plot resonant with the echo of Klan tactics during the early sixties. Various groups of skinheads across the country have engaged in harassment, assaults and murders of homosexuals and members of racial minorities, as well as acts of vandalism and desecration of synagogues and Jewish cemeteries. The Confederate Hammer Skins of Dallas have been credited with numerous such acts over the past few years and several members of skinhead groups, such as Portland, Oregon's East Side White Pride, have been convicted of charges arising from race-related murder.

Skinheads first became conspicuous in England in the early 1980s. They were an outgrowth of the punk music scene and were closely and self-consciously attached to the working class in Britain. In short order, they also appeared in the United States. Not all skins are racist, and there are some groups which are multiracial. One such organization is Skinheads Against Racial Prejudice (SHARP) which seems to be a throwback to the punk scene skinheads of the 1980s. It is probably safe to say that, although they are still primarily a blue-collar phenomenon, a preponderance of skinheads are white and most are racist. A good deal like the independent Klans, there are quite a few skinhead groups operating in America today and most have some connection to other separatist groups such as the Klan, Aryan Nations and National Alliance. Some have trained and are continuing to train with one or more militia groups. Some are Christian Identity and others are not.

Again we see the flow among the movements, with the skinheads adding the element of accession by age. Tom Metzger observes in Ridgeway's *Blood in the Face* that "there is no center" to the far-right movements in America. "It's all around but it's nowhere. It's like associations or networking. No fancy headquarters, or store fronts, or even book stores. Yet it's all over the place . . . it's a life force. Some people could call it a subculture."

Tom Metzger and his son John are the adults behind the White Aryan Resistance and Aryan Youth Movement. Though not Christian Identity, they have no qualms about accepting Identity members into their organizations. Metzger, speaking to the "un-centered" nature of the far right, has very actively connected otherwise disparate racial groups in California.

In addition to being California's premier Klansman (he was arrested with Pastor Richard Butler and several other Klansmen and Aryan Nations members for lighting crosses in Los Angeles in 1983 in public defiance of a local ordinance), Metzger is a tireless recruiter for the movements. He is particularly active in recruiting young people. Along with his son John, Metzger orchestrates "Aryan Woodstocks" from time to time in order to bring in some of the more disaffected youths who might prove appropriate candidates for the movements.

Racial rhetoric—combined with the driving, violent music (a variation of "Oi" music, originating in England and so called for the working-class Cockney greeting) of racial rockers such as Bound for Glory, Aggravated Assault, RAHOWA or RaHoWa (for Racial Holy War), Nordic Thunder and Skrewdriver—has proven more than effective for swelling the ranks of White Aryan Resistance, American Front, Aryan Youth Movement and any number of other youth-oriented and skinhead groups. Of course, such gatherings also allow garage bands to strut their stuff before an appreciative audience. Chad, a member of the Texas Aryan Nationalist skinheads, is lead guitarist in the skinhead band WHITEWASH, with klansman Jim Stinson on drums. And, as with young people of every generation, there are always more than enough groups emulating their heroes, waiting in the wings.

Skrewdriver is apparently the "Beatles" of the Aryan youth, the group that became the innovator and really got the whole thing started. Although the founder and driving force behind the racist rock band, Ian Stuart Donaldson, was killed in an auto accident in Britain in 1993, his music and its "white power" message still plays well to the macho image the skinheads have adopted. George Burdi, a Canadian (and minister with Church of the Creator) and lead singer of RAHOWA, who has been convicted of assault, pens lyrics which advise "niggers" to run while they can.

There is a lively international mail-order market for Oi. It can be obtained, along with graphics, lyrics, album covers and concert photos, over the Internet. However, although it has great appeal for the young, right-wing devotee, Oi (at least of the racial variety) is not the type of music one can generally tune into on one's radio dial. Nor is it the kind of music one can walk in and purchase off the counter at the local music superstore.

"You can't go in the store and buy Bound for Glory," complained J-2, also a Texas Aryan Nationalist skinhead, "but you can find all the nigger music you want and it's just as racist as anything we listen to."

When one considers the music of black artists like Ghetto Boys, Ice-T, Public Enemy, and other "gangsta" rappers, it is impossible to argue that the lyrics are not overtly racist, because they *are* overtly racist. The skinheads ask why such products as "Cop Killer" or "Guerrillas in the Mist" are allowed to be sold over the counter when Oi white-power rock is not?

"It's entirely inconsistent," Mark, another TAN member, adds. "How can you say 'this is wrong' for one group of people, but then act like it isn't wrong for another?"

This is indeed a bothersome question, as evidenced by publicly televised debate, talk radio, and the print media. However, more mainstream groups like Guns N' Roses, a white heavy metal group, have tested the limits of contemporary acceptable standards and have already crashed through the parameters of political correctness with lyrics which take an adversarial stance toward foreigners and blacks. In an August 1989 *The Rolling Stone* interview written by Del James, lead singer Axl Rose also notes the double standard. ''Why can black people use the word 'nigger,' '' he asks, ''but when a white guy does it . . . it's a big put-down?''

Tom Metzger obviously sees the opportunity to advance his cause among those who see such inconsistency, particularly among the youth. As cited in *Blood in the Face,* he isn't shy about discussing that opportunity. ''Whenever we're able to recruit young people or change someone's way of thinking, young or old,'' he says, ''we jump right in. If it were the Gray Panthers, it would be the same thing; whenever we see an opening, that's where we go.''

Richard Butler, too, sees the value of recruiting and organizing young people. He speaks rhapsodically of the ''Aryan Youth,'' the *Jugend* of America and the role they must play in the continued survival of the white race. His views of the skinheads are reminiscent of Hitler's notions of the Iron Youth of Germany—a relentless, single-minded force, unified by race and immersed in the Fuehrer Prinzip (leader principle). The skinheads, for Butler and for others, are the white race's best hope for the future and its only salvation.

At a Klan rally in Vidor in 1992, Charles Lee introduced a group of skinheads and made the observation, ''Everyone wants to know, 'where do they come from?' I tell them, look into a mirror. They are the product of your environment, your teachings, your lifestyles . . . they have rejected you and all you stand for. They see what you've done to them and what you're continuing to do to them and to the entire white race . . . with your integration . . . with your affirmative action . . . with your tolerance for every filthy perversion. They are what you've made them. You've turned from God and they've turned from you.''

None of the skins we met made allusions to poverty, abuse or any type of deprived childhood in their own lives. Mark, raised Catholic, describes his parents as somewhat liberal. Chad attended a private school. J-2 describes his childhood as normal. As far as they are concerned, their racialist beliefs are not grounded in childhood trauma or adolescent alienation but in awareness.

''Other races are different from us,'' Mark notes. ''Anyone who doesn't see that is a fool. They know it and we know it. We're not upset about niggers, Mexicans or even Jews wanting to stick together. They should.

And so should we. If we are to survive as races, we have to. God created us different. It's pretty clear he wouldn't have gone to all that trouble if he wanted us to mix our blood, become something else.''

Most voiced their opposition to homosexuals, foreigners, Jews, blacks and other minorities. They expressed a belief that a conspiracy exists to destroy the white race. They see themselves as defenders of their race. And, as defenders of the race, they embrace the philosophy of the White Homeland. Such a nation, in their eyes, is the only absolute way of ensuring the continued success of white Israel and the preservation of the white Christian culture against the forces of evil.

They also embrace the philosophy of the Third Reich, up to and including systematic execution of Jews, race traitors and race mixers, cripples, the profoundly retarded or anyone else who cannot pull their weight in, or might prove a drain on the idyllic Aryan bastion.

Mark's girlfriend, ''Alex,'' a seventeen-year-old girl with long blond hair and wide brown eyes, had little to say, seemingly content to stay in the background. ''I believe they're serious,'' she says of her male peers, ''but I also believe they like the attention. That doesn't mean I'm not a racist. I am. I guess I'm just not as radical as they are.''

But she, too, has her place in the grand scheme of things as proposed by the racial right. An Aryan woman is the mother of the future, a doe-eyed Eve of the New Garden, the promise of racial survival. The wives and girlfriends of the original The Order members provided locks of their hair to their men as talismans and symbols of what the struggle was about as Mathews, Pierce, Lane and the rest went into battle. The oath of The Order was taken over a girl child. The role of the Aryan woman is crucial to the movement and to the future. The role of the Aryan warrior is just as clear.

''The Bruders Schweigen [Silent Brotherhood, the official name of The Order as designated by Bob Mathews] pointed the way,'' Mark says. ''It's coming to war. A holy war for the white race, a white homeland, a future for our people.''

The violence and intimidation reported in the mainstream press hardly fits the description of what most believe war to be. It does, however, fit the description of what most would consider crime. On the other hand, as many in the movements note, the mainstream press rarely gives much consideration to veracity when reporting anything associated with the supremacists or other right-wing organizations. The fact remains that the work of the Bruders Schweigen consisted of counterfeiting, armed robbery, and at least two murders. Even though a formal declaration of war was issued against the government, it came very late in The Order's existence.

Skinhead war is somewhat different. Generally it consists of such things as painting swastikas, runes, and other Aryan symbols anywhere and everywhere in a "graffiti-media" campaign of its own. It consists of the distribution of pamphlets and the posting of fliers which have generally been lumped into the category of "hate" literature. It consists of often violent confrontations with non-whites and homosexuals. A favorite tactic in these battles is "booting."

Although the wearing of black lace-up work boots (Doc Martens) or combat boots—preferably steel-toed—began as a fashion statement and remains an element of skinhead identity, the heavy boots are also quite handy in street-fights for kicking downed adversaries. George Burdi, caught demonstrating the technique on a protestor at a RAHOWA concert, was convicted of assault and sentenced to one year in jail for the incident. This technique is also used in "fag bashing" because one does not have to come in contact with any HIV-infected serum or risk contagion with "fairy" blood seeping in through scraped knuckles.

The desecration of synagogues in Dallas, ostensibly the work of the Confederate Hammer Skins; the beating death of Mulageta Seraw, in Portland, Oregon, in 1988, to which three skinhead members of East Side White Pride pleaded guilty to reduced charges; the attack on a twenty-seven-year-old Oriental man by Aryan Youth Movement members; and the drive-by murder of a black Gulf War veteran in Dallas, Texas, are their extreme acts of war. Not just any war, but Holy War. Yahweh's war. And any means to win that war for survival is acceptable.

Some older members of the Klan, such as Charles Lee and Jim Stinson, are almost paternal when speaking of the skinheads.

"They get a little exuberant," Charles Lee says. "They haven't matured in their faith or their beliefs, so you kind of have to take that into consideration when you talk to them. Sometimes they overdo it."

One of the authors is disturbed. "I have a son about their age. I would be terribly upset if he joined the movements. Doesn't it bother other parents?"

"It does," Lee answers. "There could be violence—probably will be violence—but you have to look at a bigger picture. You lose this generation or, if you don't, you'll lose the next generation. You have to take a chance. You have to make a stand." Making a stand, for Identity Christians, applies to their political convictions as well as religious beliefs.

But Christian Identity is not the sole faith of the far right. Any number of members of the movements are adherents to more mainstream faiths, Baptist, Methodist, Catholic and others. Their versions of these faiths seem to be more reductionistic, more fundamentalist, more geared toward literal interpretations of Scriptures than one might expect to find in mainstream congregations. Still others are Dualists, or followers of rebel prophets, "Jack" Mormons, or spin-offs of the mainstream faiths as well as a few who invent their faiths as they go along.

Such as the Neo-Odinists.

Neo-Odinism is a popular movement among the skinheads, who are fascinated with Nordic/Germanic trappings to begin with. Odin is the father deity of Norse mythology. From his home, Asgard, Odin rules the old gods and goddesses, Baldur, Thor, Heimdahl, Tiu, Loki, Sif, Frig, Hel, *et al.*, in a pantheon called the Aesir, similar to that of the Greeks' Olympian gods. Thor, Norse god of thunder, is a particularly popular symbol with many of the skinheads. The Confederate Hammer Skins in one of their posters, for instance, feature a Thor character with flowing hair and beard holding aloft a hammer (apparently a carpenter's claw hammer rather than the mystical Elfin-forged battle hammer, Mjolnir). Above Thor's right shoulder is an eagle in flight, and framed in the spread wings of the eagle is the circular swastika that Mark has tattooed on his arm (which is also the crest of the 2$^{nd}$ S.S. Panzer Division).

Yggdrasil, in Norse mythology the giant ash tree whose roots and branches form a link between earth and heaven, is also the symbolic pseudonym of a prolific contributor (or contributors, if "Yggdrasil" is actually a group of writers) to the Internet of articles in a number of major supremacist web sites. The symbols, more than the faith of the Vikings, may have the most appeal for the Aryan youth. Particularly since the experiential nature and practice of that pre-Christian faith is a mystery shrouded in time. But, as among their counterparts in Germany two generations ago, the marriage of race and Nordic mysticism is still a strong draw for many skinheads and others in the movements.

But modern Odinism is not merely a fascination with the old ways nor is it actual pantheism or worship of a particular deity. David Lane, incarcerated member of The Order and author of The Fourteen Words, is—from his federal prison cell—a prolific white nationalist writer and proponent of the natural laws of Odinism or Wotanism as it is referred to in the Fourteen Word Press. "Wotansvolk," a periodical printed and distributed by Lane's wife Katja through Fourteen Word Press, goes to great lengths to describe Odinism, or Wotanism, as a racial imperative—natural and unavoidable—a philosophy underpinning a racialist world-view and an expression of the collective Aryan will. Bob Mathews of The Order had gotten pretty heavily involved in Odinism prior to his death.

Neo-Odinist devotees of the new Paganism point to the importance of the old religions and the ways they have influenced the new faiths and the culture in general and how the truths of nature are revealed in nature. The old gods and the customs of the old faiths still linger in our culture in the guise of the Yule log and the decoration of the Christmas tree (Druidism); Father Christmas (Santa Claus, a less than effectively disguised Wodin or Odin); and even the days of the week (Sun's Day, Moon's Day, Tiu's Day, Wodin's Day, Thor's Day, Frig's—or Freya's or Frey's—Day, and Saturn's Day).

Jim Stinson has his own explanation for the phenomenon. "I think they're looking for a strong God, a white God. I mean, all their lives they've been fed this line about how Christ was a Jew and how meek and gentle Christians are supposed to be. If they want a strong God, they need to look into the Bible. They need to read it right. Now there's a strong God."

Stinson becomes a little more animated as he tells the story, obviously amused. "I was talking to this guy one time and he was telling me how strong and pure the Nordic race was with Odin for its God. That the coming of the Christians made them weak." He laughs. "I told him we didn't *pray* those battle-axes out of their hands."

The symbols of the Nordic are represented in skinhead tattoos, and skinheads are almost always tattooed. This is not something unique to this particular group. Many others, such as Jim Stinson, have elected to have these statements of identity and affiliations etched into their skins.

The symbolism of certain tattoos is particularly revealing. Faceless Aryan warriors, braced and booted, framed inside a victory wreath (the wreath of the German Knight's Cross) signify the Leaderless Resistance, the anonymous Aryan working in the trenches against all odds for God and country. The boots and braces identify the warrior as a skinhead. The wreath, of course, indicates the eventual victory.

The swastika is a cross symbol of the Aryan Messiah and also a statement of kinship and solidarity with the Aryan warriors of the Third Reich. Other tattoos indicate group affiliations and memberships, sometimes ranks, and often deeds or achievements. The spider web is another common element of skinhead body art and also serves to communicate certain feats. For instance, a spider's web on the elbow may, among some groups, indicate a violent act perpetrated against an enemy, or the actual killing of an enemy. On the other hand, as Jim Stinson points out, if one is really going to get into tattoos, "What else can you tattoo on an elbow?" In any case, images of death and violence are evident everywhere in skinhead culture.

This should not be too surprising if one considers that the skinheads see themselves as the American version of the Hitler Youth and Storm-troopers in the making. In the faith where religion is race, Richard Butler maintains that the Stormtroopers of the Third Reich were the new apostles, and the Aryan gospel advanced by these apostles has passed into the hands of the skinheads.

One skins recruiting poster has a photo of S.S. Guardsmen at attention, eyes right to face their commanding officer, under the familiar caption, "We're Looking For a Few Good Men." The response address and phone number is framed between two skulls and cross-bones, the symbols of the Totenkopf (Death's Head) Division of the S.S. Another poster is of the grim reaper, naked from the waist up, carrying a scythe, with his braces hanging down from the waist of his pants. Heavily tattooed, the Reaper-Skin has the word "SKIN" across the knuckles of his right hand (a common tattoo) and a swastika between the thumb and forefinger of the left (also a common tattoo). Among the myriad of Nazi symbols there is also the spider's web across the left elbow and the word "SKINS" again on the forehead of the grinning skull.

Along with the fascination held for Nazi trappings and the religion of the ancient Norsemen, there is also the same fascination that Hitler had for Germanic runes, characters in the ancient alphabet. The lightning bolt (double-S or esstet) symbol of the S.S. is but one of many ancient Nordic symbols which are fraught with meaning for the skinheads and Neo-Odinists. For some, such fascination entails inventing a new written language, English in structure, using the alphabet of the Nordic Runes. "Some of the kids in school are even writing notes in what they call Viking," one high school teacher observed.

Variations of belief notwithstanding, the Neo-Odinists are Aryan and, as Aryans, they are kinsmen. For the Christian Identity members of the movement, there is always hope that the white man will come around in terms of belief and there is no particular need to be impatient with the more pagan brethren. And, of course, the skinheads are young.

In his 1993 Aryan Nations Congress speech, Pastor Butler notes, "A strong leader must emerge. You look at me and say 'he's too old.' Well, I am. But there are leaders out there. Perhaps there is one among you right now. Perhaps among the skinheads."

The Fuehrer Prinzip, the idea of one strong leader of the people, is one that is entirely embraced by the skinhead youth. In fact, particularly in these trying times, it is the only option that makes sense to them.

"Democracy is madness," Mark says vehemently. "It's a ridiculous system to live under. It's nothing but mob rule, and the government swings from one direction to another. Nothing's consistent."

Many skinheads believe that only through the rule of the white Aryan, through the institutionalized guidelines of Yahweh, does American society have the remotest chance for survival. And it is only through the leadership of an American Fuehrer that this situation can be brought about.

But what kind of man would make that type of leader? Why trade even the chaotic freedom of a democracy for a dictatorship?

"The leader would, of course, have to answer to the people," observes another skin. "Hitler did. It isn't at all like the Jews in the media have presented it. They act like he was some outsider or something who walked in and stole the country from the German people. That's not true. The German people wanted Hitler. He was a popular leader. They loved him."

The TAN Skins are supporters of Butler's plan for a Northwestern United States/Southwestern Canada Aryan Nation, a land absolutely free of non-white minorities, somewhere in the pristine wilderness. An idyllic land, a land of which Hitler himself might have approved.

"If you think about it, it makes sense," Mark says. "It's in a part of the country that's mostly white anyway. Other races make up less than one percent of the population and why *would* they want to live there? It's fertile land, unpolluted, where we can grow the things we need and be self-sufficient. Besides, Aryan peoples are suited to that kind of climate, ice and snow."

And what type of government would be established in the Aryan Homeland?

"Probably Fascism. It's a good form of government for white people. When you have all one race, one set of beliefs, there isn't a lot of need for votes and stuff. But it might be a republic, especially since that's what people are used to. Of course, it would be a lot different from what we have now."

Hitler's vision for Germany was undoubtedly different from what we in America have now. No matter how it is examined, history includes the truth that Hitler invaded Poland, Czechoslovakia, France, and numerous other European countries. The debate begins with the question: did he come as conqueror or liberator? Would the Aryan Homeland follow the lead of Nazi Germany?

"I don't think so," one of Mark's friends says. "I think we'll be happy just to be left alone."

Mark is not so sure. "Once we're established, which is our first goal, then we have to take a look at the rest of the world. This isn't just about America, it's about white people everywhere, white Israel. I see it as a worldwide problem.

"As a white Christian nation, I think we'd be justified in coming to the aid of our Aryan kinsmen in places like Europe or South Africa who are struggling just like we are. If we can get rid of the Jews and other races, then we can live in peace and there won't be any need to fight one another."

Mark, like Hitler, blames the Jews for all the wars that have afflicted humanity. When he says "get rid of the Jews," he means just that. Not the creation of a separate Jewish state, not deportation or relocation, but the "final solution." He looks above his head to the spreading limbs of a nearby pine tree.

"That limb there should do nicely."

But first things first. In order to establish their new order, the chosen must be united in a common cause and under a common leader. It will not be Pastor Butler. Butler, though committed enough, is like a latter-day Moses. He has devoted the greater part of his life to the Aryan cause. He has worked for years to unite the often-splintered factions of the far right into a cohesive and unified movement. Yet, standing atop the mountain, eyes turned toward the promised land he hopes to establish, he must know he will not live to abide there.

The leader, like the faithful, remains faceless at the moment—unknown, unheralded. But should that leader arrive, he will find waiting the patient minions of the Aryan youth— the skinheads—minions who will eagerly follow the banner of "Ein Volk, Ein Reich, Ein Fuehrer."

One People, One Empire, One Leader.

# CHAPTER SEVENTEEN

# Christian Patriots: Militia, the Second Amendment and Armed Society

The tree of liberty must be refreshed from time to time with the blood of patriots and tyrants.

— Thomas Jefferson

"**I** have been a Christian Patriot since my high school days," says Mike Hallimore, "and a believer in the Kingdom Identity message for nearly thirty years."

This combination of loyalties is what drives Christian patriots—love of country but distrust of those who govern it, faith in the Constitution but belief that it has been subverted by the government to serve a dark purpose rather than the citizens it was designed to protect. Lest its origin be forgotten, patriotic Christian activists remind us that the founding fathers were white Christians, many of them slave-owners. And that the Constitution is, therefore, a political and Christian document that carries both political and Christian rights and obligations.

"If you are a Christian—a real Christian—then there is no separation of church and state," says Charles Lee. "Religion *is* politics, and politics *is* religion. That's what the government wants, for Christians not to step outside the church door and see what's really going on. Keep doctrines confined to religion, not politics. That way they get the people *they* want in control.

"Your faith builds your character, your ethics, your behavior. You can't toss that aside even though there are those in the government who want us to. You have a high government official who's a proven womanizer and liar, for example, and they say 'Character is not a big deal.' That's nonsense. Character *is* important. How a person believes determines what he does. Christian patriots definitely have an agenda and a goal in mind, and their numbers are growing."

Is he speaking of militia?

"I see Christian militia as a good thing," Lee says. "In a broad sense, everyone is a member of the militia if you consider it a reserve force to draw on when the country is threatened by war. But militia also refers to the armed activists of revolutionary organizations. It is not speeches that bring about change in an oppressed nation, it is violence."

Charles Lee is prepared to embrace armed conflict. "People make absurd statements to the effect that violence for any reason is wrong. Wouldn't George Washington have gotten a laugh out of that one? There has been and always will be violence. The only question is whether it will be positive or negative violence. The American Revolution, for instance, was a war and, by necessity, violent. But it was a positive use of violent force because it resulted in freedom for the American people. I believe the same can be said about the history of the Ku Klux Klan in the Reconstruction period after the Civil War."

Cadillac John, an avid history buff, agrees. "There are three boxes that made our country great," he says. "The soap box, the ballot box, and the cartridge box."

Positive violence—righteous resistance against a malevolent force—is, with various degrees of activism, integral to the agenda of militant Christian patriots. Similarly, resistance to corruption of the Constitution by a self-serving government is the parallel agenda of a number of secular militia groups, although religion as well as racialism is often only a factor with individual members of each organization. Defense, not offense, is the avowed *raison d'être* of both types of groups, but they are quick to point out that their activism is a *reaction,* inasmuch as the government has already fired the first shot against individual freedoms.

But citizen soldiers must have arms, a safeguard foreseen by the founding fathers and addressed in the Second Amendment to the Constitution: "A well-regulated Militia, being necessary to the security of a free State, the right of the people to keep and bear Arms, shall not be infringed." The paradox comes when the malevolent force, in this case the U.S.

government, controls the people's right to keep and bear arms as well as the interpretation of "infringe." By necessity, the issue of gun control then becomes vital to both Christian and secular resistance groups.

"Every creature that walks, flies, or crawls on its belly has the right to defend itself," Militiaman Carl Haggard says. "Is a man's right any less? The government, at least the anti-gun element, would leave us all unarmed. Unable to defend our lives. Unable to defend our homes, our properties, our families. Why? Because crime exists? I don't think so.

"My right to arm myself, to act in my own self-defense, is acknowledged and guaranteed by the Constitution of the United States but it is not the Constitution that grants me that right. That right comes from God Almighty and is not subject to the whims of government."

"Gun control is the number one goal of the Clinton regime," says "Dick," a Houston gun shop owner and militiaman. "There's a conspiracy to disarm us, and the government is behind it. That's why we're always played up as dangerous to the general public. If the government can convince everyone we're a threat, they can garner the support they need to disarm us. And by 'us' I don't mean just militia members, I mean every last citizen in America."

"I'm part of the militia," Haggard explains. "You're part of the militia. Every able-bodied person in America capable of bearing arms is part of the militia. One of the arguments of the gun-grabbers who would limit our rights under the Second Amendment is that this amendment refers to the militia. They are incorrect. If you investigate the terminology as it is used not only in the Constitution but in other documents written at the time, it is clear that the reference does not solely define the militia. The armed forces are the organized militia, simply the military branch of government. They are raw force. Then there is the unorganized militia and that basically covers everyone else in the country who is not a member of the standing army."

If one listens to all the various manners in which Christian resistance groups and secular militias are defined—and the even more varied explanations of their activities—the waters are subject to becoming muddied. For instance, all Christian patriots are certainly not militant nor members of armed groups. In fact, it is likely that most citizens of the United States, whether Christian or secular, consider themselves patriots but recoil at the thought of revolution. However, any number of groups call themselves militias.

The militant White Patriots Party of North Carolina, formerly a Klan group which evolved into a paramilitary group, still supports the racialist agenda including rigidly enforced separatism. Then there were the Montana Freemen who followed the lead of Posse Comitatus and established citizen courts, and eventually declared themselves a separate nation, claiming that Yahweh had placed a protective barrier around their sanctuary to ward off their enemies, presumably the FBI. And the Viper militia, training in the Arizona desert with explosive devices in preparation for conflicts with the federal establishment.

The disparities between these types of groups are often apparent, but virtually any characteristic is present in one group or another—widely varying degrees of size and organization (or disorganization), of militancy and religious zeal, of paranoia and pugnaciousness, of racialism and inclusiveness. The media, as far as militia supporters are concerned, have done little to clarify the situation and have portrayed armed citizens as a threat to national peace and security and as possibly a diabolical force. Members of various militia organizations are presented as anti-government anarchists, paranoids, hate-mongers and racists, as well as dangerous, alienated malcontents.

Haggard insists that nothing could be further from the truth and that many Americans—including those now swelling the ranks of militia groups across the land—are finally getting beyond the bad press and are beginning to understand that the militia is a force for good. Others, such as the Christian patriots within the racialist organizations, clearly see their roles as soldiers in a revolutionary army and are ready to take action— when the time comes—against an oppressive, immoral and out-of-control federal government intent on destroying the American culture.

If one is to discuss armed society, freedom and anti-government resistance groups, it is necessary to consider two essential truths. The first is historically evident: governments can and do go bad. They can turn on the citizens, become oppressive, even tyrannical. No nation is ever exempt from that threat, and the collective experience of humankind is rife with examples.

The second truth is again obvious. An unarmed society cannot hope to defend itself against an armed military force. Whether the armed force consists of foreign invaders or domestic troops is hardly relevant to the fact that unarmed civilians cannot effectively resist an armed military.

Militia members argue that a legitimate government would take comfort in the fact that militia groups exist, and Christian groups argue that a God-fearing government would solicit Christian support. Instead, both militia and armed Christian patriots are viewed as threats. This does lead to a rather uncomfortable question regarding gun control. If the government is concerned about armed criminals, Second Amendment activists share their concern. However, if the government is concerned about armed law-abiding citizens, Second Amendment activists want to know why.

"They're not worried about crime," one militiaman states. "They're worried about me and people like me. The government wants our trust, but it's evident that they don't trust us. They fear us."

Charles Lee echoes this opinion. . . . Government *should* fear the governed. "It's kind of a backward situation in America today," he says. "A lot of people fear the federal government, and it should be the other way around. That's what the Constitution is all about. If we were going by the Constitution, I guarantee you the people who make up the federal government would be afraid, because the legislators and the politicians and the judges have been trashing it and trashing the entire concept of liberty."

Lee, who notes that the Klan has long supported the citizen's rights to bear arms, is vocal in his support of the citizens' rights to organize for defensive purposes. "Personal protection is only one reason to have an armed citizenry," he maintains. "A far more important reason is to maintain control over government. All throughout history we have seen one government after another enslave its own people, and common sense tells us it is much harder for a corrupt government to move against armed people. Today, more and more people find themselves distrustful of the federal government and are willing to defend their rights and the Constitution if need be. From what I see around me, white Americans are getting ready to defend the country from its enemies."

Enemies, from the Christian Identity perspective, include more than human adversaries. Satanic forces in their various disguises have been attempting to destroy the Adamic race since the corruption of Eve. To the Identity Christian, whoever places man's law over God's Law is an enemy. Whoever forces integration of the races is an enemy. Whoever sanctions, much less encourages, interracial marriage and the intermingling of bloodlines is an enemy. Whoever condones homosexuality and abortion/murder is an enemy. Whoever interprets separation of church and state to mean outlawing prayers in the classroom is an enemy. And anyone who views multinational, multiracial organizations such as the United Nations as benign is blind to an orchestrated step toward a Satanic

One-World Government. Even a cursory look at the government's attitudes, from a Christian Identity perspective, is enough to see that unGodly forces are at work.

Although many of their goals and tactics coincide, it is on scriptural rationale for their actions that one may draw loose distinctions between Christian Identity groups and more secular militia groups. Militias, by and large, do not consider membership on the basis of race. "I will never, *never* disallow membership for racial reasons," Haggard says. "It doesn't take much research to discover that I go out of my way to recruit minorities whenever I can. The legitimate militia does not discriminate on the basis of color or religion. There are militia members who are black and there are members who are Jewish."

"As far as I'm concerned, no one who loves the Constitution and the United States should ever be excluded because of race," one militiaman states. "Any good citizen, good patriot, is welcome. But," he adds, "it would be nice if they could speak English."

Haggard does acknowledge that some groups who call themselves militia are racist and anti-Semitic, but he does not consider them legitimate militia organizations if such beliefs are organizational principles of their groups. Haggard admits that he has visited Aryan Nations and Richard Butler, and is acquainted with Mark of the Texas Aryan Nationalist Skinheads (Mark once trained with Haggard's 1st Cavalry Militia) and with Charles Lee of White Camelia. However, he insists that his beliefs are quite different from theirs. He states that the Klansmen, skinheads, and members of Aryan Nations are entitled to their beliefs—and he believes they are sincere in their convictions—but that he is a Christian who claims no kinship with Identity Christians. "They have no charity in them," he says. "I am not a white supremacist who believes only white-skinned people have souls. We are all children of God."

He is equally clear on the demarcation between such groups as the Klan and the militia. Charles Lee, ever the promoter/recruiter, speaks with pride of the Klan as being the oldest ongoing resistance movement in America. Haggard does not deny that reality. But he does contend that the Klan is a political action organization, devoted to causes with definite outcomes in mind, while most militia are not. He contends that legitimate militia operate in the open (though membership is confidential) for legitimate defensive and beneficent purposes in case of disaster, emergency, insurrection or invasion. "Most of us are conservative, not all," he says. "Most of us are white, not all. Most of us are Christian, not all." But it must be noted, and Haggard acknowledges this as well, that there are indeed any number of racialists and separatists involved in the various militia organizations as well as throughout the ranks of self-identified Christian patriots.

Racialist ideology aside, there are issues on which the groups agree. Militia members, conservatives and Christian patriots, separatists, survivalists, and racialists, all express a deep distrust of government and point out that the founding fathers were equally leery.

"I could see it happening like this," Haggard explains, hypothesizing. "We're already being systematically disarmed piecemeal. As crime increases—and it will if our present situation is any indication—there will be some catastrophe or another that will give the government an excuse to call for even more arms control. After all, hasn't the present administration used Waco and Oklahoma City as a reason to call for 'stronger legislation' where guns are concerned?

"After the number and types of firearms available to us are limited, the catastrophic event will provide the federalists with the excuse they need to call upon the citizens to surrender the arms they have. Particularly if a law is passed. And citizens will comply. There won't be door to door search and seizures. No, when the government calls for the firearms, the *sheeple* will surrender them."

Of course, there are those in the movements who do not agree with Haggard's hypothesis, at least not completely. Many would align themselves with the idea that it is indeed well within reason to expect a bogus situation, concocted by government, to be the catalyst for the passage of laws restricting gun ownership. But as for door to door seizures of weapons?

"What the hell was Waco?" Cadillac John asks. "I don't know anything about what those people [Branch Davidians ] believed, but they had a right to be there, and as long as they weren't bothering anybody, they had a right to be armed. I haven't seen anything to back up the government's claim that the people had machine guns and all. But I do know the BATF came to them and not the other way around."

Not only do supremacists believe that Waco was a federal "gun raid," it was also a clear repression of religious freedom (albeit aimed at a heretical group, from a Christian Identity perspective). As for racialist groups, there is no lack of a political agenda as a countermeasure. And included in this agenda is preparation to resist attempts by ZOG to disarm white Americans and render them helpless to Jewish enslavement and exploitation which begins with gun control laws. For many in the movements, such tactics are something they expect to see executed with increasing frequency against those whose only crime is to demand their Constitutional rights to bear arms and believe according to the dictates of their consciences.

Cadillac John, Jim Stinson, Mark, Chad and J-2, as well as thousands of white nationalists across the country point to Waco, to Gordon Kahl, to Ruby Ridge, as examples of federal oppression where weapons and dissident voices come together.

"The police say we're better armed than they are," Jim Stinson says. "Maybe we are. I don't know. But I know I've got a right to my weapons. Maybe they should invest a little more in theirs."

Haggard, as reflected in his writing and public speaking engagements, also sees a conspiracy afoot. It is a conspiracy of "One-World-Order federalists" who, through organizations like the United Nations, intend to enslave the peoples of the world under one flag. Although he is adamant that his views are not racialist and he does not particularly view the conspirators as Zionists, he does view the plot as Satanic. A self-described "conservative Catholic," Haggard smiles as he makes the observation, "I believe in the book of Revelation. I'm not some apocalyptic kook, but what kind of Christian negates prophecy?"

For Seedline believers, the AIT's Chapter 88 "The Destiny of Our Race" gives ample evidence of the identity of the people for whom biblical prophecies are intended.

> Our purpose, our destiny, is to set an example for the world, according to God's Laws. It is morally wrong for us to try to evade this leadership by offering it to others to do in our place.
> . . . Our forefathers took an oath before Yahveh as He reaffirmed them as His Kingdom people . . . Our national transgression today is our failure to keep this vow to administer the Law of Yahveh and enforce it as the law of the land.

It is with this scriptural admonition that white Israel, the Identity Christian patriot, knows what his course must be.

Across the spectrum of militia and Christian patriot organizations, the government is seen as the problem. However, there is no consensus on how the problem is to be resolved. Although Haggard as a militiaman promotes vigilance and activism, he does not advocate unnecessary violence. Other militiamen, too, advocate political activism through organization and the vote to restore liberty to the nation. "Maybe it's a good thing that so many Americans are blind to how enslaved they've already become," one man says. "Good in the sense that we don't already have war in the streets. If folks were to suddenly realize the full extent of what the liberal government has already done to them, man, don't you know there would be violence?"

Charles Lee, like others, sees a growing awareness in white Christian America. "I believe the growth of the militia is an indication that many Americans are no longer confused about just who is responsible for the problems we are facing. The federal government has become an enemy to the survival and freedom of white Christian America. It no longer represents Americans and America's sovereignty, but seems more apt to represent foreign interests."

One thing is certain. Identity Christian patriots—white supremacists with God on their side—will not avoid violence when the time for revolution is right. Not only do they believe the time is near, they welcome it, violence and all.

"There has been very little change in world history in which violence did not play a key role," Charles Lee says. "Hoping that violence will not be a part of any future changes in America is to blind oneself to the reality of the past. America is headed for revolution. The only question that remains is, will it lead to a positive or a negative outcome?"

It is not inconceivable, should such a national schism occur, that, much like our first civil war, militia groups that have trained together may fracture and take opposite sides as politics and conscience dictate. Should such a situation come about, Identity Christian patriots of the racial right, as well as the Black Muslims and other militant ethnic organizations, hold one common belief.

Skin color will be the uniforms of the second revolution.

# CHAPTER EIGHTEEN

# Stormfront Rising: the Campaign for Hearts and Minds in the Information Age

According to the spokesman and preachers of the Christian Identity movement, the struggle to carry the true gospel, as they know it, is quite a formidable task at the present time. Pete Peters, for instance, maintains that the Jews who control the government and the media are doing everything they can to silence this truth and, since they have such powerful means at their disposal to enjoin this task, they are often quite successful.

According to Identity Christians, the truth is getting out because of the ingenuity of God's people. Circumventing the monopoly of the Jewish-controlled media, ZOG censors and FCC restrictions, the message of white Israel is being disseminated via Internet and e-mail, by fax machines and photocopiers, by shortwave and ham radio, through widespread Identity ministries' mail-order catalogues with their video and cassette tapes, books, booklets and tracts produced by independent presses and private desktop publishers—alternate routes that the media censors cannot control.

An orchestrated effort by Kingdom Identity Ministries, Ministries for America, and a large number of other Identity ministries has been mounted to recruit from specific target populations such as prisons, other faiths and denominations, or anywhere the seed of Christian Israel truth may be planted. In Branson, tables are set up where hundreds of books and pamphlets bearing the imprints of small Identity presses or bearing no printer's imprint at all are offered for sale. On the Internet, Identity and

White Nationalist home pages are growing in numbers by quantum leaps and unrestricted bounds as are the home pages of various militia and historical revisionists and on-line magazines such as *Media Bypass*. Internet chat rooms, faxes, e-mails, and all the tools of the Information Age have provided a basically unregulated medium by which the various racialist organizations can bypass the censorship of ZOG to present undiluted, uncensored, no-holds-barred truth as they see it to the American public.

The emergence of Public Access Television has provided yet an additional medium which is also proving to be a thorn in the side of those who would impede the Identity and racialist movements, as evidenced by Darrell Flinn's "The Klan in Acadiana" program airing weekly in Lafayette, Louisiana. Alternative airwaves are also a key forum for the dissident voices of the movements, and patriot shortwave broadcasts are nightly aired throughout America and the rest of the world. White Nationalism, in the information age, may just as easily be considered White Internationalism through the instant access of modern technology.

As Mike Hallimore of Kingdom Identity Ministries explains, it is the struggle for the hearts and minds of white America that is pre-eminent for the Christian Israel movement. Of course, there is and will be a physical struggle as well, but for the faithful, the "Two Seedline Conflict" will be won or lost on the spiritual plane.

"The Bible says 'My people are destroyed for lack of knowledge,'" Charles Lee states. "Knowledge of the Scriptures is the key. People cannot believe what they have not been exposed to, what they have not been taught. They cannot follow if they cannot hear the call. That's why it is so important to open the eyes of white America."

As has been noted by E. Raymond Capt, as well as the Anglo-Saxon Federation and other individuals and organizations of the Christian Israel movement, the message that is carried is not one of particular denominational doctrine. And, of course, it should be noted that most members of Christian Israel congregations have indeed been long-time members of more mainstream denominations. For instance, Charles Lee considered himself a Christian long before his introduction to Identity. Interestingly enough, many Identity Christians, including the ministers of Identity congregations, do not abjure their earlier religious affiliations and beliefs— at least in toto. Pastor Everett Ramsey, for example, is a Baptist minister and pastor of a Baptist church. Several Baptist ministers were speakers at the Branson Super Conference, and many other denominations were represented in the audience.

Capt explains that, rather than denominational ideology, the Identity movement entails a recognition and acceptance of White Israel as the historical and Scriptural Israel, the chosen people of God. He maintains that the concept transcends denominational variances and is not a question of Catholic versus Baptist versus Presbyterian versus Methodist ideology. Mike Hallimore agrees. "It's not like a 'new' religion," he says. "Accepting the truth of Identity doesn't mean that you turn your back on your faith. Identity is just added to the pre-existing beliefs and it makes those beliefs come alive in a way they never have before. The difference is between a partial truth and a whole truth." If this is the case, then it easily follows that other Christians—at least white Christians—could prove receptive to the idea of Christian Israel. As Charles Lee has noted, every white person in the world is a potential convert—if they can only hear the word.

Although there is widespread rejection of Identity tenets on the part of what Hallimore refers to as "Christian*dumb*," he, like other members of the movements, are convinced that this is a knee-jerk reaction based on the spurious conventional teachings that the Jews constitute true Israel and that Christ Himself was a Jew. Thus, it stands to reason that outreach ministries would engage in an effort to reach other white Christians who have not heard the message of Christian Israel and therefore have had no opportunity to either embrace or reject it.

Even if the larger portion of mainstream Christendom is intent on cutting Identity Christians from the fold of the redeemed, a primary goal of many Identity ministries is to bring their erring brothers to the truth of the Covenant People. To this end, Pastor Ramsey's organization, Faith Baptist Church and Ministries, for instance, sponsors an "Adopt a Pastor" program.

The "Adopt a Pastor" program is designed to carry the message of Christian Israel to other pastors and bring them into the growing kingdom of God. Thus, these leaders are identified, sought out and recruited in fulfillment of the obligation of evangelism inherent in the Christian faith. In a May 1997 newsletter published by Faith Baptist Church and Ministries, Pastor Ramsey notes, "The 'Adopt a Pastor' program will move on to more pastors. We have ministered to 5,000 pastors, many who have responded very positively. More pastors are becoming aware of the message of who we are and the need for spiritual revival in the land."

The true believer must be willing to seize upon every opportunity to offer the truth to those born to the elect, regardless of religious affiliation, wherever the opportunity presents itself. Michael Hallimore makes the point that both pastors and members of many congregations are receptive to the doctrines of Identity because it is a historic part of their faiths. An undated pamphlet *For the Benefit of our Pentecostal Brethren!* by Curtis Clair Ewing and George Southwick, speaks to the historical and instrumental role American Pentecostal Churches played in sponsoring the Christian Israel movement in the late nineteenth and early twentieth centuries. Hallimore makes the same claim. "Of course the Pentecostal Church used to teach Identity," he says. "Baptists used to teach it. Methodists used to teach it. This is true Christianity."

However, outreach efforts are not limited to members or leaders of Christian congregations. One of the main thrusts of Kingdom Identity Ministries, for example, is a prison ministry. A number of Identity Christians, because of actions based on their beliefs, have run afoul of the system and consequently found themselves in federal or state prison. In fact, a number of speakers and attendees at the Branson Super Conference spoke of their incarceration as a matter of pride and a badge of honor. The shame involved in such incarceration, for these individuals, is a shame that rests directly upon the government which places the Laws of God in a subordinate position to the laws of man. Thus, it is reasoned, those faithful who suffer imprisonment for actions based on scriptural beliefs and principles are worthy of honor and, for many, are prisoners of war. In the eyes of the Identity faithful, if the agents of ZOG think these individuals have been neutralized then they are sadly mistaken. As in the case of the apostles of old, the cells of the faithful become the pulpits of the faith.

In 1994 at the Texas Department of Criminal Justice facility at Tennessee Colony, Texas, inmate Riley Ray Fultz and several other incarcerated men founded, incorporated and chartered the Church of Aryan Christian Heritage. Although the church itself is impossible to separate from the Texas Aryan Brotherhood (a white prison gang of which Fultz is a member), it is organized around the scriptural principles of Identity and is recognized by the state as a legitimate religious organization.

But there is another factor which must be considered in the prison ministries which is more pragmatic in nature. Lee is very candid in discussing the practical aspects of white racialist organizations within the walls. "If the government had its way, I'd be in prison right now," he says. "There's a huge non-white population in the penitentiary. How long do you think a Grand Dragon of the Ku Klux Klan would last in that general population? Any prison sentence I got would be the same as the death penalty. Any white man who goes to prison needs someone to watch his back."

Oddly enough—although recruitment efforts, at a glance, are touchy situations—racialist ideology also has its share of adherents among white police officers who are supportive of the cause. The history of the Klan includes members of various police organizations who were also Klansmen. However, it is manifestly evident that though such supporters and believers within these organizations are valuable indeed, spreading the word within the law enforcement agencies is certainly not without risk. Thus such converts and supporters are often incidental rather than a result of an organized attempt to bring them into the fold.

In addition to being spread via prison ministries and recruitment among church congregations, the Identity message is also offered to those who attend gun shows where any number of right-wing, racialist or other political organizations may be represented. Militia groups, the John Birch Society, Second Amendment supporters, and others often set up booths and offer a wide variety of products to passersby, including books, pamphlets, audio and video tapes and personal one-on-one witnessing. At "Preparedness Expos" across the country, one might encounter such people as John Trochmann of the Militia of Montana, who in 1997 made a tour of the United States speaking at such events. Or Louis Beam, who reportedly attended a gun show at George R. Brown Convention Center in Houston, Texas, in April of 1997.

As one strolls the aisles amid the various displays, one can choose from a wide variety of weaponry, including rifles, shotguns, handguns, blowguns, knives and swords as well as other military equipment and paraphernalia such as gas masks, tents, MRE's (Meals Ready to Eat), flags, camouflage uniforms and anything the survivalist, revolutionary or military buff might need. But there is also a lively business in literature. At every such event one is likely to find copies of the *Anarchist's Cookbook,* a volume that provides step-by-step instructions for the construction of explosive devices which can be manufactured with easily acquired household material. Or *The Turner Diaries,* by Andrew MacDonald (a.k.a. William Pierce) a novel of the coming race war and the martyr/hero Earl Turner. Or Pierce's latest work, *Hunter.* Yeager *(Jaeger* means "Hunter" in German) is the hero of the work and spends most of his time hunting down and killing racially mixed couples and Jews. The fictional Yeager is based on the short yet bloody career of Joseph Paul Franklin—né James Clayton Vaughn, Jr.—who was convicted of shooting down racially mixed couples in the late seventies and is presently incarcerated for those crimes. One is almost certain to find one or two versions of the infamous *Protocols of the Learned Elders of Zion* which documents the methodology of the alleged Jewish plot for world domination.

There are also volumes which address Identity doctrine—E. Raymond Capt's scholarly works, and books authored by Everett Ramsey, Charles Weisman, Bertrand Comparet, Richard Hoskins and dozens of others who are sometimes surprisingly prolific authors. The fact that many of these works are unregistered with the U.S. Copyright Office and the Library of Congress is largely immaterial and, in fact, is an advantage inasmuch as censorship is therefore not an issue. These books, tracts and pamphlets articulate the perceived truths of the racialist right—the truth of Christian Israel, the truth about ZOG, the truth about the Jews, the truths about the so-called Holocaust, about the much-maligned Third Reich, and all the truths of the movements which adherents maintain are impossible to present through conventional outlets.

And they are impossible to present through conventional outlets precisely because these outlets are controlled by the very groups Identity Christians are attempting to expose. Since this organized and expected propagandistic control allows the establishment conspirators to reach millions, combating the efforts of ZOG is a most daunting task.

To this end, Dr. William Pierce's National Alliance created its own press, National Vanguard Books in Arlington, Virginia, which turns out an amazing amount of racialist literature. Aryan Nations Press, Javelin Press, Aryan Truth Network, Richard Hoskins's Virginia Press, Kingdom Identity Press and numerous other Christian Patriot alternatives work toward the reeducation of white America, which is a necessary first step to bringing about the appropriate race-consciousness necessary for white activism.

National Vanguard publishes Pierce's books *The Turner Diaries* and *Hunter,* as well as other works such as *Which Way Western Man?* by William G. Simpson and *The Might of the West* by Lawrence R. Brown. Periodicals are also published for a very exclusive far-right audience. Publications such as *National Vanguard,* which advertises "more of Earl Turner's ideas," is published bi-monthly. *Attack!* and the *Best of Attack!* and *National Vanguard* are also distributed through this press.

For a younger reading audience, National Vanguard is now publishing comic books to spread the message of Aryan truth and the philosophy of the National Alliance, and is also marketing "segregated" children's stories which were published prior to World War II and are devoid of any integrationist, affirmative action agendas. Aryan Nations also has a growing children's section of publications which promote white pride and the faith of Identity among Aryan children. Kingdom Identity Ministries' children's section lists reprints of McGuffey's Reader, Aesop's Fables and other character-building books, as well as offers to parents a wooden "Rod of Correction" imprinted with scriptural verses.

Holocaust revisionism is a hot topic in many of these publications. Called "Holocaust deniers" by their Jewish and establishment foes, the authors and distributors of revisionist literature attempt to provide alternative and, the racialists insist, accurate versions of the "myth" of the Jewish Holocaust. For instance, over the past several decades, Americans have been bombarded with the horror stories of the Jewish experience during World War II. The stark and horrifying images of massive stacks of emaciated bodies—the zombie-like living skeletons draped in striped uniforms, peering from behind the barbed wire of Auschwitz, Bergen-Belsen, Sobibor, Dachau, Treblinka and other alleged "death" camps—have moved many Americans to pity for the Jew, hatred for the Aryan soldiers of the Third Reich. The official position of Aryan Nations and like organizations such as Canada's Heritage Front is that this is precisely the response such propaganda is intended to provoke.

Eustace Mullins's 1984 *The Secret Holocaust* (Aryan Truth Network) makes the claim that the Holocaust never happened and offers controversial evidence to support the allegations that the photos taken in the death camps—supposedly of "dead Jews"—were actually photos of dead Germans who were victims of the Jews. In fact, the claims offer no irrefutable supporting facts at all. Fred A. Leuchter is hailed—at least by racialists—as the world's foremost expert on gas chambers. His 1988 *The Leuchter Report* debunks claims of mass gassings at the so-called "death camps." This work offers equally questionable and hotly debated scientific proof that such events did not occur and could not have occurred at those sites, and is frequently taken to task by Jewish, Christian and other "establishment" and watchdog organizations such as the Nizkor project. Scholarly and historical merit notwithstanding, such works denouncing the Holocaust as myth and as a propaganda device of ZOG are widely accepted as fact among the racialist right.

Other widely read anti-Semitic publications include *Billions for the Bankers, Debts for the People* by Pastor Sheldon Emry (Aryan Truth Network, no print date); *The Bible: Handbook for Survivalists, Racists, Tax Protestors. Militants and Right-Wing Extremists,* as well as *The Real Hate Group,* both by Pastor Pete Peters of the LaPorte Church of Christ, LaPorte, Colorado (Scriptures for America Worldwide, no print dates); and the periodical *Liberty Bell,* (Liberty Bell Publications) which includes such contributors as William Pierce.

Pastor Van Herrell, a Christian Identity minister from Tennessee, has recently completed the *New Testament, Anointed Standard Translation* (Herrell Brothers Publishing House, 1995). This new translation is doing quite well among members of the movements. Identity believers maintain that this edition more clearly articulates the true message of Identity and Two-Seedline doctrine as found in the Scriptures.

But the late twentieth century was the age of instant access, the information super-highway, the international communications network—the Internet. This relatively new technology has provided the racialists with the means to spread their message and ZOG has no real means at present of controlling it. White nationalism has gone high tech and members and potential members can rally without ever meeting face to face. Anyone with a computer, telephone line and modem can join a discussion group and post a message with no editing or regulating. Transmission is global with virtually no time lag between messages and replies, and a cyber-rally of uncountable attendance can host a thousand-way conversation while each participant sits in his own living room a continent away from the others.

However, it must be noted that, particularly as an unregulated entity, the Internet is every bit as much a disinformation highway as it is an information highway. There are virtually no controls to prevent anyone with the time, talent and creativity from designing and disseminating any information, accurate or not, under the guise of fact, complete with bogus documentation. This is something which soon becomes apparent to any reasonable person who spends much time in cyberspace. Thus, if one searches for Christian Identity, it is quite possible to access sites such as Kingdom Identity Ministries or America's Promise Ministries, or other Identity sites which promote the message of white Israel—or the Nizkor Project, which denigrates it—or Southern Poverty Law Center's Klan-watch, which tracks it. It should come as no surprise to find that those on opposite sides of an issue level accusations of dishonesty and distortion of facts at the other, and these certainly do. The battle of words in cyberspace is a pitched, heated, and ongoing conflict.

But this medium of communication, along with shortwave radio broadcasts, is growing in popularity among the ''armchair militia members'' and ''closet revolutionaries'' who never go to meetings or weapons training but turn on the computer or radio to read or listen to extremist messages. Thus, a number of soldiers of the racialist right may very well prove to be loners who are not formally attached to any organization. This does not mean they may not prove in the long run to be quite dedicated. Nor does it mean they may not prove, in the long run, to be very dangerous indeed.

However, the medium with the most versatility is, of course, the computer screen, with its potential for text with varied font styles, eye-catching graphics and color, sound and, for those with the right equipment, chat mode and voice communication. But its uniqueness is the capacity for interaction between the message on the screen and the ability of the reader to reply immediately without fear of censorship. There is a sense of anonymity—essentially false, as a number of Americans are discovering—associated with the Internet. It is therefore not surprising that this is the favorite hangout of many ''cyber separatists,'' one that is growing rapidly. Anyone with the right equipment can run a computer bulletin board from his bedroom, and it takes no more equipment to log onto the Internet and send the message around the globe.

The information base made possible by Internet also serves to create a worldwide link through which organizations such as militia, Klans, skinheads, patriots and other groups are but a keystroke away. In addition, a user may click into mayhem manuals replete with bomb recipes, click again into white or black separatists selling their particular message of supremacy, click to an enrollment screen and add his name to the list of subscribers. This system also includes private and public e-mail, discussion forums, news groups, mailing lists, file transfers, and any number of other services on a worldwide net, many of which are proving quite useful to the white separatists.

Don Black, a former Klansman imprisoned for his role in a plot to launch an armed invasion of the Caribbean Island of Dominica in the early eighties (which garnered Black a three-year stint in jail), publishes an Internet *White Patriot's List,* for example, which is a seventeen-page smorgasbord of groups and information of interest to white separatists.

His list includes American Front, Aryan Nations, General Jack T. Mohr's Crusade for Christ and Country, Confederate Hammerskins, British Hammerskins, Christian Posse Comitatus, Northern (Canadian) Hammer Skins, David Duke (the allegedly former white supremacist), Pastor Robert Hallstrom's Gospel of the Kingdom, Mike Hallimore's Kingdom Identity Ministries, Dave Barker's America's Promise Ministries and other Identity congregations, and a detailed (but by no means complete) list of various Klans, neo-Odinist and other pre-Christian Aryan religious organizations.

Besides contact information, merchandise is also offered in Mr. Black's communication. One can browse through publishers of white nationalist books and literature as well as the racialist Oi music of such skinhead rockers as Bound for Glory, White Terror, Midtown Boot Boys, Nordic Thunder, Das Reich, Max Resist and the Hooligans, Aggravated Assault, Aryan, RaHoWa and, of course, *Skrewdriver:Live!* which is a perennial favorite. In this respect, communications services have created a ''yellow pages'' for the acolytes, neophytes and wannabes of the far right.

A vast array of topics and links dear to racialist hearts are packaged in colorful electronic periodicals such as *Stormfront, The New Order, National Alliance* and an ever-growing number of cyber magazines and alternative news sites. It would seem there is enough to satisfy the most eclectic of far-right tastes at any sitting.

Many of these publications, virulently racial and anti-government, are put together in sophisticated packages with remarkably beautiful graphics. And many of these Internet missives seem to promote violence and revolution. However, in order to avoid direct action on the part of the government and prosecution on sedition charges, language used by the revolutionary groups is studiously vague and circular.

Of course, those in the movements who surf the net are quite aware of the risks of sounding too seditious, just as they are quite aware that anyone with knowledge of the systems can access and monitor information thrown into the public domain. And as might be expected—by those on the racialist right, anyway—the lap-dog legislators of ZOG are scampering to pull the plug on these most unpolitically correct web sites. ZOG is also eager to use whatever information it can seize from such sites—as evidenced by a 1997 court order allowing the recovery of the private e-mail messages of the separatist Republic of Texas members. Such information, the racialists maintain, will be used to destroy individual dissidents and organizations. Thus, computer sharpies on the dissident side of Internet are indeed challenging ZOG to keep up with their latest toy/ploy to outwit censors, and government censors are pedaling ever harder to outwit the sharpies. Encrypting communications on the Internet would foil prying ZOG eyes, but it would also foil the movements' recruitment of new members, inasmuch as no one could read the documents onscreen. Screens full of gibberish—which is all that the public would see—would probably turn off users so that they would also miss the web sites not encrypted.

Louis Beam, in his Internet essay "The Conspiracy to Erect an Electronic Iron Curtain," published in *Stormfront,* speaks to the issue of government censorship of the Net and Jewish involvement in that effort. It is, he contends, ironic that groups such as the ADL who publicly tout diversity would be so intent on silencing voices which challenge mainstream positions and world views. He also states that it is odd that the same people who oppose firearms in the hands of honest citizens also fear information in the minds of the people and maintains that information bans "only affect people who desire to think for themselves." Beam notes that the truth "is anti-semitic" and the "government is erecting a police state." And he proudly asserts that if speaking truth and opposing tyranny fall within the realm of anti-Semitism and government opposition, "then I am both."

The ability to uncover personal data—birth, marriage, medical records, education, income, financial dealings, church affiliation, occupation, social and leisure activities, driving record, insurance information, credit card records and more—is a very real threat to all citizens. For a person with computer savvy, virtually any computerized record anywhere can be unearthed and stored for future use. In the right hands—or the wrong ones—this can be a powerful tool and an even more powerful weapon.

Of course, in addition to attempts to regulate white nationalist sites out of existence, there are organizations such as the Nizkor Project, the ADL, the Southern Poverty Law Center and other watchdog organizations which follow the activities of the racialists and are active in an information campaign of their own. Nizkor, for instance, devotes a good deal of its time and efforts in challenging the information offered at racialist sites, which are regularly monitored and discredited by such organizations. And the Southern Poverty Law Center, whose most prominent spokesman is Morris Dees, posts a complete list of racialist organizations, their leaders and activities and updates of ongoing court cases and events throughout the nation and the world.

Of course, talk radio is a popular medium and the success of conservative hosts such as Michael Reagan and Rush Limbaugh bear witness to the extent that the populist conservative formats are accepted. And Reagan and Limbaugh, along with G. Gordon Liddy and others, have been taken to task by more left-leaning members of the government for promoting "hatred and divisiveness" over AM airwaves. Still, these programs command a large audience share. And there are programs—some of which take an even sharper right to tiptoe along the network acceptability line—broadcast over such entities as the Eagle Radio Network where stringent Constitutionalists and more radical Libertarian voices are also acceptable.

But these individuals, no matter how hard-nosed they may be perceived by their listening audiences, are the watered-down Jewish-approved voices that Michael Hallimore refers to as Kosher Conservatives. "They are never going to come right out and say the races need separate territories," he says. "They will never honestly discuss the Jewish role in the destruction of our culture. They can't. They're part of it."

To circumvent the controls of ZOG, white nationalists and Identity Christians, who lay it all on the line as far as Hallimore and other members of the movements are concerned, have fallen back on the old technology of shortwave radio to spread the word of what they are about. Pastor Pete Peters broadcasts his "Scriptures for America" radio program four to five nights weekly on shortwave to reach white patriots with the message of Christian Israel. Dr. William Pierce, of National Alliance, broadcasts "American Dissident Voices" to reach white America with the truth of National Socialism and to blister the regime of Bill Clinton—and his toadies such as Janet Reno—with vituperative alternative views on national events. Militia spokesmen and supporters such as Mark (Mark from Michigan) Koernke take to the airwaves to preach the doctrines of training, preparedness and resistance—and to issue the call to arms. From Canada, Wolfgang Droege and the Heritage Front broadcasts its message across national lines into the United States and U.S. sources reciprocate. At the Branson Super Conference, Pastor Rick Strawcutter exhorts the faithful to consider setting up their own shortwave programs in their individual areas to create a seamless network of like-minded voices preaching the doctrine of Identity.

Television, however, is still the primary source of information for citizens of the United States. In the twenty-plus years that it has been available, cable television has offered a veritable cornucopia of input to the American public. There is something for every taste from pay-per-view pornography and sporting events, to the shopping network, to the ever-growing twenty-four-hour news channels such as CNN. Of course, the three major networks remain, and there are those such as WGN, TBS and FOX which are of the super network variety.

However, the differences between the various networks are superficial as far as the racialist right is concerned. As has been noted, the members of the movement feel that all such outlets are more or less ZOG establishment propaganda machines and are hardly worth noting as far as any subject of consequence is concerned. The same may be said of the various religious networks. Although conventional network programming falls short of the racialists' fairness mark, there is one television outlet that they feel has distinct possibilities: public access television.

Public access was created by legislation passed in the 1980s to ensure fairness in the expression of ideas and to provide alternative programming for the public. For the most part, public access is a wide-open forum with few restrictions regarding taste, subject matter, or other guidelines which rule network television. Of course, pornography—child or otherwise—or material presented in violation of state, federal or local law is prohibited, but, other than those exceptions, one can find almost anything on public access.

Darrell Flinn and his wife Anna Lynn of the White Kamellia Knights of Lafayette, Louisiana, are veterans of the network talk shows and video journal programs such as "Hard Copy." They are also the producers of the public access program "The Klan in Acadiana." The Flinns have certainly done their part to test the limits of public access through their format of panel discussions, call-in segments, alternative news reports, interviews with various guests and the occasional diversion of skits which by no means shy away from extremely dark humor.

In one segment, Flinn conducts a "scientific experiment" to explain the phenomenon of black church fires across the country. His tongue-in-cheek hypothesis is demonstrated with a block of wood and Jerri-Curl. Flinn hams it up as he explains his theory of the spontaneous combustion of wood products exposed to years of African American hair-care products. As the wooden block bursts into flame, Flinn smiles broadly into the camera.

Flinn maintains that such portrayals of blacks is no worse than the treatment whites receive nightly on network television.

"If someone tunes in and doesn't like what they see," he says, "they're more than welcome to change the channel or turn off the set. There's no law that I'm aware of that requires a person to watch television or any particular program."

Objectionable humor notwithstanding, the Flinns take their program quite seriously, and public and vehement conflicts with their detractors have made the couple rather high-profile in Lafayette. According to Flinn, guests, panel discussions, and the advancement of racialist ideas have led station management and local government to try to rein them in. Most recently, Flinn is involved in a legal entanglement in which he has been accused of violating local ordinances on air. The law in question is a state ''mask law'' dating back to the 1920s which is clearly aimed at the Klan. The law states that, with the exception of Mardi Gras and Halloween, it is illegal to wear a mask in public and was intended to prevent Klan members from gathering publicly under the cloak of anonymity.

The Flinns ran afoul of this ordinance in 1996 when they had three guests on a program who insisted on concealing their faces. As Flinn explains it, one of the guests, a local fireman, feared reprisals from his employers should they discover his particular political views. ''This isn't an outrageous fear or some kind of paranoia,'' Flinn explains. ''The man was afraid he'd have his ability and willingness to perform his job questioned, that there would be repercussions from his supervisors and co-workers—and there were. He was afraid he would lose his job and be held up to ridicule in the community. White people know this, if they're honest with themselves. If they say what they really believe, what's really on their minds, they're going to be crucified for it.''

And, Flinn maintains, the individual in question was found out and did indeed suffer the expected consequences of appearing on the program, although he was not fired from his job. But Flinn is also quick to point out the inequalities involved in making an issue of masks on the program. ''It's still a Klan law,'' he says. ''Selectively enforced.''

He argues that objectionable subject matter and beliefs are all over public access, including the black supremacist message of Nation of Islam. ''The Snake Pit,'' another program on the Lafayette station, according to Flinn's assessment, is at least equally offensive to the American public. Tax rebels, homosexuals, atheists—all are protected and granted both air time and favored status which white racialist organizations do not enjoy.

Flinn also speaks to more mainstream programs, talk shows and news reports which regularly conceal the identities of their guests to save the guests from retaliations, embarrassment, or negative consequences of their appearances. ''It's done both nationally and locally,'' Flinn says. ''How often do you see any host of any program charged with a crime for something like this? I don't wear a mask, Anna doesn't wear a mask, but if we want to take precautions to protect our guests, then we're criminals. In my mind, it's clearly discriminatory.''

At the time of this writing, the Flinns are awaiting the decision of city government on whether or not the charge is going to be pursued any further. Flinn does not think it will be. ''All we have to do is be good and all will be forgiven,'' he says. ''Until we say or do something else to rattle their cages.''

Flinn, as well as other racialists, maintains that as the establishment moves to silence them and regulate them out of existence, the movements will continue to find alternative methods to spread the word. The struggle for hearts and minds will continue.

But the struggle, for the true believer, is also for souls. The message of Identity is the Word of God. In their eyes, no attempts on the part of ZOG will ever silence that word as it is spread to the elect. The alternate voices of the racialist right will continue to challenge the Satanic policies of government, expose the conspiracies of ZOG, proclaim the establishment of the New Kingdom, seek out the lost sheep of True Israel, White Israel, and speak to the coming of Yashua, Yahweh of Hosts.

# CHAPTER NINETEEN

# The Dogs of War: Leaderless Resistance and the New Revolutionaries

> And Caesar's spirit, ranging for revenge,
> With Ate by his side come hot from hell,
> Shall in these confines with a monarch's voice
> Cry 'Havoc' and let slip the dogs of war; . . .
> Shakespeare, *Julius Caesar*

What was Timothy McVeigh thinking?
The surprisingly speedy trial and conviction of the key Oklahoma City bomber did not answer this question to the satisfaction of many Americans. And, for many if not most of us, it is a question that nags our consciousness like a willful child demanding attention. McVeigh, it seems, was an angry man. He was angry about Ruby Ridge. He was angry about Waco. He did not like what he saw happening in the United States. He was unhappy about the direction in which his country was going. He felt oppressed and abused by the government and felt he personally had to do something.

And indeed he did do something.

In 1978 William Pierce wrote the fictional *The Turner Diaries* in which a federal building was bombed. In 1995 after reading the book, Timothy McVeigh did just that, in the process killing 168 innocent Americans, which, according to the racialists, was unfortunate but unavoidable in wartime. Like the fictional Earl Turner, one angry man defied the Evil Empire, ZOG, the Synagogue of Satan. By choosing the anniversary of the Waco disaster to create a new disaster in Oklahoma City, McVeigh established a new symbol for the militant right to bear as a standard into the continuing battle.

Before April 19, 1995, it was David Koresh who was for many in the movements the symbol of resistance to government oppression. Certainly, he was a symbol of righteous resistance for McVeigh. Why did this man, David (Vernon Dean Howell) Koresh, who was not Identity or even overtly militant, so capture the minds of the militant right? Defending his beliefs with his life, David Koresh and the Branch Davidians not only defied the United States government, they forced the government to reveal to the world its ineptitude, its disregard for human life, its arrogance, its duplicity. David Koresh, as far as his supporters in the movements are concerned, tore the mask from the pretender government. David Koresh exposed the face of ZOG.

White Christian patriots consider their battle plan reciprocal, since they intend to defend the nation as strongly as the Evil Empire is plotting to destroy it. Taking up the Davidian mantle of resistance, including the knowledge that innocents must be sacrificed, men like Timothy McVeigh add their name to the list of patriot martyrs.

Many throughout history have resorted to similar violent measures to rouse their countrymen to action, a course not all historians agree is the most effective means. Timothy McVeigh is not the first, nor will he be the last, to turn to violence in order to create change.

Truman R. Clark, a professor of history at Tomball College near Houston, claims that if these men had studied history, they would have known their acts would not start a revolution. In his 8 June 1997 *Houston Chronicle* article ''McVeigh, Other Would-Be Revolutionaries Ignored History,'' Clark cites other incidents such as the 1920 Wall Street bombing against the capitalist bankers and the 1910 Los Angeles Times bombing against the virulently anti-union publisher Harrison Gray Otis, the murders committed by Charlie Manson and the bank robberies of the Symbionese Liberation Army led by Donald ''Cinque'' DeFreeze, all abortive attempts to start a revolution. If the bombers had known their history, Clark says, they would have known their violent acts wouldn't accomplish anything or motivate anyone.

Many Americans will readily agree with Clark, others just as surely will not. Many will voice no public opinion. They will speak of nothing controversial, join no revolutionary organizations. They will pay their taxes and express no overt anger at government policies. Instead, they will quietly sit at home reading *The Turner Diaries* and vitriolic anti-government essays on the *Stormfront* web site, study the Bible and listen to White Power messages on shortwave radio. Some will act on their own to fulfill the predictions made by others, more violence will be in the news, and again the search will be on. But in the ranks of the leaderless resistance, there are no organizations to identify, no chains of command, no leaders to blame.

McVeigh, it was argued by the prosecution, was steeped in conspiracy theory and the radical thinking of the far right. McVeigh, the prosecution contended, was guilty of 168 counts of premeditated murder through which he hoped to start a revolution. And in the judgment of most Americans, McVeigh was guilty of murder, although unsuccessful in this attempt to provoke armed revolt. Still, the detonation of the explosive device and the devastating consequences are now stamped upon the contemporary American mind with indelible ink. Though we Americans may, as is our national wont, put it behind us and move forward, we as a nation will not forget the heretofore most savage and destructive expression of civil and political dissatisfaction ever perpetrated by one alienated individual within our borders. And, of course, it is quite tempting to take comfort in the knowledge that McVeigh was simply one alienated individual.

Comforting, but not true.

"As far as I'm concerned," says Cadillac John, "Oklahoma City is just another example of the leaderless resistance. I don't feel bad about what happened in Oklahoma. It was bound to happen and it's going to happen again and again. Americans are getting fed up and, once they do, they don't need anybody to tell them what to do."

Cadillac John, like many on the racialist right, disagrees with the government's position that McVeigh, in addition to seeking revenge for Waco and Ruby Ridge, hoped to start a revolution. In fact, many maintain that a revolution is already under way and has been for some time. Timothy McVeigh, in their eyes, is but one of many soldiers, nameless and faceless for the most part, who are fighting and will continue to fight the war against ZOG, against One-World Government, against the Evil Empire. Such nameless and faceless warriors are the soldiers of the Leaderless

Resistance. And, as one member of the movements notes, "There are thousands of Timothy McVeighs out there."

Of course, as previously noted, not all revolutionaries are bombers and out for blood. Not all seek warfare in the streets or an armed overthrow of the existing system. However, this does not mean that non-violent organizations may not employ some of the tactics of leaderless resistance or that they are not dedicated to their particular cause. Such is certainly not the case. Posse Comitatus and the Montana Freemen, although both express a willingness to use violent force when push comes to shove, have resisted the might of government by challenging the government's right to enforce certain laws and standards on individual citizens. Both organizations have, for instance, formed citizen courts as alternatives to the present judicial system. Both have issued warrants for federal, local and state officials, both recognize no higher legislative power than county government, both tie up the courts with liens and lawsuits and often work within established frameworks such as the legal system, alternative media, and other areas to give the government a fit under its own rules.

Some of these revolutionary tactics may best be described as harassment tactics through which the system is challenged in such a manner that it must confront itself. For instance, the Constitutionalists pore over legal documents, laws, legislation and countless volumes of case studies, comb government policy, tie up the courts, overturn decisions and basically make the agents of ZOG either eat their own words or effect positive changes.

The Republic of Texas, for instance, a non-racialist separatist group claims that Texas was brought into the Union illegally, that there was no proper annexation of the sovereign territory. And, since Texas was illegally annexed, federal law does not apply in the state, which is in reality still a sovereign territory although occupied by a foreign and illegal government. A former Deputy Harris County Attorney who has investigated Republic of Texas notes, "Like it or not, they raise some valid Constitutional issues." Members of ROT issue their own identification, refuse to pay taxes, refuse to carry a DPS driver's license, issue their own license plates and have embarked on a campaign of filing lawsuits against state, local and federal government agencies, issuing challenges and depositions to government officials, and filing property liens which have snarled the courts in a most significant manner. Former State Attorney

General Dan Morales went public with his intent to vigorously prosecute those whom he accuses of filing "frivolous" claims and suits against the state with the intention of creating problems for the court system and government.

One member of the Republic of Texas finds this amusing. "Yeah, right," he says laughing. "You know why Dan Morales won't do anything about any of this? He *can't* do anything about it. Unless of course, they want to pass fair laws, tear down this sewer of a legal system we have and replace it with a system beneficial to the welfare and well-being of the citizens. It's their system. No one is doing anything at all illegal."

In the long run, such organizations may have a more realistic chance of creating changes within the system than do the armed revolutionaries of the leaderless resistance. However, the odds regarding success do little to inhibit the zeal of the warrior activists of the racialist right.

Timothy McVeigh, purportedly a student of the *The Turner Diaries* and other racialist literature, apparently understood the concept of leaderless resistance well. Leaderless resistance is exactly what one might imagine— that is, if one imagines small, armed, militant groups, independent of each other, autonomous, but all fighting for the same cause. The concept of leaderless resistance as practiced by the supremacist movements can be credited, according to Louis Beam, to the late Col. Ulius Louis Amoss, a former Naval intelligence officer, although there is scriptural basis for such resistance as well. In Beam's article titled "Leaderless Resistance" in the final issue of his publication *The Seditionist* (Issue 12, February 1992), he notes that Amoss was the first to write on the theories of this type of "cell" organization for groups he felt would be resisting a Communist takeover of the United States.

Leaderless resistance is an alternative organizational structure which lends itself to independent revolutionary action apart from any central control. Beam notes that in conventional power structures, there is pyramidal hierarchy, in effect, a pecking order or chain of command "diagrammatically represented with the mass at the bottom and the leader at the top." This structure is also seen in organizations such as the Ku Klux Klan and militia groups modeled after military organizations. Once such organizations are identified by agents of the federal government, the pyramid structure or chain of command is worse than useless. In fact, it is a positive detriment to any revolutionary function at all:

In the pyramid type of organization, an infiltrator can destroy anything which is beneath his level of infiltration and often those above him as well. If the traitor has infiltrated at the top, then the entire organization from top down is compromised and may be traduced at will.

Both Beam and Charles Lee are familiar with this type of infiltration. "The feds decided a long time ago that one of the best ways to bring down an organization is not only to infiltrate it, but to place agents in position of leadership," Lee notes. "In more than twenty years with the Klan, I've seen more than one betrayal . . . and, even though I know it's possible and even likely, it's something you never really get used to. I expect traitors, but it's still painful. These people are turning against their own kind."

It is undoubtedly true that compromised Klansmen have provided a great deal of information to the federal agencies whose task it is to monitor them. And, of course, the Klan and other organizations have indeed experienced their share of federal infiltrators. The history of this type of infiltration, although reasonably justified in the eyes of both law enforcement agencies and the public at large, is ostensibly to gather information on revolutionary groups or others who might pose a threat to the peace and security of the nation. But there are many in the movements who believe that these agents, finding no revolutionary or illegal activities among their target organizations, are certainly not above creating situations which can be used to destroy the groups they have infiltrated.

Carl Haggard, Commanding General of the United States Special Field Forces Militia, tells anyone who will listen that the militia movement is not about white supremacy nor is it about revolution. However, he also notes that more often than not, the government takes an adversarial position toward the militia and, in effect, acts toward them as if they were a hostile force rather than honest patriotic citizens. To this end, government infiltrators invade legitimate militia groups with the intention of destroying them and, once inside, act accordingly. Haggard constantly urges members of such groups to be aware of this destructive practice and to avoid attempts on the part of the government agents and others, including racialists, who would compromise the integrity of the militia organizations.

But there are any number of groups in America today which are undoubtedly revolutionary, and some militia groups are included among them. Some, like Aryan Nations, have overtly declared their "state of war" with the powers that be and have a stated agenda of a separate homeland.

Others, such as the now-defunct The Order and National Alliance have an agenda which includes the dismantling or overthrow of the present government. However, it is an extremely formidable task to carry on a guerrilla war against such a resourceful foe as the federal government when the front-line forces of the resistance are centrally organized in a chain of command that follows the pyramid structure.

This organizational problem was experienced by West Virginia's Mountaineer Militia. Seven members of the Mountaineers, led by Floyd Ray Looker, were arrested in October 1996 in connection with an alleged plot to bomb the FBI's National Information Center building, a repository for fingerprint files. FBI sources confirmed that they had been monitoring the group from the inside for quite some time and acted when they did because they were aware of the group's plan to transport a large amount of explosives across state lines. The decision to make arrests was made in large part because federal agents feared losing track of the explosives and placing the public at risk.

The pervasiveness of federal access to resistance organizations is a reality.

As far as Beam is concerned, any resistance organization which has centralized leadership and a hierarchical chain of command (such as a militia) is vulnerable to compromise through infiltration. He contends that federal resources are such that once they identify any organization or any individual as a threat, the days of that organization or individual are numbered. However, in established resistance groups where organization is extant, the government has a vested interest in keeping all its revolutionary "eggs" in one basket. And as long as all the eggs are in one basket, or in a limited number of baskets, they are much easier to account for.

"If I had it all to do over again," Charles Lee states, "I probably would not go public. Don't get me wrong, I don't regret joining the Klan and I certainly don't regret standing up for what I believe in. But it's been pretty tough at times. Sometimes I don't remember what it's like to not have someone breathing down my neck and watching my every move."

The members of the movements do note that leaders such as Charles Lee and long-time members of groups such as the Klan or Aryan Nations have gained a notoriety in law enforcement circles that precludes a normal life and inhibits any "terroristic" activism in which they might otherwise engage.

"I do not advocate lawlessness," Lee notes. "I do not encourage people to threaten, kill, bomb or any of the other things I've been accused of. Like that Dan Morales thing. But—even if I wanted to—I couldn't. I'm too high-profile. It's absolutely suicidal for any racialist who's been identified by the government to consider, much less act upon an impulse like that.''

Lee contends, as do most of our subjects, that the downfall of many white Christian patriots has come about because those individuals do or say something to attract attention to themselves. Gordon Kahl, for instance, made the mistake of recruiting for Posse Comitatus and appearing on television urging taxpayers to stop paying taxes and resign from the government. In addition to becoming high-profile, many make the mistake of trusting too easily. The small cells of the leaderless resistance scheme of organization address both of these problems.

Anonymity is the shield and first line of defense for such small revolutionary cells. There is no high profile inasmuch as there is no public recruiting. There are no rallies, conventions, gatherings or outspoken leaders. Where such a system is extant, law enforcement often has an extremely difficult time determining a starting point for any investigation. The racialists maintain that the best and most effective tool such agencies have to use against them is the inside informant. In the small cells of the leaderless resistance, where recruitment is done very carefully and selectively by those who compose the cells, such risk of infiltration is kept to a minimum. Even where there is successful infiltration of a cell, only this small unit of resistance is compromised and not the movement as a whole.

If one follows this line of reasoning, then it makes sense that, as Beam observes, the last thing those who monitor and compromise the activities of revolutionary groups would like to see is a ''thousand different small phantom cells opposing them.'' And, if this is the last thing the government wants, the forces of the racial right are anxious to make sure that such resistance is the first thing the government gets. Thus, the leaderless resistance, consisting of small cells of one to seven individuals with no centralized leadership, already recognizes the enemy—the government, ZOG, the players in the One-World conspiracy. And it is the contention of those on the racial right that once the enemy is identified, then no other instruction is needed.

Richard Hoskins, in *Vigilantes of Christendom,* uses Bob Mathews's group as an example of both the strengths and the weaknesses of the cell and its leaders to explain leaderless resistance. Hoskins notes that Mathews recruited a small group of men into the organization he called the Bruders Schweigen (Silent Brotherhood). Bound by a sacred oath and modeled after "the Order," a fictional leaderless resistance cell from William Pierce's *The Turner Diaries,* Bob Mathews's revolutionary force met with immediate and surprising success.

The Order's war against the government included printing and passing counterfeit money to compromise the economy, forging identification documents, purchasing arms and land for arms training, robbing banks and armored cars to finance the revolution and distributing these funds to racialist organizations across the country, killing the Jewish talk show host and blasphemer Allan Berg, and other much-publicized activities which marked their brief albeit notorious career. The salient issue, however, is just how silent was the Silent Brotherhood? The small cell—nine in all—were silent indeed, and very effective, although they exceeded what is considered the maximum appropriate number of seven. Law enforcement officials in the Pacific Northwest were left scratching their heads with no idea where to even begin investigating the wraith-like group of revolutionaries which appeared, acted and disappeared again without leaving as much as a footprint.

But, as Hoskins notes, Mathews's fatal flaw came when he "confused numbers with might." As long as Mathews and company were a small cell, they were virtually invulnerable. But Mathews began to recruit. He brought more members on board than he could effectively handle and, as is often the case in such situations, one of them—Tom Martinez—was a Judas.

And because Mathews brought the Judas on board, the organization was compromised. Mathews, thirty-one at the time of his death, paid the ultimate price for failing to follow his own game plan. But Mathews was not the only one brought down by his indiscretion. By the time the trials were over, member Bruce Pierce was sentenced to 250 years in federal prison, Randy Duey 100 years, David Lane 190 years. Did the punishment fit the crimes? Not as far as the members of the movements are concerned. The Order members who did not remain silent, who cooperated with the government and testified against their former comrades, received much lighter sentences and have all been released from prison. The prisoners still languishing in the "federal gulags," considered by the movements to be prisoners of war, are those who kept the blood oath of silence.

Had Mathews elected not to expand, had he elected to distribute funds anonymously, to keep things close to the vest, many in the movements believe he would be alive today. But, as both Hoskins and Lee note, hindsight is twenty-twenty. Hoskins does point out in his book that nothing is in vain when Aryan Christians seize opportunities to grow and learn. Thus, The Order is not just an example of the impact that a small group of dedicated individuals can have in furthering the agenda of the racialist right, but it also serves as illustration of pitfalls to be avoided by the new wave of Christian revolutionaries who will undoubtedly follow in their footsteps. And already there are such organizations active in the country today.

In a two-part CBS Evening News, "Eye on America" interview, October 14 and 15, 1996, Dan Rather spoke with Walter Theode (or Thody), a member of the group calling themselves the Phineas Priesthood. Theode is presently serving a 39-year sentence for two armed robberies he committed to finance the activities of another branch of the Phineas Priesthood. The organization, in keeping with the philosophy of leaderless resistance of which it is a part, is an organization only in the loosest sense. When Rather asked how many members the Phineas Priesthood has, Theode hypothesized in regard to the size of the total organization, "I'd say there are probably no more than two hundred." And that this small membership is scattered in independent cells. "The Phineas Priesthood," Theode said, "is not and never has been, a centralized organization."

Rather responded, "And that makes it hard for law enforcement to deal with?"

"Very definitely."

Theode spoke of the deaths in the Oklahoma City bombing as "killings" rather than murder. He noted the difference as "The only thing that would make it murder is if you don't consider it a war." And, for the separatists of the racialist right, it is most definitely a war.

It is important to note that Theode's organization, the Phineas Priesthood, although it takes its name from the story of Phinehas and the race mixers Zimri and Cozbi in the book of Numbers, does not define the concept of the modern Phineas priest. A Phineas priest is defined by actions which are based on a zeal for God, and the priest is then considered an enforcer of God's Law. Inclusion in the Priesthood of Phineas—the scriptural priesthood, not the revolutionary group—does not require a particular political belief or theological training, nor does it require membership in any particular church or organization. It does require a knowledge of the Word and the Law of God. It does require being moved by the Holy Spirit, by Yahweh. And it requires action. As God announced when Phinehas used his javelin:

> Phinehas the son of Eleazar, the son Aaron the priest, has turned back My wrath from the children of Israel, because he was zealous with My zeal among them, so that I did not consume the children of Israel in My zeal. (NUMBERS 25:11)

Thus, if men such as Timothy McVeigh and Terry Nichols, neither of whom have claimed Identity beliefs, were moved to outrage by a realization of the evil inherent in the government, and if this outrage led to violent action, righteous and justifiable by scriptural criteria, then they have participated in the *function* of Phineas priests. This is true even if they were unaware of the Spirit and how it moved them. Their works, more than any ideology, training, or ceremony, have identified them. Some in the movements would venture to state they have claimed the mantle of the priesthood in the past. But, as Richard Hoskins notes in *Vigilantes of Christendom,* those who consciously enforce God's Law in defiance of man's law are the *true* inheritors of the title Phineas priest. And the Phineas Priesthood ties in very nicely with the concept of leaderless resistance which also is described by the Scriptures.

In the book of Ezekiel the prophet experiences a vision. Yahweh opens the eyes of Ezekiel to the abominations and iniquities perpetrated by the children of Israel who have turned from the Word, from the Law, and have allowed "strangers" (non-whites/non-Christians) to live among them and intermarry, have yielded to un-Godly government, and are engaging in widespread acts of blasphemy and self-destruction:

> Then He said to me, "have you seen this, O son of man? Is it a trivial thing to the house of Judah to commit the abominations which they commit here? For they have filled the land with violence; then they have returned to provoke Me to anger. Indeed they put the branch to their nose.
>
> Therefore I also will act in fury. My eye will not spare nor will I have pity; and though they cry in my ears with a loud voice, I will not hear them." (EZEKIEL 8:17–18)

The widespread abominations described in the passage are certainly likened to the United States of today for the faithful of the Church Militant.

And, as Yahweh has revealed to the prophet the problems in the land of the Israelites, He also describes the solution:

> Then He called out in my hearing . . . "Let those who have charge over the city draw near, each with a deadly weapon in his hand." And . . . six men came . . . One man among them . . . had a writer's inkhorn at his side . . . They went in and stood beside the bronze altar.  (EZEKIEL 9:1-2)

According to Hoskins, the Book of Ezekiel describes the perfect number for the enforcement of God's law—seven. And among the six men who constitute the cell is the scribe who identifies the enemies of the Lord and marks the faithful. The seventh member, always present among the faithful, is Yahweh of Hosts ever guiding the group in its divine purpose. The purpose is clearly defined in the following passage:

> To the others He said in my hearing, "Go after him [the scribe] through the city and kill; do not let your eye spare, nor have any pity.

> Utterly slay old and young men, maidens and little children and women; but do not come near anyone on whom is the mark [made by the scribe to identify the faithful]; and begin at My sanctuary. So they began with the elders who were before the temple."

> Then He said to them, "Defile the temple, and fill the courts with the slain. Go out!" And they went out and killed in the city.  (EZEKIEL 9:1-7)

Thus, the methods and the motivations of the priests of Phineas are often in complete alignment with the mission of the leaderless resistance. Hoskins claims that the Phineas priests have always been among Aryan Israel and have always risen to enforce God's Law among those who would flaunt it. Their commitment to the Word is absolute: God's Law prescribes death for race mixers, Phineas priests put them to death. God's Law prescribes death for usury, Phineas priests execute usurers. God's Law prescribes death for blasphemers, Phineas priests destroy those who blaspheme. God's Law prescribes death for homosexuals, Phineas priests carry out the sentence. This is the Law as commanded by the Scriptures.

It is a widespread belief among the movements that many of the ills of the world result from failure to enforce scriptural law. Such failures are serious affronts to Yahweh and usually result in catastrophe for White Israel. Allowing in the "stranger" has resulted in oppressive and tyrannical government as freedoms and property are lost to the money-lenders. Strangers have visited White Israel with plague. The children of God have adopted the ways of the stranger and turned from Yahweh. Crime is rampant. Social upheaval is rampant. The only hope for the future is knowledge of the Law and willingness to enforce it.

But not all White Israel people accept Phineas priests as God's appointed enforcers, or even acknowledge their scriptural legitimacy. The Phineas Priesthood falls only within the militant Seedline faction of Identity, a two-tiered concept that inspires controversy on both levels. Regarding the Phineas Priesthood, one non-Seedline minister cites the same verses from Numbers 25 as proof that God was only commending Phineas as worthy of a place in history, not authorizing a gang of "Phineas hoods." These so-called Phineas priests, the minister says, are no more than self-appointed hoodlums who clothe their lawlessness in mistranslated or misunderstood scriptures.

Hoskins notes that adherence to scriptural principles and the knowledge of the Laws of God are key elements which those in the movements cannot afford to overlook. To do so is to court disaster. This, he maintains is another reason The Order was doomed to failure. Bob Mathews was an Odinist, not a Christian. He did not fully understand the risks involved in working with individuals who were not dedicated Christians, who did not put the Word first.

In *Vigilantes of Christendom,* Hoskins includes communications from both Bruce Pierce and Richard Scutari, two imprisoned Order members to make his point. Hoskins describes how he wrote to Bruce Pierce and inquired what Pierce would do differently if he could. Pierce responded that he had come to the conclusion that "working with others is a sure sign of eventual failure." He also was unequivocal in stating that under no circumstances would he ever again cast his lot with non-Christians. Pierce is quoted in Hoskins's work as stating, "Not only would they have to be Christians, but they would have to Identify with God's Law and believe the Law-commands of God, and their life would have to manifest those beliefs."

Along the same lines, Richard Scutari responds to Hoskins's question "Would you do it again?" Scutari, too, is unequivocal in his response. "In a heartbeat! But without the stupid mistakes. I have dedicated my life to God's Laws, the meat of the Word. The motivating forces come from Laws, the meat of the Word." This, too, is the mark of a true priest of Phineas—one who knows the Word, and the Word Made Flesh and who listens to the voice of God within him—one who hears the voice and follows—with zeal. Scutari further states, "The motivating forces come from deep within my soul and I would not be much of a man if I did not act on what every fiber in my body tells me is right."

Thus, for many members of the movement, the call to Phineas priesthood is more conscription than volunteerism. It is being touched by God Himself. As Mike Hallimore notes, Phineas priests are moved by the Holy Spirit. One who executes race-mixers simply because he does not like race mixing, for instance, is not functioning as a priest of Phineas. However, one who is zealous to fulfill the commandments of God—like Phinehas of the Book of Numbers who, filled with the Holy Spirit and righteous anger, takes up the javelin and enforces the will of the Creator—this is a true Phineas priest.

Hoskins and others have observed that throughout American history, our society, based on Christian principles, has been not only intolerant of un-Christian activities, always perceived as abominations, but absolutely hostile toward them. Only in modern times have the American people rolled over to creditors who enslave not only the individual, but the nation. Only in recent years have we been willing to tolerate the intermarriages with "strangers" which are common today. Only in the past few decades have Americans stood for the slander of the Church and Christianity itself by blasphemers who wish to deny the true religion, who wish to separate the state from its divine basis. To engage in such abominations—forbidden by Yahweh—was to become lawless. To support such activities was to become a renegade. And to engage in lawlessness, to become a renegade was to die.

Hoskins maintains that this was because in former times white Christians, inwardly seething with righteous rage, would arise to enforce the Laws of God. Open homosexuals would simply disappear. Mixed-race couples would be found dead. Banks would be robbed and the wealth redistributed. Renegades, those who were "of the blood" yet violated the Law, who turned against their own people in their lawlessness, who adopted the ways of the stranger, were forced to pay very careful attention to what they did and said because they knew their days were numbered. This was the influence of the Phineas Priesthood.

Such zealots, whether they are in the phantom cells of the leaderless resistance or acting alone, are certainly a force to be reckoned with and undoubtedly a thorn in the side of the agents of ZOG. But they mostly pose a threat to anyone who violates the Laws of Yahweh, who has the temerity to insult the true God of the world, who blasphemes against Him or the faith.

Hoskins makes the observation that, even today, a renegade gives careful attention to a speaker who complains of a violation of God's Law. ''The renegade is never sure,'' he says, ''whether the one speaking is a harmless malcontent or a priest. The difference is the difference between life and death.''

# CHAPTER TWENTY

# Signs of the Times: The Future of America

And they [the disciples] asked him, saying, Master, but when shall these things be: and what sign will there be when these things shall come to pass?

And he [Jesus] said . . . the time draweth near . . . ye shall hear of wars and rumours of wars. . . . nation shall rise against nation, and kingdom against kingdom: And great earthquakes shall be in diverse places and famines, and pestilences: and fearful sights and great signs shall there be from heaven. . . . And there shall be signs in the sun, and in the moon, and in the stars: and upon the earth distress of nations, with perplexity: the sea and the waves roaring. . . . And when these things begin to come to pass, then look up, and lift up your heads; for your redemption draweth nigh. (LUKE 21:7–11, 25, 28)

In the last years of the twentieth century, true believers saw a record number of fearful sights and great signs—comets both familiar and newly discovered, new stars, new galaxies, old theories shattered. Man's footprints on the moon. Wheel tracks on Mars. Sunspots powerful enough to disrupt electrical circuits on the earth. Wars and rumors of wars, pictures of starving children and emaciated bodies. Diseases virulent and resistant to antibiotics. Flesh-eating viruses and radioactive wastelands. Global warming. Weather disturbances unseasonable and unpredicted, anomalies in the records of the National Weather Service. High Richter-scale earthquakes. Unprecedented clusters of tornados and forest fires, of monsoons and floods, of hurricanes and tsunamis, unaccustomed high levels of snowfall and rainfall—or the opposite—of entire countries laid waste by drought and famine.

Major environmental changes, global in nature and scope, are signs of the end times, the return of Christ. The apocalyptic interpretation of such phenomena, particularly for the Identity Christian, reveals the presence of other signs of the end times—the presence of false prophets, the agents of the anti-Christ. It is not surprising to many Americans, even those who are not Identity, that the federal government slants facts and falsifies reports. But it is somewhat surprising to consider weather reports significant in this arena.

"There's actually not much global warming, not nearly as catastrophic as the reports indicate," says a prominent meteorologist who has worked with the National Weather Service for decades. "Global temperature is half a degree or so warmer, but it hasn't been proved that man is responsible for that.

"I don't think the weather is worse than it used to be. We have about a hundred years of good records. There were some pretty devastating hurricanes in the late 1800s where thousands of lives were lost and, of course, the 1900 storm in Galveston where 6000 people were killed. Actually, the last twenty to thirty years, as far as hurricanes go, we've been in a fairly quiet period.

"It's the government that collects the data. Weather satellites, buoys and such. It was in 1988 that a NASA researcher, based on his numerical model, reported an increase in global warming. Environmentalists jumped at it, applying for government grants to do more research."

We ask why the weather should be represented as more ominous than it actually is. "Political, economic, and religious agenda, maybe," he says. "To foster world unity. You have to scare people on a global issue, something common to all of them, to get them to cooperate. People don't get together if they aren't scared of something." One-World government? we ask. "World *unity,*" he answers, then adds, "Have you heard of Gary Allen's book *None Dare Call it Conspiracy?*"

We had. Only a couple of weeks earlier, as we sat with two Klansmen at a diner in South Houston, one of them pulled out a dog-eared, yellowed paperback and laid it on the table. "You need to read this," he told us. We leafed through it, a 1971 edition of *None Dare Call it Conspiracy* that had seen some heavy service.

The book is on the reading list of many in the movements, but they *do* dare call it conspiracy because that is exactly what they see. When the U.S. government reports that all nations must unite under one governmental umbrella or face global extinction, as far as the movements are concerned it is another indication that one-worlders are using any means at hand, including weather reports, to accomplish their goal.

"It's all because of [the] United Nations," says Cadillac John, "the New World Order. You know [the] United Nations has that thing out in front, that they'll beat swords into plowshares? Well, they can't. In Psalm 127 it says except the Lord build the house, they that build it labor in vain.

"It's all there in the Bible, what'll happen when God's people disobey His commandments. In Micah, Chapter 5, God tells them that He'll throw down the seagates against their enemies. He'll break their pride and power. He'll throw down their war horses and His people will be overcome.

"You think it isn't happening? Read the papers. Our war horses are being thrown down every day. Airplanes and helicopters all over the world have been falling out of the skies, engines quitting, planes catching on fire, pilots making stupid errors and screwing themselves and their whole damn cargo into the ground.

"The seagates against our enemies, we're losing those, too. The Subic Bay and the Philippines—we've lost those. The Suez Canal was given up a long time before that, and now we're losing the Panama Canal. But not because we're losing them in battle. We're *giving* them away. As far as I'm concerned, Jimmy Carter and Bill Clinton are guilty of the highest treason against this government of anybody I've ever seen. Look at Clinton. Foreign policy lays in ruins while he commits adultery in the Oval Office, and he's worrying about a legacy. He left one, all right. This kind of leadership has got to stop. The only way it's going to stop is when people wake up and see what's going on."

Does not prophecy describe the conditions that herald the end times? To this, the faithful say amen. And they are equally clear that the prophecies also predict false prophets, false teachers who will intentionally misinterpret these signs in order to mislead the children of God. All perverting the Scriptures. All intending to bring about the reign of the Beast. All strangers and renegades bent on destroying White Israel. All harbingers of the end times. Omens, ever a part of the Christian faith, are also found in the heavens and are equally open to misinterpretation by such false prophets.

"I've been upset for years by those who claim to be prophets," says Covenant pastor George Southwick in a January 2000 sermon entitled "America: Prophets and Judgment." "The Bible is both prophecy and history. I'm amazed at the lack of understanding of preachers and people who claim great visitations of God and prophesy the most dreadful things to come upon America. The movement from 1999 to the year 2000 was a watermark, a time when people claimed the worst, and what happened? Nothing. I know a preacher that absolutely believed that Jesus was coming in 1984 and wrote a book about it. It didn't happen. And yet he goes right on with all his prognostications, with his fumblings of scriptures, and people believe it."

"As for prophecies," Mike Hallimore says, "I generally avoid the topic because I have seen so many false prophecies and predictions made over the years. . . . No one knows the exact method by which a prophecy will be fulfilled until after it has taken place. We are told that no man knows the day nor hour of His return, yet we do know that we are living in the last days."

Pastor Pete Peters' two-part sermon entitled "Signs of the Times" at the 1997 Branson conference examines the significance of heavenly phenomena such as UFOs and the comet Hale-Bopp. He contends that people are fascinated by UFOs and speaks to the phenomenon. Peters also confesses that at one point, he himself was fascinated by UFOs and bought every book he could find on the subject. He also notes that, once he found Christ, he threw them all out. Yet Peters does view UFOism as prophetic, an omen that describes for the faithful the shaky spiritual ground on which many white Christians tread.

Identity Christians do not believe in the Rapture, the mass migration of the faithful to heaven before the tribulation. Nor do they believe—as the Heaven's Gate cult did—that there will be extraterrestrial involvement in spiritual matters such as a mass migration of souls on a spaceship following the tail of a comet. Peters does, however, see similarities between Heaven's Gate and most Judeo-Christian churches today—both of whom tolerate corruption—and he ties both to the end times.

The thirty-nine members of Heaven's Gate, according to Peters, were not only castrated physically but spiritually as well. When the comet appeared in 1997, they saw it as a sign from heaven to kill themselves, free their souls from their bodies and board a spacecraft they believed followed the comet. Peters expresses sympathetic feelings for the Heaven's Gate members who were so egregiously misled by their false prophet.

Dr. Phillip Arnold of Houston's Reunion Institute is a scholar of first-century apocalyptic Christian theology, ancient religious groups that believed in Jesus as Messiah but continued to obey Old Testament laws. In Rice University's Winter 1997 issue of *Sallyport,* author David Medina's article ''Doctor of Doctrines'' examines Arnold's practical application of his knowledge to modern alternate religious groups out of the mainstream. In part, this includes David Koresh and his followers. The violent outcome at Waco could have been avoided, Arnold feels, if the FBI had only tried to understand the religious beliefs of the Branch Davidians and their interpretation of biblical signs.

In early 1993, Medina reports that Arnold was stunned by TV reports about Waco, the symbolism of ''a thirty-three-year-old carpenter, an illegitimate son who was claiming to be the Messiah,'' whose apocalyptic visions were of the seven seals mentioned in the Book of Revelation. In Revelation, an angel offers a sacred book secured with seven seals. The only person with the power to break the seals is the Lamb, usually thought to be Jesus. Koresh believed himself to be that Lamb, and that it was his responsibility to teach the world the meaning of the seals.

''FBI agents considered David's talk Bible babble,'' Medina quotes Arnold as saying, ''The government didn't understand that the Davidians were motivated by an obedience to God that was more important than obedience to man's laws.''

Arnold gives Medina this account of his own involvement. In an attempt to intervene and solve the crisis peacefully, during the Branch Davidian stand-off, he went to Waco. Three times he approached the FBI with offers to help. Three times he was ignored, but an FBI agent did tell him that Koresh believed that ''the fifth seal was about to be fulfilled,'' which Arnold recognized as a very real prelude to catastrophe.

When Arnold was denied permission to speak to Koresh, he went on a Dallas radio show and spoke of Koresh's prophetic beliefs. Koresh heard the radio shows and wanted to speak to Arnold, but again the FBI denied permission. Arnold and a colleague then appeared on KGBS Dallas, a radio station the Davidians listened to every day and, using religious language, the two tried to convince Koresh that he had not gotten his message out to the world and that he (Koresh) needed to write a book explaining the seals. Arnold then gave a tape of the broadcast to Koresh's lawyer, Houston attorney Dick DeGuerin, who took the tape to Koresh.

On April 14, Medina reported that Koresh told the FBI he had received word from God to surrender but only after he had written his interpretation of the seven seals. Five days later, on April 19, 1993, government tanks fired tear gas into the Davidian compound and television cameras showed the world the catastrophe as it happened. Koresh and the majority of the Branch Davidians died in the fire that ensued. According to the article:

> Two days later, Arnold appeared on Ted Koppel's *Nightline* with an FBI agent who said that the FBI had irrefutable evidence that Koresh was not writing the seals. At the time Arnold did not have any evidence to counter the agent's claim. Later that year, however, Branch Davidian survivor Ruth Riddle gave DeGuerin and Arnold a computer disk that contained the first chapter with a preface and introduction written by Koresh. "After I studied Koresh's manuscript, I was convinced he would have completed the entire essay in about two weeks," says Arnold.
>
> Arnold also appeared on *Larry King Live* and then testified at a 1995 congressional hearing whose findings criticized the FBI for mishandling the situation and for not consulting religion experts.   (Medina, "Doctor of Doctrines")

Apparently the FBI did learn something from the encounter. Three years later in the spring of 1996 when the Freemen stand-off in Jordan, Montana, was beginning to look like another potential Waco disaster, the FBI called on Arnold. Although the Freemen, a religious group, did not allow outsiders into their house during the 81-day stand-off, Arnold interpreted important religious concepts to the FBI. This time the FBI listened to a religion expert while applying basic law enforcement techniques. The result on June 13, 1996, was a peaceful surrender.

Phillip Arnold's purpose, the article states, is not to justify religious zealots or to defend aberrant behavior, but to explain alternate religious ideologies that are out of the mainstream. For this purpose he founded the Religion-Crisis Task Force, which consists of about sixty religion and social science experts who provide information about religious beliefs to law enforcement and media.

Klanwatch, a watchdog organization of the Southern Poverty Law Center, believes that there is a growing need for such an organization as Arnold's. "As the year 2000 approaches," says the June 1997 edition on SPLC's web site, "there is a risk that many in the growing Identity movement will attempt to bring their apocalyptic vision to reality through violence." In the same edition of SPLC's "Racist Identity Sect Fuels Nationwide Movement," Klanwatch reports that the single most dangerous element in the growing militia movement is "the expanding network of Identity followers. For them, this is a holy war, one they intend to fight to the finish.''

Joel Dyer, who has studied the rural roots of the anti-government movement for seven years, agrees. Dyer says in his 1997 book *Harvest of Rage: Why Oklahoma City Is Only the Beginning:*

> The terrible truth is that the radical Identity adherents are substantial in number, and they are becoming more influential. . . . They are well organized and heavily armed—and they are fully committed to a holy war that has already been declared. . . . The coming holy war being devised by religion-motivated antigovernment radicals—convinced that globalization represents the coming of the Antichrist and subsequently the end of the world is as inevitable and unavoidable as the global marketplace itself.

Identity Christians do see the millennium as a time of conflict and change. However, they have a different take on the subject than do Dyer, Arnold, Klanwatch, SPLC, or any of the watchdog organizations who fear increased violence from the Identity believers. As Cadillac John and dozens of our other subjects have maintained all along, the war is not of their making. Simply being who they are and believing what they believe is enough to provoke the Satanic government into action. Whereas they agree that their struggle is a holy war and one they do intend to fight to the finish, they also point out that it is holy war for the other side as well. From the beginning of time, the struggle has been a struggle for survival between the Children of Light and the Children of Darkness that both sides intend to win.

"We are traveling the same road," Charles Lee states grimly, "but we are going in different directions. Our fates have always been tied together. Maybe neither side ever wanted it to be that way, but that's the way it is."

Phillip Arnold expected to be busy as the millennium approached. "As we get nearer to the year 2000," he said, "radical action taken by alternative religious groups will break out in unexpected places. . . . The millennium is a time when all religious groups—including mainstream denominations—seek a sign from God."

The 1996 birth of a red heifer in Israel where there have been no red cattle for two thousand years? Read Numbers 19. A proposed space station that resembles "a wheel in the middle of a wheel"? Read Ezekiel 1. The hydrogen bomb? Read Revelation 6:12–14. The 1996 relocation of Jacob's

Pillar Stone? Read Ezekiel 21:27. Wars and rumors of war, distress between nations, hurricanes and floods and famine and earthquake and plague? Read any newspaper. The signs are clear—to those who see them as such. The Millennium will undoubtedly bring an increase in these omens and an increase in active responses to them as both the Children of Light and the Children of Darkness recognize the implications of these events and their true significance.

Arnold notes that in both Judaism and in Christianity, important events occur every thousand years. In 1000 B.C. King David established his kingdom to begin the unbroken lineage promised by Yahweh. One thousand years later, Yashua the Christ arrived as the Savior of mankind. One thousand years after that, William the Conqueror took England and established the British throne—a continuation of the lineage and Throne of David. With the coming of the new millennium, a harbinger of the end of time to some true believers. The world will register another thousand-year mark. The pages of this book are filled with signs and predictions and prophecies, some of which have already proved themselves.

Phineas priests and the leaderless resistance recognize the signs and their activism increases accordingly. The Atlanta bombings at Olympic Park, a lesbian nightclub, and an abortion clinic have been claimed by the Army of God. A new tactic in the latter bombings entails the use of secondary anti-personnel devices. In short, the damage of the first explosion is compounded by another bomb designed to kill and maim investigators and rescue workers. News commentators report that federal agents have yet to determine if the Army of God is actually an organized group or a single individual. The consensus among the movements, however, is that it really does not matter. The nature of the movement and its success or failure does not depend on numbers, but upon the dedication and zeal of those who would raise their arms to strike back against the enemies of Yahweh.

In 1990, Richard Hoskins wrote in his *Vigilantes of Christendom* that "the Phineas Priesthood in the near future may become a central fact in your life." In 1996, surveillance cameras in a Spokane bank took photographs of armed Phineas priests as they robbed the bank. Borrowing an old tactic of The Order, the robbers detonated a bomb to draw attention away from the holdup. The bank robbers left behind a sermon-like apocalyptic warning with their distinctive signature. A hodge-podge of scriptural quotations and references linked together, the missive reads, in part:

Greetings:

Thus says Yahweh, Behold, I will rise up against Babylon and against them that dwell in the midst of them that rise up against me, a destroying wind . . .

Yahweh has brought forth our righteousness: come and let us declare in Sion the work of Yahweh our Elohim. Make bright the arrows, gather the shields . . . prepare the ambushes: for Yahweh hath both devised and done that which He spake against the inhabitants of Babylon.

. . . Thou Israel art my battle ax and weapons of war; for with you will I break in pieces the nations, and with you will I destroy kingdoms; And with you will I break in pieces the horse and his rider; and with you will I break in pieces the chariot and his rider; With you also will I break in pieces man and woman . . . with you will I break in pieces captains and rulers . . . Behold. I am against you, O destroying mountain . . . they shall not take of you a stone for a corner, nor a stone for foundations; but you shall be desolate forever, says Yahweh.

. . . Come out of her my people, that you be not partakers of her sins and that you receive not of her plagues. For her sins have reached unto heaven, and Yahweh has remembered her iniquities . . . her plagues shall come in one day, death and mourning and famine; and she shall be utterly burned with fire: for strong is Yahweh Elohim who judges her.

Let the high praises of Yahweh be in their mouth, and a two-edged sword in their hand; to execute vengeance upon the heathen, and punishments upon the people: To bind their kings with chains, and their nobles with fetters of iron: To execute upon them the judgement written: this honor have all His saints. Praise You Yahweh.

Flee you usurer from the face of our land, and all that would not that the Master reign over them, for the end of Babylon is come. Praise Yahweh!

Authorities arrested three Sandpoint, Idaho, men in the case: Robert S. Berry, a 42-year-old, self-employed mechanic; 51-year-old Verne Jay Merrell, a former nuclear engineer; and 45-year-old Charles H. Barbee, former AT&T employee who most recently made his living buying and selling military surplus items. A dozen charges were brought against the three, including the bombings of the Spokesman-Review newspaper office and a Planned Parenthood Office, use of force in a bank robbery on two occasions, car theft, and possession of explosives in the commission of a crime. Of the twelve charges, the men were found guilty of conspiracy, transportation across a state line of a stolen vehicle (two counts) and possession of unlawful firearms. The jury had no decision on the other eight charges.

Merrell testified during the trial, referring to himself as an "ambassador to Yahweh," whom he claims commanded him to be armed. That Merrell is Identity Christian is beyond denial. He claims to be of the tribe of Judah and therefore not a Phineas priest because Phinehas was of the tribe of Levi. However, Merrell also contends that Phinehas did have the authority to put the race-mixers to death and to enforce God's Law. And according to God's Law, usurers are worthy of death for charging interest on loaned money. Therefore, from this line of reasoning, targeting such sinners for robbery and relieving them of false idols (U.S. currency) hardly constitutes theft. Merrell maintained that banks, immoral laws and abortions are a threat to the United States and that such laws and practices, overtly contradictory to the Laws of God cannot, in good consciousness, be obeyed.

The true believers of the racialist right expect to see more resistance on the part of white Christians. More bombings of abortion clinics. More executions of race-mixers and homosexuals. More righteous defilements of the temples of the Synagogue of Satan—banks, finance companies and other institutions of usury. More attempts to enforce true law, Yahweh's Law, among the lawless. More fulfilment of the prophecies. More signs of the times.

# EPILOGUE

# The Final Chapter

August 9, 1990. Houston, Texas. Fifteen-year-old Hung Truong, a Vietnamese immigrant spending a night with a friend, was walking to a convenience store in the early hours of the morning. A group of skinheads including Derek Ian Hilla and Kevin M. Allison, both aged eighteen, accosted the teens, attacking and stomping the Asian youth.

Truong died the following morning.

The two skinheads were convicted. In court, Allison testified that the last words he heard from Hung Truong were "God forgive me for coming to this country. I'm so sorry."

Thus goes the holy war in America.

In Springfield, Tennessee, two black youths were found guilty of killing nineteen-year-old Michael Westerman. Freddie Morrow and Damien Darden, both eighteen years of age, were sentenced to life in prison. Westerman, a white, was allegedly killed for displaying a Confederate flag on his truck. In Fayetteville, North Carolina, James Burmeister II, a white member of the elite 82nd Airborne was found guilty of murdering a black couple, Michael James and Jackie Burden. At the end of their workday, Burmeister and a fellow white soldier changed into their skinhead attire. Burmeister then killed James and Burden reportedly "because they were black." In New York City, two black men, twenty-one-year-old Lemrick Nelson and forty-three-year-old Charles Price, were convicted of violating the civil rights of Holocaust scholar Yankel Rosenbaum. Nelson was convicted of stabbing Rosenbaum as he walked down the street, and Price of inciting a crowd to "go get the Jew."

So goes the nature of race relations in the United States.

In Oklahoma, Willie Ray Lampley, pastor of a fringe church, is arrested along with three accomplices in a plot to detonate a bomb at the Greenway Plaza building in Houston which houses an office of the ADL. In California, a federal courthouse and a federal bank are targeted for bombs. In Alabama, a federal judge is killed by a letter-bomb. In Washington, three Phineas Priests rob a federal bank; in court one declares, "Yahweh is my defense." In Reno, Nevada, an explosive device is found triggered but undetonated at the Internal Revenue Service offices. In Atlanta's Olympic Stadium, a bomb explodes among a crowd of concert-goers; an abortion clinic and a gay bar are bombed, and "The Army of God" claims credit for the acts. Across the nation, society divides along racial lines about the Confederate flag, about the songs "Dixie" and "Carry Me Back to Old Virginia," about the books *Huckleberry Finn* and *To Kill a Mockingbird,* about the Declaration of Independence. Synagogues are desecrated. Black churches burn.

In 1995, more than 8,000 hate crimes were reported to the FBI: 61% related to racial bias, 16% to religious bias, 13% to sexual orientation, 10% to ethnic or national origins. Crimes are still being committed against foreigners, homosexuals, interracial organizations, those involved in interracial relationships or marriages, those who participate in or support abortions, agents and offices of the federal government. The furor continues over Ruby Ridge, Waco, Oklahoma City, the L.A. riots, prayer in schools, affirmative action, AIDS, welfare, government, immigration, and all the ills that have plagued us for decades.

Such is life in twentieth-century America.

The contributors to this book acknowledge that such problems exist. But they insist that violence committed by any person claiming to be Identity should be attributed, instead, to a fringe group. Across the board, our interviewees deny that the true teachings of Identity promote hate or advocate violence.

But in the interest of inclusiveness, all groups—the fringe, the ill advised and the ill informed, the fanatics and the nuts, the newsworthy and the impostors—must be included in any serious discussion, especially if they claim to be acting under directions from God.

Still the movements continue to grow. Lines blur between distinct organizations, agendas are often concealed in rhetoric, membership in some groups relies on the continuing alienation and disaffection of a significant segment of white society, membership in others is based on heartfelt religious beliefs. All, we hope, have been given their say.

This is the final chapter because a book has to stop somewhere, not because there is no more to discuss. The authors are still not racists, Identity Christians, or white supremacists. But we are much more knowledgeable than when we first began this work and, we hope, wiser. We have attempted to present an inside look at the racial right and other right-wing movements in the words and from the perspectives of members of those organizations. We hope we have been successful.

But we also feel that this work raises many more questions than it answers. Questions such as, with the burgeoning evidence of Christian Identity on the world scene, why haven't mainstream ministers of the various orthodox Christian denominations researched, taught, questioned, even challenged the message of Aryan Israel?

The answers are simple. They don't know about it, they don't want to acknowledge it, perhaps some agree with it, or—as many Identity Christians believe—their intent is to suppress it.

During the course of our research, we spoke with a number of non-Identity Christians, several ministers, many laymen, and a professor of comparative theology. None of them knew about Christian Identity, the "Seedline Doctrine," Covenant theology, or British Israelism. Most of them were as ignorant of the movement as the authors themselves were prior to studying what Identity Christians believe. During our research, we were surprised to discover that not only is the concept of White Israel *not* new, but evidence of the belief can be found in plays of Shakespeare, in poems of English poet William Blake, in sixteenth-century history books, in the Pilgrims' sermons and hymns, in Church of England and Puritan prayer books, in the early twentieth-century American Pentecostal movement.

The reference is there. We looked it up. Why were the authors not taught about this concept in our churches as we were growing up?

Equally as baffling, if the concept of White Israel has been around for so many centuries, why haven't Americans been more informed by Identity Christians themselves about their beliefs? Methodists and Baptists and Catholics and other denominations loudly proclaim the tenets of their faith to the world, undeterred by the possibility that they will be misunderstood or criticized or reported wrongly.

The question remains. Where is the theological debate on this issue?

Why are the pulpits silent? Where are the programs on Christian networks? Where are the books in Christian bookstores? Where are the documentaries on educational and network channels? Honest debate and serious discussion will not come through inviting a few robed Klansmen or red-braced skinheads onto a talk show to be thrown to the salivating audience and hooted down before any dialogue can transpire.

Mike Hallimore, one of our more meticulous advisors, would welcome such honest debate. "No matter how you read it," he says, "the Bible speaks to a chosen people. The Scriptures show the chosen people to be someone other than the Jews. We would be happy to debate this with anyone on the basis of the Scriptures and let the chips fall where they may."

The authors produced this work looking over our shoulders, wondering when Christian Identity was going to explode onto the media scene. There are related works being produced, and the number of trade books and articles that mention Christian Identity is increasing, but we are astounded at how often the reporting of mainstream media misses the point. We have watched hours of network programming and documentaries that focused on hatred, particularly racial and anti-government hatred, as the driving impetus behind the separatist movements. While we cannot negate the importance of that element, we were baffled about why the scriptural basis for their beliefs was not included as a significant factor.

We were equally astounded that hours of air time were given to the militias and resistance groups while only seconds and minutes addressed, and in a very superficial way, the concept of leaderless resistance. Press was given to individuals and to groups, to their weapons and their actions, but not investigation into the spiritual beliefs that underpin those actions.

We hope to see the situation change in the coming years, for we feel very strongly that this subject merits serious public dialogue. We hope to see this system of beliefs seriously addressed from the mainstream pulpit and by the leaders of the religious right. And by the media if they will listen to what is really being said. We especially hope to see a clearer demarcation made between the inclusive and the exclusive varieties of faith.

It was impossible for the authors, as we conducted our research and found the degree to which the racial right is discounted as only a more or less annoying element by the rest of American society, not to think of Berlin and Paris in the twenties when the upper-crust German aristocracy spoke of the upstarts in the proletarian movements, particularly the

Freikorps and the Nazi Party, in equally disparaging terms. It is impossible not to see the parallels between modern America with its racial right and the Parisian intellectuals who sat in their cafes discounting the quaint new leader of *les allemands*—the former paper-hanger, the little corporal with his dark lock of unruly hair and Charlie Chaplin mustache—who was causing such a futile disturbance.

The world learned. When the real might of the country—the butchers, bakers, and candlestick makers, the policemen, firemen, housewives and ironworkers—come together under a banner of faith, of victor-identity, of chosenness, perhaps it serves the world to take notice. It is certainly in the best interest of whatever minority groups are the target of their rage to sit up and take notice.

But how does a society proceed at this point? How shall federal agencies combat a threat to the integrity of the state while still preserving the laws which protect *all* American citizens, even those dedicated to the destruction of that system?

An organization dedicated to the establishment of a Christian theocracy *is* a threat to a constitutional republic. A movement dedicated to the establishment of a racial homeland is most definitely a threat to those not of that race.

What can or should be done at this point, or even what is possible, is largely a question of one's perspective, the balance between personal conviction and national welfare, the determination to make clear one's stand on issues, one's beliefs and one's visions for America.

Charles Lee, speaking from the convictions afforded by his faith, is satisfied to let the plot unfold as it is destined. "The future is carved in stone and there is no way anyone can change it," he states with confidence. "All things in the Scriptures will come to pass in God's time."

# AUTHORS' NOTES

From John R. Craig:

How does a nation of free men monitor movements which aggressively advocate the violent overthrow of the United States government (and claim that God commands the execution of their enemies) without violating their rights to free expression? At what point does freedom of religion become treason or sedition? Where does a democratic government cross the line in identifying the legal or illegal, if those activities take place under the umbrella of "religious freedom"?

In order to secure accurate information about these beliefs, I found it necessary to draw on my over thirty years of contacts and resources as an investigator. My co-authors and I assured our public and private sources of our best efforts to objectively record their beliefs, aims and goals without our personal commentary. It was difficult to convince these subjects that we are researchers, not propagandists or apologists.

The Anglo/Christian Identity-Aryan Nations system of beliefs demands a hearing and careful evaluation, if for no other reason, because of its extreme violent structure and the growing number of practitioners. The American public has recently witnessed violence from but a few ardent advocates. Certainly, not all followers of the Anglo-Christian Identity movement would build bombs or perpetrate heinous crimes. But a public that understands these beliefs can more accurately categorize their acts of violence and perhaps safeguard citizen liberties more effectively.

Three Aryans wrote this book about other Aryans who have boldly staked their religious claims to the "whole" of society. We appreciate their candor, but they do not speak for all of us.

As an orthodox, conservative Christian, Son of the South, and grandson of a former Klansman, I can assure the reader that my contribution to this writing was difficult to complete without my personal comments and reflections. Our word to those who opened the secret religious sanctuaries of their beliefs and plan of action had to be maintained. That was the deal we struck in order to get the information vital to this book.

I remain convinced that in a free democratic society the articles of establishment of that nation bestows on each member the same rights and responsibilities. Liberty guarantees each citizen the right to live his life in complete and absolute freedom as long as that citizen lives his life free of criminality. I challenge those citizens who disagree with this most basic concept of democracy to either change our articles of establishment at the ballot box or meet the rest of us in a field of battle.

I dedicate my efforts on this book in honor of Robert B. Thieme, Jr., pastor of Berachah Church, Houston, Texas. My earthly mentor who helped me separate lies from truth. And in memory of Felix Mucasey and in honor of his family. An immigrant Jew who fled tyranny, he befriended a young Christian boy and taught me some very important lessons in life.


From Myra Barnes:


Adjectives have been a problem for me in the preparation of this book, from the four-letter variety that aren't normally a part of my conversation to the racial epithets to the innocuous words describing actions I dislike. Our interviewees have been aware from the first that certain topics are personally distasteful to us, and we appreciate that they still cooperated. We hope they recognize our painstaking efforts to remain clinically objective in putting their views onto paper.

The word *Israel* has been a problem at times, too, in that its grammatical environment has had to be carefully tailored to indicate definition. *Israel* is a geographical Middle Eastern territory. *Israel* is a citizenship. *Israel* is an ancient biblical tribe. *Israel* is the renamed Jacob. *Israel* is a lineage.

*Israel,* used by Jews, refers to themselves. *Israel,* used by Identity Christians, refers to the white race. *Israel* is traditionally a noun, but when our sources call themselves "the Israel people," *Israel* is an adjective.

Inaccuracy also bothers me, but I freely confess to correcting a few spelling lapses in correspondence and purposely neglecting to place "[sic]" in quoted material. Fervor supersedes spelling at times (a theory I would not admit to my Senior English students). Many times I preferred to quote an author's words instead of paraphrasing with our own, but we couldn't. We were faithful to the sense of the passage, but nothing can reproduce the flavor of an author's own words—the groups he honors with a capital letter and those he relegates to lowercase, the way he shouts in capitals and whispers in 10-point font and sieg-heils a signoff with a bolded !88!

Most of the information in this book is unavailable in libraries, although we did use some newspapers and magazines as secondary support. Periodicals are a nation's pulse, but as recently as a couple of years ago, events involving the subjects of this book were listed in research guides under the general heading of "Ku Klux Klan" or "Neo-Nazi" or "Militia," titles that were accurate only up to a point. Even into early-1998, a majority of these articles miss the vital element that drives the people they write about.

"Christian Identity" is now listed as a heading in *Reader's Guide to Periodical Literature.* That's a start. But not until the religious beliefs of white Christian supremacists and patriots and separatists are figured into their motivations will the world begin to grasp the intensity of their determination.

We authors consider the preparation of this book a labor well worth the thousands of hours it cost us, but we have admittedly worked with conflicting emotions. The first time an interviewee referred to *Soldiers of God* as "our book," that pleased me. Despite our ideological differences, this has been a joint effort and we have worked well together. Besides white supremacy, we talked about our children, about car repairs and current events, about the food and coffee over which we coordinated our notes.

In many ways, the 1997 conference in Branson was a high point in this project that made it all come together. For one accustomed to library research and scholarly footnotes (and the routine of Southern Baptist revivals), for me it was an entry into a new world albeit not always a comfortable one. I'll remember the registration table and my puzzlement at a photograph with the notice ''This man is not welcome'' and the courteous lady in pink who explained. I'll remember the pretty young Mennonite woman who told me how she made her headcovering, then the young man who made a hasty retreat when he discovered I was a writer. Of all the families sitting through hours of meetings, I never saw a child corrected or one that needed correction. I'll remember Ray Capt's scholarly expertise, his support and gentle guidance. I'll especially remember a gracious lady who gave me a much-needed hug. I'll remember taking my coffee into the hallway during a break and listening to a young man play Bach's ''Jesu Joy of Man's Desiring,'' and I'll never forget the sweet sound of the Boatwrights' magnificent dulcimers. I especially enjoyed the music, but I confess to some uneasy moments. We greatly appreciate Mike Hallimore's explanations and his allowing us to quote from the AIT and showing us around, but he did much more. Mike's acceptance of us helped calm any disquiet I might have felt during the meetings, and for that I'm grateful.

During the years we have worked on this project, our research has taken place in restaurants and parks and gun shows instead of libraries— with Charles and Jim and John, Mike and Bob, Mark and Chad and young men much like my son might have been—and each time I learned more than I expected to. It's a small conversational step, I discovered, between ''He takes cream in his coffee'' and ''He's in federal prison.''

Since the first edition of Soldiers of God in 1998, a question I've been asked often is, ''Weren't you afraid?''

With the major contributors to this book, no. I've spent hours on the phone with them; we've shared meals; I've been in their homes; I've met their wives and children and girlfriends; I've watched the skinheads graduate from college and enter into careers. Without exception, the encounters have been congenial, comfortable, non-threatening.

At gatherings that included strangers, well, sometimes. A skinhead rally is not for the faint-hearted. Or a cross-lighting in the backwoods with forty hooded Klansmen. Or an Identity meeting with armed security guards, one in particular. But sticky moments have been rare. On the whole I've felt at ease and, most of the time, welcome.

I will never again watch the evening news without ambivalence, remembering the pleasant company across the table, yet hoping I never see them on the national news. Some of the white supremacists we met in the preparation of this book are extremely vocal about their beliefs. Others believe softly and carry a mighty big stick.

From Howard Bushart:

The first draft of *Soldiers of God* was completed January 15, 1996. Martin Luther King, Jr.'s official holiday. I think that somehow fitting. The project has since been reworked and updated and is now complete. But I still find my ears perking up at the news reports on militia and other elements of the radical right—and sometimes I recognize the names of people involved. I still read newspaper and magazine articles with an eye for their inclusionary value even though I know I'm finished including. But it is not simply from force of habit. Perhaps the interest continues because the innocence has been lost.

From time to time, this has been an extremely difficult book to put together. The people we interviewed are the kind of people I've been around all my life, a good deal more prejudiced and certainly a little more steeped in religion than the average Southern Baptist, but blue-collar, Southern stock. My feelings toward them have been ambivalent to say the least. I have been unsettled at times, alternating between feeling comfortable and uncomfortable with them, between anger and sadness, confusion and fascination and, as a friend pointed out, subject to mood swings throughout the project.

But personal feelings and appositional philosophies notwithstanding, we all seemed to muddle through somehow and I believe we have accomplished what we set out to do. Our subjects explained their beliefs to us and we presented those beliefs as objectively as we could. We appreciate their cooperation. Still, it was difficult to reconcile the realities of my life with their realities.

It was very difficult, for instance, to listen to Mark, Chad and J-2 speak of the euthanization of the "unproductive" disabled, then drive home to care for my son who is a stroke victim. To listen to the talk of the racial holy war, then encounter face to face the Truong family's pain over dinner.

It has been difficult to listen to the theories of the "soullessness" of non-whites, then argue it from a Christian Identity point of view. I couldn't help but think about my colleagues, Lynette, Vanessa, Janice, Shirley, Francene—whom I esteem highly—and how the material in this book would undoubtedly be hurtful to them. I couldn't help but think of my students—of whom I am so Godawfully proud—Colleen, Sherman, Rudy, Samsook, Toni, Adolfo and others who are out there every day doing their level best to make the often hostile terrain of life a little more passable for others. Bright, devoted, energetic, caring, if these are lacking souls, then I know of none who can claim the title.

I couldn't help but think of Carey Levin, a Jew, who probably more than anyone else on the planet is responsible for the fact that I'm still drawing the occasional breath; who years ago—against my better judgment—pulled me back from the brink when I was at my self-destructive worst. A small feat perhaps in some eyes, but I'm grateful.

I couldn't help but think of Leonard McCaghren and Bill Larrimore and any number of other veterans of the European War who have fascinated me throughout the years with their stories. And who never doubted for one minute that they shot the right people.

At the same time, I was surprised to find I enjoyed talking with Charles and with Cadillac—who, if he isn't careful, strays from the party line and can sound awfully egalitarian—and with Jim, too. I admired the soft-spoken earnestness of Mike Hallimore and the thoughtful sincerity of E. Raymond Capt as they patiently explained some key point or another to me. I often wonder what they might have been under other circumstances. Mark, Chad, J-2, Alex, I wonder what they might yet become.

Occasionally someone who was aware of the project would look at me, frown and ask, "How can you stand those people?" or "Don't you hate them?" Honestly, I started the project prepared to hate them. I don't. If nothing else, I've learned I have no room in my life for that particular emotion. I am grateful for the opportunity this work provided me to encounter my own beliefs. The soldiers of God took me places inside myself I haven't visited in years, places I had forgotten even existed.

While roaming about in there, I had the opportunity to have a values check of sorts. They are not bad.

# BIBLIOGRAPHY
# AND SELECTED READING

Abernathy, J. ''Feds Target the Internet.'' *PC World,* 13 (May 1995), 68–69.

Aho, James A. *The Politics of Righteousness: Idaho Christian Patriotism.* Seattle: University of Washington Press, 1990. Reprint by Reaktion Books, University of Washington Press, 1995. [see review by Wills, G.]

———. *This Thing of Darkness: A Sociology of the Enemy.* Seattle, University of Washington Press, 1994. [see review by Wills, G.]

Allen, Gary. *None Dare Call It Conspiracy.* Cutchogue NY: Buccaneer Books, 1990. [previous imprint: Rossmore, California: Concord Press, 1971.]

Allen, Jennifer. ''Young, White and Surrounded.'' [Fourth Reich skins race war plottings in Los Angeles] *Rolling Stone* (30 June 1994), 54–56.

*American Institute of Theology* Correspondence Bible Course. The American Institute of Theology [formerly of Newhall, California], 1970. [300-page Bible study guide] a division of Kingdom Identity Ministries, P. O. Box 1021, Harrison, Arkansas 72602. Director Michael K. Hallimore.

''Are Scrolls Still Hidden in Qumran?'' [possible cache of red heifer's ashes from ancient times] Jerusalem Ministries International. Everett, Washington. (http://www.halcyon.com/rlovest/bfp/qumrandig.html)

Armstrong, Herbert W. *Mystery of the Ages.* New York: Dodd, Mead & Company, 1985. [Not available from Dodd, Mead & Company. The book is out of print, but copies are available from Philadelphia Church of God, Inc., P. O. Box 3700, Edmond OK 73083.]

Aryan Nations World Headquarters. Hayden Lake, Idaho. (http://www. nidlink.com/~aryanvic) [Church of Jesus Christ Christian, Aryan Nations, Hayden Lake ID 83835, E-mail: aryannhq@nidlink.com]

Asin, Stephanie. "Probation Given for Role in Murder: Defendant Convicted in Gay Man's Slaying." *Houston Chronicle,* 28 June 1997, 1A.

Bardwell, S. K. "Bomb-Making Recipes Found in Teen's Home." [teen loses fingers in explosion of Internet bomb] *Houston Chronicle,* 16 April 1996, 20A.

———. "2 Claiming to Be Neo-Nazis Held in Murder of Gay Man." *Houston Chronicle,* 5 January 1996, 1A, 6A.

Barkun, Michael. "Militias, Christian Identity and the Radical Right." *The Christian Century,* 112 (2–9 August 1995), 738–740.

———. *Religion and the Racist Right: The Origins of the Christian Identity Movement.* Chapel Hill: University of North Carolina Press, 1994.

Barlow, John Perry. "A Declaration of Independence of Cyberspace." *The Humanist,* 56 (May/June 1996), 18–19.

Barnes, Edward. "A Rare Visit with the Rebel of Ruby Ridge." [life of separatist Randy Weaver since the 1992 shootout with federal agents] *Time,* 145 (29 May 1995), 24.

Baum, Geraldine. "Preserving Modern Judaism." *Houston Chronicle,* 6 January 1996, 1E–2E.

Beam, L[ouis] R. "The Conspiracy to Erect an Electronic Iron Curtain." [essay; Internet surveillance and censorship as part of a government plot] Internet as of June 1996: (http://www.stormfront.org/stormfront/iron__cur.htm)

———. "Leaderless Resistance." *The Seditionist,* February 1992. Reprint on Internet: (http://www.io./com/~wlp/aryan-page/misc-lr.html) [Internet reprint signed Louis R. Beam Jr.]

Berlet, C. "The Right Rides High." *The Progressive,* 58 (October 1994), 22–29.

Bernstein, Jonathan. "TV Shows Exploit Weak, Encourage Hatemongers." *Houston Chronicle,* 14 November 1996, 37A.

Bielski, Vince. "Armed and Dangerous." [wise use movement meets the militias] *Sierra,* 80 (September/October 1995), 33–34.

Biema, David Van. *See* Van Biema, David.

Blackman, Philip. *Mishnayoth.* New York: The Judaica Press, Inc., 1963. [The *Mishnah.* Seven-book series with Hebrew text, English translation, introductions, notes, supplement, appendix, indexes, addenda, corrigenda.]

Blood, Michael. "Publisher: It's Awful, So Read It: Race-War Novel in Paperback Soon." [publisher of white supremacist book *The Anarchist Cookbook* to reprint *The Turner Diaries,* calls it "ignorant, nauseating and bigoted."] *Houston Chronicle,* 26 April 1996, 13A.

Bloom, Allan. *The Closing of the American Mind: How Higher Education Has Failed Democracy and Impoverished the Souls of Today's Students.* New York: Simon and Schuster, 1987.

Bock, Alan W. "Ambush at Ruby Ridge." [the Christian Identity Movement] *Reason,* 25 (October 1993), 22–28.

———. "Ties That Blind." *National Review,* 47 (15 May 1995), 24–25.

———. "Weekend Warriors." *National Review,* 47 (29 May 1995), 39–42.

"Bomb Could Have Been Meant for Retired ATF Agent." [bomb with note in Alabama] *Houston Chronicle,* 4 January 1995, 4A.

"Bomb Found in Reno." *Houston Chronicle,* 19 December 1995, 16A.

Bovard, James. "Hear No Evil." *The American Spectator,* 29 (January 1996), 40–44+.

———. *Lost Rights: The Destruction of American Liberty.* New York: St. Martins' Press, 1994.

———. *Shakedown: How the Government Screws You from A to Z.* New York: Viking Penguin, 1995.

Boyd, Robert S. "Color's Only Skin Deep." [More scientists rejecting race concept, saying it's a social idea with no biological reality] *Houston Chronicle,* 11 November 1996, 8D.

Braeden, Charles S. *These Also Believe: A Study of Modern American Cults and Minority Religious Movements.* New York: Macmillan, 1949.

Bray, Michael. *A Time to Kill.* Advocates for Life Publications. [Published between 1994 and 1997. Our photocopy is incomplete.]

Brooke, James. "Matchmaker Mines Militia Movement." [Patriots' personal ads] *New York Times,* 14 February 1997.

Brown, Lawrence R. *The Might of the West.* Arlington, Virginia: National Vanguard Books, n.d.

Brown, Tony. *Black Lies, White Lies: The Truth According to Tony Brown.* New York: William Morrow, 1995.

Burleigh, Nina. "The Movement's Sympathetic Ears on Capitol Hill." [support given to citizen militias by Helen Chenoweth and Steve Stockman] *Time,* 145 (8 May 1995), 66.

Butler, Richard G. Personal correspondence, 2 February 1996.

"Calling for South to Secede: Confederate Flags Waved Before Clinton's Visit." *Houston Post* (AP), 5 March 2000, 9A. [In protest to President Clinton's proposed march in Selma, Alabama, to commemorate "Bloody Sunday" of the Civil Rights Movement, Kilt-wearing bagpipers played "Dixie" to honor "people with authentic Christian sensibilities."]

Capt, E. Raymond. *Jacob's Pillar: A Biblical Historical Study.* [tracing the Stone of Destiny, or Stone of Scone] Thousand Oaks, CA: Artisan Sales, 1992. Listed in the Aryan Nations' and most ministries' catalogs. Also by Hoffman Publishing Company (www.bacnet.com/artisan.html).

————. *Missing Links Discovered in Assyrian Tablets.* [study of Assyrian tablets that reveal the fate of the Lost Tribes of Israel] Thousand Oaks, CA: Artisan Sales, 1985.

————. Personal interviews and correspondence.

————. "The Traditions of Glastonbury." [archeological search for Jesus's missing years age 13–30] Muskogee OK: Artisan Sales, 1983. Videotape "The Traditions of Glastonbury" with E. Raymond Capt filmed on location, available from Capt's Covenant Media Productions, PO Box 1497, Thousand Oaks, California 91358-0497.

Carter, Dan T. *The Politics of Rage: George Wallace, the Origins of the New Conservatism, and the Transformation of American Politics.* New York: Simon and Schuster, 1995.

Chideya, Farai. "Women Who Love to Hate: Anatomy of a Female Racist." *Mademoiselle,* 100 (August 1994), 134–137.

Chidley, Joe. "Spreading Hate on the Internet." *Maclean's,* 108 (8 May 1995), 37.

Christian Israel Covenant Church, Ministries. Waneta Quick Stop Box 348. 4155 Deep Lake-Boundary Road, Colville WA 99114.

Christian Research Institute. P. O. Box 500, San Juan Capistrano CA 92693. (http://www.equip.org/)

Clark, Truman R. "McVeigh, Other Would-Be Revolutionaries Ignored History." *Houston Chronicle,* 8 June 1997, 4C.

Coates, James. *Armed and Dangerous, the Rise of the Survivalist Right.* New York: Hill and Wang, 1987.

Cohen, A. *Everyman's Talmud.* New York: E. P. Dutton, 1949.

Comparet, Bertrand L. *Your Heritage: An Identification of the True Israel Through Biblical and Historical Sources.* Harrison, Arkansas: Kingdom Identity Ministries, [n. d.]

"Computer Screen: Explore Alternatives to Restricting Electronic Speech." *Houston Chronicle,* 12 December 1995, 26A.

Cooper, Marc. "Camouflage Days, E-Mail Nights." *The Nation,* 261 (23 October 1995), 464–466.

———. "Montana's Mother of All Militias." [Militia of Montana] *The Nation,* 260 (22 May 1995), 714.

———. "Oklahoma City Backfire: the N. R. A. Takes Cover in the G.O.P." *The Nation,* 260 (19 June 1995), 877–882.

Coplon, Jeff. "Skinhead Nation." *Rolling Stone* (1 December 1986).

Corcoran, James. *Bitter Harvest: Gordon Kahl and the Posse Comitatus: Murder in the Heartland.* New York: Viking, 1990.

———. *Bitter Harvest: The Birth of Paramilitary Terrorism in the Heartland.* New York: Viking Penguin, 1995.

Corn, David. "The New Minutemen. [patriot movement] *The Nation,* 262 (6 May 1996), 4–5.

———. "Playing with Fire." [right's antigovernment rhetoric spurs on paranoid militia groups] *The Nation,* 260 (15 May 1995), 657–658.

Coulson, Danny O. and Elaine Shannon. *No Heroes: Inside the FBI's Secret Counter-Terror Force.* New York: Pocket Books, 1999.

Covenant Media Productions. P. O. Box 1497, Thousand Oaks CA 91358-0497.

*The Covenant People.* Merrimac, Massachusetts: Destiny Publisher, n.d.

Criss, Nicholas C., and T. Gregory Gillan. "Beam Says His 'New Right' Has Middle East Links." *Houston Chronicle,* 2 April 1989, 16A.

Dager, Albert James. "Kingdom Theology." (http://webcom.net/~bhph95/kingdoml.htm) Reprint of an multi-part article in *Media Spotlight* beginning in April 1986. This 80-page, six-part investigation into various branches of Kingdom Theology includes Christian Identity, Kingdom Identity, and Nation of Yahweh. Parts 2–6 are hyperlinked to Part 1.

*Danger: Extremism: The Major Vehicles and Voices on America's Far-Right Fringe.* Edited by Research Director Alan M. Schwartz. New York: Anti-Defamation League, 1996.

Davidson, Osha G. *The Best of Enemies: From Prejudice to Friendship in the Post Civil-Rights South.* [Ku Klux Klan] New York: Simon and Schuster Trade, 1996.

Dawson, Patrick, Douglas Waller, and Richard Woodbury. "State of Siege." [Montana's Freemen, comparison to Waco] *Time,* 147 (8 April 1996), 24–27.

"Declaration of Arbroath." English and Latin versions available on the Internet. Titled "Scottish Declaration of Independence," also available in Aryan Nations catalog.

Dees, Morris, with James Corcoran. *Gathering Storm: America's Militia Threat.* New York: HarperCollins, 1996. [see Matthews, B., for supremacist's review of book]

Dees, Morris, with Steve Fiffer. *Hate on Trial: The Case Against America's Most Dangerous Neo-Nazi.* New York: Villard, 1993.

Diamond, Sara. "Patriot Games." [Patriot movement groups in California] *The Progressive,* 59 (September 1995), 26–28.

Dobb, Edwin. "Not in Our Town!" [skinheads; residents in Billings, Montana, battle anti-Semitism] *Reader's Digest,* 145 (November 1994), 96–100.

Dority, Barbara. "Ratings and the V-Chip." [discussion of 1 February 1996 passage of Communications Decency Act as massive federal censorship of Internet and more] *The Humanist,* 56 (May/June 1996), 16–19.

Doskosh, P. "The Mind of the Militias." *Psychology Today,* 28 (July/August 1995), 12–14.

Douglas, John, and Mark Olshaker. *Mind Hunter.* New York: Scribner, 1995.

Dowd, Ann Riley. "The Net's Surprising Swing to the Right." *Fortune,* 132 (10 July 1995), 113–115.

Drosnin, Michael. *The Bible Code.* New York: Simon & Schuster, 1997.

Dyer, Joel. *Harvest of Rage: Why Oklahoma City Is Only the Beginning.* Boulder, Colorado: Westview Press, 1997.

Dyer, R. A. "Local Office Was Likely Bombing Target." [ADL office in Houston] *Houston Chronicle,* 15 November 1995, 25A.

————. "Slaying Leaves Deep Scars: Man Grieves for Lost Companion." [followup of Bardwell and the German Peace Corps; murder of homosexual] *Houston Chronicle,* 6 January 1996, 25A, 27A.

Egan, Timothy. "Lawmaker's a Heroine to the Far Right: Idaho Republican Loves the Old Days." [Rep. Helen Chenowith, Klan, militias, One-World conspiracy, Idaho's role] *Houston Chronicle,* 15 January 1996, 1A, 4A.

Elder, Isabel Hill. *Celt, Druid and Culdee.* (Foreward [sic] by Lord Brabazon of Tara) Thousand Oaks CA: Artisan Sales, 1990. [Reprint of 1973 Edition by Covenant Publishing Company, Britain]

El Niño Theme Page: Frequently Asked Questions about Climate and El Niño. NOAA/PMEL/TAO Project Office 1997. Text: Michael J. McPhaden and Nancy N. Soreide. Updated monthly. Internet.

Elshtain, J. B. "Revolutionary Pulaski." [residents organize against the Aryan Nations and the KKK in Tennessee] *Commonweal,* 117 (6 April 1990), 206–207.

Emry, Sheldon. *Billions for the Bankers and Debts for the People.* Sandpoint, Idaho: America's Promise Ministries, n.d.

Epperson, A. Ralph. *The New World Order.* Tucson, Arizona: Publius Press, 1990.

————. *The Unseen Hand: An Introduction to the Conspiratorial View of History.* Tucson, Arizona: Publius Press, 1985.

Ewing, Curtis Clair and George Southwick. *For the Benefit of Our Pentecostal Brethren!* The Covenant Peoples Advocates (n.p., n.d.)

————. "A Study Into the Meaning of the Word Gentile as Used in the Bible." Harrison, Arkansas: Kingdom Identity Ministries, n.d. [Ewing's addendum says that this study material has appeared twice before in leading religious magazines, but he does not identify the magazines.]

Ezekiel, Raphael S., *The Racist Mind: Portraits of Neo-Nazis and Klansmen.* New York: Viking Penguin, 1995.

"The Far Right Is Upon Us." [threat of citizen militias] *The Progressive,* 59 (June 1995), 8–10.

Farley, Christopher John. "A Nest of Vipers." [Viper Militia] *Time,* 148, (15 July 1996), 24–25.

————. "Patriot Games." [gun-toting white men are forming militias] *Time,* 144 (19 December 1994), 48–49.

Fehrenback, T. R. *Lone Star: A History of Texas and the Texans.* [historical basis of Republic of Texas movement] New York: Wings Books, a Random House Company, 1991.

Finklestein, Louis, ed. *The Jews: Their History, Culture, and Religion.* Third edition. New York: Harper & Row, 1960. [Two-volume collection of 42 essays, plus appendix and index.]

————. *The Jewish Religion.* New York: Schocken Books, 1960.

Fischer, M. A. "Gerry Spence vs. Janet Reno." [attorney in Ruby Ridge case wants to prosecute FBI agents for the Weaver murders] *Gentlemen's Quarterly,* 66 (January 1996), 96–103.

Flinn, Anna Lynn. Personal Interviews 1995–98.

Flinn, Darrell. Personal interviews, 1995–98.

Flint, Jerry. "What's a Trilaterial Commission?" *Forbes* (24 November 1980), 45–49.

Flynn, Kevin, and Gary Gerhardt. *The Silent Brotherhood: Inside America's Racist Underground.* New York: Free Press, 1989.

Ford, Henry, Sr. *The International Jew: The World's Foremost Problem.* London: n.d. [1948].

Foster, Jim, and Donna Hales. "FBI Expected to Bring Charges Against Three: Suspect is Head of Universal Church of God." [Willie Ray Lampley, bomb] *Muskogee (Oklahoma) Daily Phoenix,* 13 November 1995, 1A–2A.

Foster, Jim. "Suspect Says He Was Entrapped: Agents List Ingredients for Alleged Explosive: 4 or 5 Buildings Allegedly Targeted." *Muskogee (Oklahoma) Daily Phoenix,* 14 November 1995, 1A–2A.

Franks, Zarko. "Death Row Inmate Silent on Secret Aryan Brotherhood." [interview with James "Cosmo" Briddle] *Houston Chronicle,* 6 July 1982.

Freemantle, Tony. "We Didn't Have a Ball in Year of 'Great Divide.'" *Houston Chronicle,* 31 December 1995, 1A.

Frens, Robert. "AIDS 1994." [AIDS as God's judgment against homosexuals] *Liberty Bell* (August 1990), 46.

Friedlander, Saul. *Nazi Germany and the Jews.* New York: HarperCollins, 1997.

Fry, Kristi. "Bomb Plot Case to Unfold Today: Religious Leader Finds Arrests Ironic: Lampley Had Visited Elohim City in May." *Muskogee (Oklahoma) Daily Phoenix,* 13 November 1995, 1A–2A.

Gamwell, Franklin I. "Affirmative Action: Is It Democratic?" *Christian Century,* 113 (24 January 1996), 77–80.

Gardner, Tom. "2 Jailed in Attempt to Bomb IRS Office: Device Fizzled Outside Nevada Building." *Houston Chronicle,* 29 December 1995, 2A.

———. "2 Suspects Are Strange Bedfellows: Nevada Co-Workers Held Without Bail." *Houston Chronicle,* 30 December 1995, 19A.

Gibson, James William. *Warrior Dreams: Paramilitary Culture and Manhood in Post-Vietnam America.* New York: Hill and Wang, 1994. [title also listed as *Warrior Dreams: Violence and Manhood in Post-Vietnam America.* See Wills for review]

Glastris, Paul. "Patriot Games." [militia movement's devotion to language of the nation's founding documents] *The Washington Monthly,* 27 (June 1995), 23–26.

Gleick, J. "dirtytricks@campaign96.org." [persuasive uses of Internet, World Wide Web] *The New York Times Magazine,* 3 September 1995, 20.

Gorman, Christine. "Pssst! Calling All Paranoids." [militia movement] *Time,* 145 (8 May 1995), 69.

Gray, C. "As Nazi As They Wanna Be." *Saturday Night,* 109 (March 1994), 24–26.

Grunberger, Richard. *Hitler's SS.* New York: Dorset Press, 1970.

Haggard, Carl D. "Remember the Alamo! Remember Waco!" [videotape] A Speech, with Introduction by Carl D. Haggard at Boerne, Texas, October 22, 1994. The Committee for the Bill of Rights.

Haggard, Carl D., and Nancy Haggard. "A Well-Regulated and Legal Militia: Constitution, Common Law and Common Sense Make the Case for Militias." *Soldier of Fortune* (May 1995).

Hale, William M. Deposition. No. B-940, 489C. District Court of Orange County, Texas, 163rd Judicial District. Orange, Texas. May 3, 1996.

Hales, Donna, and Kristi Fry. "FBI Informant Says He Had to Protect Public: Bomb Test Was Set for Sunday, According to Informant," *Muskogee (Oklahoma) Daily Phoenix,* 14 November 1995, 1A–2A.

———. "4th Bomb-Plot Suspect Surrenders: Man Was Former Pilot for

Hillary Clinton, Sam Walton.'' *Muskogee (Oklahoma) Daily Phoenix,* 15 November 1995, 1A, 6A.

Hallimore, M[ichael] K. ''God's Great Race.'' Harrison, Arkansas: Kingdom Identity Ministries, [n.d.]

——. Personal interviews and correspondence 1995–1998.

Hanegraaff, Hank. *Christianity and Crisis.* Eugene, Oregon: Harvest House Publishers, 1993.

Hasselbach, Ingo, and Tom Reiss. *Fuehrer-Ex: Memoirs of a Former Neo-Nazi.* New York: Random House, 1996.

——. ''How Nazis Are Made.'' *The New Yorker,* 71 (8 January 1996), 36–57.

Hawtin, George R. *The Abrahamic Covenant.* [tracing the Aryan race from Abraham to the twentieth-century British throne] Thousand Oaks CA: Artisan Sales, 1988.

''Hearts of Hate: The Battle for Young Minds.'' [skinheads] Television documentary. *The Learning Channel,* 6 January 1996.

Hedges, Michael. ''Violent Crime Waits to Explode, Report Says: Recent Drops seen as Lull Before Storm.'' *Houston Chronicle,* 6 January 1996, 17A.

Herrell, Van S. *New Testament, Anointed Standard Version.* Kodak, Tennessee: Herrell Brothers Publishing House, 1995.

Herrnstein, Richard J., and Charles Murray. *The Bell Curve: Intelligence and Class Structure in American Life.* New York: Free Press, 1994.

Higham, Charles. *American Swastika.* New York: Doubleday, 1985.

Hill, Jim, and Rand Cheadle. *The Bible Tells Me So: Uses and Abuses of Holy Scripture.* New York: Anchor Books/Doubleday, 1996.

Hines, Cragg. ''Decline in Minority Enrollment Stuns Clinton.'' *Houston Chronicle,* 11 June 1997, 21A.

Hoskins, Richard Kelly. *Our Nordic Race.* Lynchburg, Virginia: The Virginia Publishing Company, 1958.

——. *Vigilantes of Christendom: The Story of the Phineas Priesthood.* [Subtitle extension: As the Kamikaze is to the Japanese, As the Shiite is to Islam, As the Zionist is to the Jew, so the Phineas priest is to Christendom] Lynchburg, Virginia: The Virginia Publishing Company, 1990.

"Internet Firm Cuts Access to Neo-Nazi Sites." [Germany's Internet providers try to block access to more than 200 hate-group discussion forums originating in the U.S.] *Houston Chronicle,* 27 January 1996, 25A.

Jackson, David S. "Skinhead Against Skinhead." *Time,* 142 (9 August 1995), 42.

Jackson, Thomas. "What is Racism." Internet as of December 1995: (http://stormfront.wat.com/stormfront/whatisra.htm) [originally published in *American Renaissance,* Volume 2, Number 8].

Jasper, William F. " 'Counciling' Mr. Clinton: The CFR Offers Its Advice to the New President." *The New American* (25 January 1993), 5–13.

Jaworski, Leon. *After Fifteen Years.* Houston: Gulf Publishing Company, 1961.

Johnson, Denis. "The Militia in Me." *Esquire,* 124 (July 1995), 38–45.

Johnston, David. "Senate Panel Denounces 'Mistakes' at Ruby Ridge." *Houston Chronicle,* 22 December 1995, 5A.

"Judge Blamed for Hate Suspect Avoiding Trial." [Jewish groups claim German judge too lenient on man who says the Holocaust was a hoax] *Houston Chronicle,* 13 January 1966, 28A.

Kahl, Joan Britton. "Death and Taxes." [Widow of Gordon Kahl, Joan Kahl Britton tells her eyewitness account of the Gordon Kahl conflict with the government] Both audio and videocassette. Available from Kingdom Identity Ministries, Harrison, Arkansas.

Kaplan, Jeffrey. "A Guide to the Radical Right." *The Christian Century,* 112 (2–9 August 1995), 741–744.

Keegan, John. *Waffen SS: The Asphalt Soldiers.* New York: Ballantine Books, 1970.

Keith, Jim. *OKBOMB! Conspiracy and Cover-up.* Lilburn, Georgia: IllumiNet Press, 1996.

King, P. " 'Vipers' in the 'Burbs." [Viper Militia] *Newsweek,* 128 (15 July 1996), 20–23.

Kingdom Identity Ministries. P. O. Box 1021. Harrison, Arkansas 72602. Statement of Beliefs, catalog and booklist (http://www.kingidentity.com).

Klaidman, Daniel, and Michael Isikoff. "The Fed's Quiet War." [strategy to combat the militia threat] *Newsweek,* 127 (22 April 1996), 47.

Klaidman, Daniel, and Stryker McGuire. "Inside a Nest of Vipers." [Viper Militia] *Newsweek,* 128 (22 July 1996), 65.

Kleim, Milton John, Jr. "National Socialism Primer." Second Edition Updated 04/17/95. 19-page *Stormfront* document: (http://204.137.145. 254/~tintin/ns/nsprimer.html) FAQ section good for general information; 8-page bibliography containing phone numbers, AM and shortwave radio stations, music distributors, URL info, written material and publishers pertinent to the movements. [About Kleim: see ADL Research Report "Hate Group Recruitment on the Internet," 1995.]

Kovel, Joel. *White Racism: a Psychohistory.* New York: Columbia University Press, 1984.

Kraft, Dina. "Rare Red Heifer's Birth Stirs Bizarre Israeli Theological Fight." [reference to Biblical prophecy in Numbers 19:1–10] *Houston Chronicle,* 27 May 1997, 21A.

Lacayo, Richard. "Anatomy of a Disaster." [Ruby Ridge] *Time,* 146 (28 August 1995), 36–37.

Lambert, Wade. "Militias Are Joining Jury-Power Activists to Fight Government." *The Wall Street Journal,* 25 May 1995, A1, A5.

Lancaster, John. "Gadhafi and Farrakhan to Sway U.S., Libyan Says." [Farrakhan seeks support from Libya in mobilizing a black army to establish a separate black state within the U. S.; black separatism] *Houston Chronicle,* 26 January 1996, 18A.

Lanier, Jaron. "Would Be Unthinkable to Censor the Internet." *Houston Chronicle,* 4 January 1995, 23A.

Lapham, Lewis H. "Seen but Not Heard." [message of the Oklahoma bombing] *Harper's Magazine,* 291 (July 1995), 29–36.

LaPierre, Wayne R. *Guns, Crime, and Freedom.* New York: HarperCollins, 1995. [see Wills for review]

Lee, Charles. Personal interviews, 1995–98.

———. Personal notes, untitled, undated and unpublished.

Leo, John. "A Chilling Wave of Racism: From L. A. to Boston, the Skinheads Are on the March." *Times,* 131 (25 January 1988), 57.

Leuchter, Fred. *The Leuchter Report: The End of a Myth: A Report on the Alleged Execution Gas Chambers at Auschwitz, Birkenau and Majdanek, Poland by an Execution Equipment Expert.* Shushan, New York: Samisdat Publishers, Ltd., 1988. [Also available on Internet.]

Levin, Jack, and J. McDevitt. *Hate Crimes: The Rising Tide of Bigotry and Bloodshed.* New York: Plenum, 1993.

Levitas, Daniel. "Militia Forum." [Senate subcommittee hearing] *The Nation,* 261 (10 July 1995), 42.

———. "Sleeping with the Enemy: A. D. L. and the Christian Right." *The Nation,* 260 (19 June 1995), 882–888.

Lewin, Leonard L. *Report from Iron Mountain on the Possibility and Desirability of Peace.* New York: Dial Press, 1967. [later revealed as a hoax; *see* Navasky for hoax; see Wills for 1995 review].

Lewis, Bernard. *Semites & Anti-Semites.* New York: W. W. Norton & Co., 1986.

Lind, Michael. *The Next American Nation: The New Nationalism and the Fourth American Revolution.* New York: Free Press, 1995.

"The Long Shadow." *Newsweek,* 115 (7 May 1990), 34–44.

"Lost Right." [danger of expanded police power] *National Review,* 47 (10 July 1995), 14–15.

Macdonald, Andrew. [William L. Pierce] *Hunter.* Hillsboro, W. Virginia: National Vanguard Books, 1989.

———. [William L. Pierce] *The Turner Diaries.* Arlington, Virginia: National Vanguard Books, 1978. Reprint: New York: Barricade Books, 1996. [See Wills for review]

Mann, Charles. "Regulating Cyberspace." *Science,* 268 (5 May 1995), 628–629.

"The Marriage License: Issued by God or the State?" Harrison, Arkansas: Kingdom Identity Ministries, [n.d.]

Martin, Guy. "The Short Life and Solitary Death of a Young Nazi." *Esquire,* 120 (September 1993), 95–101.

Martin, Steve J., and Sheldon Ekland-Olson. *Texas Prisons: The Walls Came Tumbling Down.* Austin: Texas Monthly Press, 1987. [information on the Texas Aryan Brotherhood]

Matthews, Bob. "Report for the Rest of Us." [supremacist's review of Morris Dees' *Gathering Storm*] Internet review: (http://www.anwhq.com/ deebook.html)

Maxwell, Joe, and Andrés Tapia. "Guns and Bibles." [militia extremists] *Christianity Today,* 39 (19 June 1995), 34–37.

McDonald, Marci. "The Enemy Within: The Far Right's Racist War Against Society is Opening New Fronts Across Canada." *Maclean's,* 108 (8 May 1995), 34–40.

McVay, Ken. "The Nizkor Project." (webmaster@nizkor.org), 3 September 1996. [Endnote #44 in *Web of Hate* says the Nizkor ("remember") Project is devoted to countering the claims of Holocaust deniers and neo-Nazis. *Nizkor,* operated by Ken McVay, has the largest archive of Holocaust-related material on the Internet.] Internet address for *Nizkor:* (http://www.almanac.bc.ca/)

Medina, David D. "Doctor of Doctrines: Revelation, Knowledge, and Understanding are Phillip Arnold's Articles of Faith." *Sallyport* (Winter 1997), 14–19. [publication of Rice University]

Methvin, Eugene M. "Anti-Terrorism: How Far?" [we have a right to protect ourselves from terrorists] *Natinal Review,* 47 (10 July 1995), 32–39.

Metzger, Tom. Interview on *Investigative Reports.* Arts and Entertainment Television Network, September 1995.

Metzger, Tom and John Metzger. White Aryan Resistance Hate Page. Internet as of June 1996: (http://www.users.ct.com/crash/m/metzger)

"Militias More Volatile than Ever, Report Says." *Houston Chronicle,* 12 April 1996, 2A.

Miller, Timothy, ed. *America's Alternative Religions.* Albany: State University of New York Press, 1995.

Mollins, Carl. "At Home with a Racist Guru." [National Alliance leader William Pierce] *Maclean's,* 108 (8 May 1995), 42–43.

Montalbano, William D. "Stone of Scone Takes the High Road Home." *Los Angeles Times,* 16 November 1996.

Morgan, R. W. *St. Paul in Britain: The Origin of British Christianity.* Thousand Oaks CA: Artisan Sales, 1984. Reprint of an 1860 edition.

Morganthau, T. "The View from the Far Right." [Militia movement] *Newsweek,* 125 (1 May 1995), 36–39.

Mullins, Eustace. *The Secret Holocaust: A Primer for the Aryan Nations Movement.* Dallas: Aryan Truth Network, 1984.

"The Muslim Program." *The Final Call,* 14 (2 August 1995), 39.

Myers, Lawrence W. " 'Chosen People': Inside the Mind of Christian Identity." *Media Bypass,* 4 (July 1996), 20–24.

Myers, Walter Dean. *Malcolm X: By Any Means Necessary.* New York: Scholastic, 1993.

Navasky, Victor. "Anatomy of a Hoax." [radical anti-government groups believe phony *Report from Iron Mountain* by Leonard Lewin] *The Nation,* 260 (12 June 1995), 815–817.

Nelson, Jack. *Terror in the Night: The Klan's Campaign Against the Jews.* New York: Simon and Schuster Trade, 1993.

Nelson, Joyce. "The Trilateral Connection." *Canadian Forum,* (December 1993), 5–9.

"Net Surfing as a Political Tool." *Fortune,* 132 (10 July 1995), 114.

Neubarth, Michael. Editorial. "Healthy, Wholesome, and Helpful." [Internet is *not* "a dangerous world of bomb information."] *Internet World,* 7 (February 1996), 6.

"Nichols' Father, Brother Upset Over Wife's Book." [Terry Nichols] *Muskogee (Oklahoma) Daily Phoenix,* 13 November 1995, 2A.

Noble, Kerry. *Tabernacle of Hate: Why They Bombed Oklahoma City.* Ontario: Voyageur Press, 1998.

"Officials Probe Bomb Found at Nevada IRS Office." *Houston Chronicle,* 22 December 1995, 23A.

Oliver, Revilo P. "Christianity—Religion of the West." Internet as of December 1995: (http://204.137.145.254/~...n/whitenat/religion.html)

"On the Moderate Fringe." [David S. Jackson's interview with James "Bo" Gritz] *Time,* 145 (26 June 1995), 62.

"On Jews, Homosexuals, and Race Traitors." [Internet; title appears only on opening read-only screen menu; no title or author on the printable on-line article that begins with quote from "Sinners in the Hands of an Angry God" by Jonathan Edwards] Internet as of June 1996: (http://www.io.com/~wp/aryan-page/sinner.html)

Ostling, R. "A Sinister Search for 'Identity.'" *Time,* 128 (20 October 1986), 74.

"Overcoming Internet Surveillance." By "A. C." Internet as of December 1996: (http://www.io.com/~rlogsdon/aryan-page/cng/cens.html) [signature "A. C." is assumed to be Reuben Logsdon, an illusive Internet contributor]

Pagel, Jean. "Defendents Accused of Shooting Blacks to Ignite Race War." *Houston Chronicle,* 6 November 1995, 11A.

"Paper Says McVeigh Had Political 'Note.'" *Houston Chronicle,* 5 November 1995, 11A.

Parmenter, Denver. Interview on *Turning Point.* ABC Television Network, 5 September 1995.

"Patriots and Profits." Television documentary. CNN 29 October 1995.

Peters, Pete. " *The Bible: Handbook for Survivalists, Racists, Tax Protestors, Militants and Right-Wing Extremists.* " La Porte, Colorado: Scriptures for America, n.d. Read-only on Peters's Scriptures for America World-wide and LaPorte Church of Christ web site (http://www.logoplex.com/shops/sfa). Israel-Identity FAQ at (http://ra.nilenet.com/~tmw/faq.html).

———. *The Real Hate Group.* LaPorte, Colorado: Scriptures for America, [n.d.]

Pfaff, William. *The Wrath of Nations: Civilization and the Furies of Nationalism.* New York: Simon and Schuster, 1993.

Pierce, Bruce. Interview on *Turning Point.* ABC Television Network, 5 October 1995.

Pierce, William L. "Nationalists, Jews and the Fate of Eastern Europe." *Liberty Bell,* 17 (August 1990), 27–42.

———. [As Andrew Macdonald]. *Hunter.* Hillsboro, W. Virginia: National Vanguard Books, 1989.

———. [As Andrew Macdonald]. *The Turner Diaries.* Arlington, Virginia: National Vanguard Books, 1978. Reprint: New York: Barricade Books, 1996.

———. Interview. *"The Turner Diaries:* William Pierce, Ph.D.," *Sixty Minutes,* CBS Television Network, 19 May 1996.

Powell, William. *Anarchist Cookbook.* New York: Barricade Books, 1990.

Pranaitis, I. B., Rev. *The Talmud Unmasked: The Secret Rabbinical Teachers Concerning Christians.* St. Petersburg, Russia: Kozlowsky, Imperial Academy of Sciences, 1892. Translated from Russian into English by Leo H. Lehmann in 1939. English version published 1939 (no publishing information available). *The Talmud Unmasked: Part II* added in English by Col. E. N. Sanctuary in 1941; *Part II* published singly in a limited edition in 1941 (no publishing information available) and reprinted more fully in the late 1970s (no publisher or exact date available). *Talmud Unmasked Part II* added to the original text in 1972. Complete text reprinted by Christian Defense League 1985.

"Prisoner Hangs Self After Arrest Over Killer Bean Extract." [connection between paramilitary group, terrorism and imported castor bean toxin ricin; no known antidote] *Houston Chronicle,* 24 December 1995, 2A.

"Proposed Recitation of Declaration Protested." *Houston Chronicle* (AP), 1 March 2000, 12A. [Blacks in New Jersey protest forcing school children to recite the Declaration of Independence, calling it exclusionary and insensitive.]

*The Protocols of the Meetings of the Learned Elders of Zion.* [Some editions omit *"of the Meetings"* in the title] Translated from the Russian Text by Victor E. Marsden, n. p., 1934. Assumed by some groups to be a hoax, various versions are listed in Identity catalogs. A version of *Protocols* is available under the heading " 'Jew' World Order" on Joe Bunkley's 1st WWW BANNED MEDIA PAGE, 2nd Edition, 16 August 1995. Internet (http://www.gsu.edu/~hisjwbx/#air)

Pyle, Richard. " 'The Bible Code': Theologians Are Taking a Skeptical Attitude at New Book's Premise." *Houston Chronicle,* 28 June 1997, 3E.

Ramo, Joshua Cooper. "Crime Online." [Illegal activities conducted via Internet using encrypted messages; encryption methods investigated] *Time Digital* (Fall Special 1996), 54–58.

Reavis, Dick J. *The Ashes of Waco: An Investigation.* New York: Simon and Schuster, 1995. [see Wills for review]

"Report Shows Hate Groups Growing in United States." *Jet,* 77 (29 January 1990), 22.

Richards, Charles. "Film Cites New View of Waco Siege: Branch Davidian Inferno Blamed on FBI in Video Documentary." *Houston Chronicle,* 23 April 1997, 2A.

Richissin, Todd, and Craig Whitlock. "Pair Didn't Hide Hate Behavior: Accused Killers Flaunted White Supremacy Views in Army." *Houston Chronicle,* 18 December, 1995, 6A.

Ridgeway, James. *Blood in the Face: The Ku Klux Klan, Aryan Nations, Nazi Skinheads, and the Rise of a New White Culture.* New York: Thunder's Mouth Press, 1990. Reprint: New York: Thunder's Mouth Press, 1995.

"Road to Oklahoma." Television documentary. *CNN Presents.* CNN 19 November 1995.

Robertson, Pat. *The New World Order.* Dallas: Word Publishing, 1991.

Robinson, Russ. "Cyberlaw, Censorship, and the Internet." CompuServe, CNNFORUM, 13 January 1996. [Robinson is CompuServe's director of public relations.]

Rockefeller, David. "The Trilateral Commission Explained." *The Saturday Evening Post,* (October 1980), 36–38, 84.

Ross, L. J. "Anti-Abortionists and White Supremacists Make Common Cause." *The Progressive,* 58 (October 1994), 24–25.

Roth, Bennett. "Panel Warned of Possible Militia Surge." *Houston Chronicle,* 3 November 1995, 5A.

Rusk, Roger. *The Other End of the World.* Knoxville, Tennessee: Plantation House, Inc., 1988. [also Le Book Co., Inc., P. O. Box 866007, Plano, Texas]

Safran, Claire. "Not in Our Town!" [Billings, Montana, residents fight hate groups after anti-Semitic attacks] *Redbook,* 184 (November 1994), 81–83.

Sahagun, Louis. "Other Groups Threaten Violence If Agents Attack Montana [Freeman] Militia." *Houston Chronicle,* 5 April 1996, 18A.

Sandel, Michael J. *Democracy's Discontent: America in Search of a Public Philosophy.* Cambridge, Massachusetts: Belknap Press of Harvard University Press, 1996.

Scheer, Robert. "Trilateral Pass." *The Nation,* 260 (19 June 1995), 874.

Schroder, Eugene, and Micki Nellis. *Constitution: Fact or Fiction.* Cleburne, Texas: Buffalo Creek Press, 1995.

Schurman, K. "Living in a Global Village: Is Society Ready?" [effects of Internet] *PC Novice,* 6 (September 1995), 80–92.

"Scottish Declaration of Independence." See "Declaration of Arbroath."

Sereny, Gitta. *Albert Speer: His Battle with Truth.* New York: Knopf, 1995.

*The Servant People: Anglo-Saxon Identity and Responsibility.* Merrimac, Massachusetts: Destiny Publishers, n.d.

Shahak, Israel. *Jewish History, Jewish Religion: The Weight of Three Thousand Years.* [Pluto Middle Eastern Ser.] Boulder, Colorado: Westview, 1994.

Shapiro, Joseph P. "An Epidemic of Fear and Loathing: Bar Codes, Black Helicopters and Martial Law." [conspiracies, anti-government groups] *U. S. News & World Report,* 118 (8 May 1995), 37–41.

Sherry, Michael S. *In the Shadow of War: The United States Since the 1930's.* New Haven, Connecticut: Yale University Press, 1995. [see Wills for review]

Shockley, William B. *Shockley on Eugenics and Race: The Application of Science to the Solution of Human Problems.* Washington, D.C.: Scott-Townsend, 1992.

"The Sign on the Cross," [KKK] *America,* 173(15–22 July 1995), 3.

Simpson, William G. *Which Way Western Man?* Arlington, Virginia: National Vanguard Books, n.d.

*The Skinhead International: A Worldwide Survey of Neo-Nazi Skinheads.* New York: Anti-Defamation League, 1995.

"Skinhead Ties to Soldiers." [82nd Airborne] *Houston Chronicle,* 21 December 1995, 23A.

Slatalla, Michelle, and Joshua Quittmer. *Masters of Deception: The Gang that Ruled Cyberspace.* New York: HarperCollins, 1995.

Smolowe, Jill. "Enemies of the State." [right wing militia] *Time,* 145 (8 May 1995), 58–64.

Spence, Gerry. *From Freedom to Slavery: The Rebirth of Tyranny in America.* New York: St. Martin's Paperbacks, 1995.

"Stars, Stripes, and Swastikas." [skinheads in 82nd Airborne] Television documentary. *Prime Time Live.* ABC, 13 March 1996.

Stern, Kenneth S. *A Force upon the Plain: The American Militia Movement and the Politics of Hate.* New York: Simon and Schuster, 1996.

———. "Militia Mania: A Growing Danger." *USA Today,* 124 (January 1996), 12–14.

Stiles, T. J. " 'Freemen' the Latest Chapter in a Bloody History." [the American West as the seat of fundamentalism, right-wing religious movements, Christian Identity] *Houston Chronicle,* 11 April 1996, 25A.

Stiles, T. J., ed. *In Their Own Words: Warriors and Pioneers.* [traces development of fundamentalist religious movements in the American West; early Christian Identity] New York: Perigree Books, Berkley Publishing Group, 1996.

Stimson, Eva. "White Supremacists Take On Trappings of Religion." *Christianity Today,* 30 (8 August 1986), 30–31.

Stinson, Jim. Personal interviews, 1995–98.

Stone, Brad. "Home Is Where the Web Is." *Newsweek,* 125 (Fall/Winter 1995), 67–72.

"Stone of Scone Due in Scotland Today." [the historic Stone of Scone, or

Jacob's Pillar, on which Scottish kings were crowned, is returned to Scotland after 700 years] *The New York Times* (15 November 1996), A6.

"Survivalists: Gun Militias in America." Television documentary. The Learning Channel, 6 January 1996.

Swartz, Mimi. "Vidor: In Black and White." [Charles Lee on cover: "Unmasking the Truth About Texas's Most Hate-Filled Town"] *Texas Monthly,* 21 (December 1993), 130–136, 158–166.

Tabor, James D., and Eugene V. Gallagher. *Why Waco?: Cults and the Battle for Religious Freedom in America.* Los Angeles: University of California Press, 1995. [see Wills for review]

Talty, S. "The Method of a Neo-Nazi Mogul." [George Burdi] *The New York Times Magazine,* 25 February 1996, 40–43.

Tanner, M. "Extreme Prejudice: How the Media Misrepresent the Militia Movement." *Reason,* 27 (July 1995), 42–50.

Tharp, Mike. "The Rise of Citizen Militias." *U. S. News & World Report,* 117(15 August 1994), 34–35.

———. "Thunder on the Far Right." *U. S. News & World Report,* 118 (1 May 1995), 36.

Thellin, "Cadillac" John. Personal interviews, 1995–98.

Thieme, R. B., Jr. *Anti-Semitism.* Houston: R. B. Thieme, Jr., Bible Ministries, 1991.

———. *Divine Establishment.* Houston: R. B. Thieme, Jr., Bible Ministries, 1988.

———. *The Divine Outline of History: Dispensations and the Church.* Houston: R. B. Thieme, Jr., Bible Ministries, 1989.

Thomas, Mark. *The Watchman: The Voice of the Christian Posse Comitatus in Pennsylvania.* [Internet magazine. hard copy edition, also; jointly with Church of Jesus Christ Christian, Aryan Nations] (http://www2.stormfront.org/watchman/intex.html) [Thomas is a Christian Identity minister ordained by Pastor Richard Butler at Aryan Nations 1990.]

Thomas, Pierre. "Identity of Letter's Author Sought: Federal Agents Detail Apparent Links Among 3 Atlanta Bombings." [Letter signed 'Army of God' claims to be violent opponent of abortion, homosexuality and the federal government; article reprints portion of letter] *Houston Chronicle,* 10 June 1997, 4A.

Thompson, Helen. "Freedom Fighter." [NAACP and KKK] *Texas Monthly,* 23 (March 1995), 50.

Thompson, Linda D. "Waco, the Big Lie," and "Waco II, the Big Lie Continues." [videotapes, anti-government] Indianapolis, Indiana: American Justice Federation, 1994.

Todorov, Tsvetan. *The Conquest of America.* N.p.: Peter Smith, 1995.

"Too Close to Home." [testimony by judge and citizens of Montana, Washington and California about harassment and threats by militia members before Oklahoma City bombing] *The New Yorker,* 71 (24 July 1995), 29.

*United States Code, Annotated,* Section 18, Chapter 115 "Treason, Sedition, and Subversive Activities," 1994. §2381 "Treason," §2382 "Misprision of treason," §2383 "Rebellion or insurrection," §2384 "Seditious conspiracy."

Van Biema, David. "Militias." [message of Mark Koernke] *Time,* 145 (26 June 1995), 56–62.

———. "When White Makes Right." [skinheads] *Time,* 142 (9 August 1993), 40–42.

Van Impe, Jack. *666 Conspiracy: The United States of Europe and the New World Order.* Video casssette. Jack Van Impe Ministries, Trinity Broadcasting Network, 1995.

Voll, Daniel. "At Home with M. O. M." [a week in the life of the Militia of Montana] *Esquire,* 24 (July 1995), 46–49.

Von Vulcan, Joshua Friedrich. *Brothers of the Robe: A Story of Unbridled Valor and Resistance to Racial Extinction.* Noxon, Montana: Javelin Press, 1996.

Wade, Wyn Craig. *The Fiery Cross: The Ku Klux Klan in America.* New York: Simon & Schuster, 1987.

Wagner, Dennis. "FBI Amtrak Probe Makes Enemies." [Witness, note citing "Sons of Gestapo," FBI's investigation] *Houston Chronicle,* 15 January 1995, 2A.

Wallace, Terry. "Dallas Official Sparks New Controversy: Price Defends Racial Remarks." *Houston Chronicle,* 11 January 1996, 31A.

Walt, Kathy. "Professor's Words Prompt Irate Reactions." *Houston Chronicle,* 12 September 1997, 37A.

Walter, Jess. " 'Every Knee Shall Bow.' " [Ruby Ridge, cover story] *Newsweek,* 126 (28 August 1995), 28–32.

———. *Every Knee Shall Bow: The Truth and Tragedy of Ruby Ridge and the Randy Weaver Family.* New York: Regan Books, 1995.

Warner, James K. "Land of the Zog." (Aryan Truth Network, n.d.)

*The Web of Hate: Extremists Exploit the Internet.* New York: Anti-Defamation League, 1996. Prepared and written by David S. Hoffman, Research Analyst, Research and Evaluation Department, Civil Rights Division. This 60-page book reproduces pages from Internet hate areas, addresses topics of white supremacists, Identity Christian pastors, KKK, skinheads, militias and other groups. Includes a glossary, bibliography, and URL list. The Anti-Defamation League's web page address: (http://www.adl.org).

Weiss, Philip. "Outcasts Digging In for the Apocalypse." [survivalists, radical right militias] *Time,* 145 (1 May 1995), 48–49.

West, Phil. " 'They Deserved to Die': Pair Get Life in Prison for Killing Man Who Flew Rebel Flag." [Confederate flag on the back of a pickup truck] *Houston Chronicle,* 13 January 1996, 21A.

Wells, Robert. *Anarchist Handbook.* Miami, Florida: J. O. Flores [Volume 1 (1985), Volume 2 (1991), Volume 3 (1991)].

"Who Is Larry Pratt?" [views of Pat Buchanan's former campaign co-chairman] *The New Republic,* 214 (11 March 1996), 9.

Wiley, John K. "Spokane Bombings, Bank Heist Resemble Tactics of Supremacists." [The Order, Aryan Nations, note left at bank "Greetings from Yahweh."] *Houston Chronicle,* 3 April 1996, 4A.

*William L. Pierce: Novelist of Hate.* [about Pierce's books *The Turner Diaries* and *Hunter]* New York: Anti-Defamation League, 1995.

Wills, Garry. "The New Revolutionaries." [cover story; review of *The Turner Diaries* and eight more extremist books] *The New York Review of Books,* 42 (10 August 1995), 159–160.

Witkin, Gordon. "The Fight to Bear Arms." *U. S. News & World Report,* 118 (22 May 1995), 28–30.

———. "One Man's Story." [testimony of Randy Weaver] *U. S. News & World Report,* 119 (18 September 1995), 22.

Yggdrasil. "White Nationalism—Key Concepts." Internet as of December 1995: (http://204/137.145.254/~...n/whitenat/concepts.html).

*Young Nazi Killers: The Rising Skinhead Danger.* New York: AntiDefamation League, 1993.

# Index

abortion, 152
Abrahamic Covenant, 50-51
*Abrahamic Covenant, The* (Hawtin), 54, 57, 60, 72
Acquired Immunodeficiency Syndrome (AIDS), 80, 126, 153, 155-56
Adamic Covenant, 47-50
Adamites and pre-Adamites, 35, 43, 46, 48, 139, 144
affirmative action, 7, 138, 150
African Methodist Episcopal Church, 205
Allen, Gary, 260-61
Allison, Kevin M., 269
"American Dissident Voices" (radio program), 16, 197, 238
American Front, 194, 207, 235
*American Institute of Theology* (AIT) Correspondence Bible Course, 45-58, 64, 75, 76, 78-79, 86-87, 113, 143-44, 224
American Nazi Party, 192
Americans With Disabilities Act, 153
America's Promise Ministries, 21, 234, 236
Amoss, Ulius Louis, 247
*Anarchist's Cookbook*, 231
Angelic Conflict doctrine, 43, 80, 134
Anglo-Israelism, 34, 44, 55, 56, 57, 60, 63, 72
Anglo-Saxon Federation of America, 55, 56-57, 191, 228
Anti-Defamation League (ADL), 56, 108, 110-11, 112, 118, 182, 237
anti-Semitism, 8, 33-34, 57, 190-91, 233-34, 237
*Anti-Semitism* (Thieme), 36, 103
Arnold, Phillip, 263, 264, 265, 266
Aryan Brotherhood, 2, 134, 194, 195
Aryan Nations, 2, 8, 24, 28, 29-30, 134, 175, 186, 189-203, 235; Aryan Nations, 3; Beam's speeches at, 4, 5, 99; Butler and, 3, 8, 28, 29, 82, 99, 117, 186, 189-200; Christian Identity doctrine, 38; Jewish Holocaust, 233; McVeigh's ties to, 119; Oath of Allegiance, 10; racial equality, 141; Ruby Ridge incident and, 14; Seedline doctrine, 76, 82, 86; skinheads and, 206, 214; Statement of Beliefs of Aryan Nations/Church of Jesus Christ Christian, 82-84
Aryan Youth Movement, 206, 207, 210
Aryans, 33, 36, 44
Asin, Stefanie, 158
Associated Press reports: Branch Davidians incident in, 18; Waco tragedy in, 17
atheism, 22, 173
*Attack!*, 232

Bailey, David, 25
Bakker, Jim, 99, 167
banking, 107-8, 131-33, 153
Barbee, Charles H., 267
Barker, Ray, 49-50, 51, 58, 66, 68, 85, 105, 122, 133-34
Barley, David, 21, 90
Beam, Louis R., 3, 4-5, 9, 19, 99, 125, 166, 197, 231; Branch Davidian incident and, 16;

Gordon Kahl incident, 27; government infiltration/leaderless resistance, 247, 248, 249, 250; Identity doctrine, 21; on the Internet, 237; nickname for Ellison, 117; White Camelia Knights, 175, 185
Bean, Daniel Christopher, 157, 158
Berg, Allan, 251
Berry, Robert S., 267
*Best of Attack!*, 232
Bethel Baptist Church, 84
*Bible: Handbook for Survivalists, Racists, Tax Protestors, Militants and Right-Wing Extremists, The* (Peters), 92-95, 234
Bible, 37; AIT Correspondence Bible Course, 45-58, 64, 75, 76, 78-79, 86-87, 113, 143-44, 224; book of Daniel, 95; book of Ezekiel, 46-47, 66, 253-54, 265, 266; book of Genesis, 59; book of Luke, 259; book of Numbers, 146, 252-53, 256; book of Revelation, 129-30, 148, 263, 265; Christian Identity and Bible study, 39-43; gentiles in the, 78-79; homosexuality, 156-57; King James Version, 40, 62, 66, 155, 193; Old and New Testaments, 34, 36, 38, 40, 42, 43, 61, 104-5; racism and hatred in the, 105
Bible Educator Ministry, 53
*Billions for the Bankers, Debts for the People* (Emry), 131-32, 234
*Birth of a Nation* (movie), 159
*Bitter Harvest* (Corcoran), 163
Black, Don, 235-36
blacks, 35; AIDS, 155; race relations, 136-37, 139, 140-41, 142-43; slavery, 34; television portrayal of, 239; on welfare, 149
blood, 144, 145, 194
*Blood in the Face: The Ku Klux Klan, Aryan Nations, Nazi Skinheads, and the Rise of a New White Culture* (Ridgeway), 26, 27, 108, 110, 206, 208
*Book of Common Prayer, The*, 33-34
booting, 210
Braeden, Charles S., 63
Branch Davidians (Waco, TX), 15-19, 81, 116, 119, 125, 223, 244, 263-64
Branson Super Conference of Christian Israel Churches, 89-92, 94, 97, 98-99, 127, 161, 176, 224, 228-29, 229-30, 238, 262
British Israelism, 33, 36, 38, 44, 54, 133-34
British throne and the stone, 59-72
Britton, Neumann, 5, 21, 27, 101, 125, 186, 190, 192, 196, 200
Brown, Jonathon, 90-91
Brown, Lawrence R., 232
Brown Shirts, 190
Brown, Tonya, 91
Bruggeman, James, 28, 90
Burden, Jackie, 269
Burdi, George, 207, 210
Bureau of Alcohol, Tobacco and Firearms (BATF), U.S.: Branch Davidian incident,